LEGACY CITIES

CONTINUITY AND CHANGE

LEGACY CITIES

AMID DECLINE AND REVIVAL

EDITED BY

J. ROSIE TIGHE & STEPHANIE RYBERG-WEBSTER

UNIVERSITY OF PITTSBURGH PRESS

Published by the University of Pittsburgh Press, Pittsburgh, Pa., 15260

Manufactured in the United States of America
Printed on acid-free paper
10 9 8 7 6 5 4 3 2 1

ISBN 13: 978-0-8229-4563-5
ISBN 10: 0-8229-4563-0

Cataloging-in-Publication data is available from the Library of Congress

Cover photo: *Cleveland Skyline from South with Steel Mills*, Paul Duda
Cover design: Joel W. Coggins

CONTENTS

PART 2: The Legacy of Decline in Cleveland

PART 3: Strategies for Mitigating Decline in Cleveland

ACKNOWLEDGMENTS

This book is the result of nearly two years of discussion and collaboration and would not have been possible without the support of many individuals. First, we want to thank all of the contributors for dedicating their time and effort in producing thoughtful and engaging chapters. Our colleagues at Cleveland State's Levin College of Urban Affairs greatly assisted the development of the book concept and its evolution. In particular, we thank Robert Gleeson for supporting a college-wide brown-bag lunch series in the spring of 2016 that brought together faculty and research staff for an open discussion of legacy cities and the need for this volume.

We are also extremely grateful to the Levin College women's fund for providing financial support for the project. Maxine Goodman Levin, our college's namesake, established the women's fund to support the research and scholarly careers of female faculty. In particular, we thank Roland V. Anglin, dean of the Levin College of Urban Affairs, Lora Levin, chair, and the entire women's fund board for their ongoing support.

We also thank our publisher, the University of Pittsburgh Press, and in particular our editor, Sandy Crooms, for early and unwavering support of this project. Alex Nielsen also provided excellent copyediting on a tight deadline.

Finally, we are ever thankful to our families and friends for their support throughout this project.

LEGACY CITIES

INTRODUCTION

The Legacies of Legacy Cities

STEPHANIE RYBERG-WEBSTER AND J. ROSIE TIGHE

Legacy cities, also commonly referred to as shrinking, Rust Belt, or postindustrial cities, are places that have experienced sustained population loss and economic contraction. Although legacy cities exist around the globe—most notably in former manufacturing powerhouses in Germany, the United Kingdom, France, and Japan, this book focuses on the US context, with a particular emphasis on Cleveland, Ohio. While research on cities that have sustained considerable population decline resulting from economic change has been happening for decades, a surge of scholarly work in the United States began in earnest in the twenty-first century. Coined by the American Assembly in 2011, the term *legacy* evokes these cities' positive heritage and assets as well as their continuing burdens and challenges. This volume explores the multiple, complex, and, at times, competing legacies of legacy cities and the ways in which those legacies shape contemporary urban policy, planning, and administration. We emphasize the continuity and tensions between the past, present, and future of legacy cities, addressing their definitive cultural, historical, physical, social, environmental, and economic conditions. This volume builds upon a scholarly and popular interest in legacy cities (Farley 2000; Galster 2012; Binelli 2012; Maraniss 2016; Dewar and Thomas 2013; Leduff 2013; Ryan 2012). We focus primarily on Cleveland, a prototypical legacy city that has received significantly less attention in the legacy/shrinking cities literature compared to the more extreme case of Detroit.

This volume explores not only the commonalities across legacy cities in terms of industrial heritage and population decline but also their differences. Much of the popular and scholarly discussion focuses on the ongoing challenges and distress facing cities like Detroit and Cleveland; other cities (Philadelphia, Pittsburgh, and Chicago, for example) have had modest population increases, and many are experiencing some level of renaissance in their downtown cores and select neighborhoods. And while the specific future of legacy cities is uncertain, their contribution to the development of the nation is unquestionable, and their resilience through the sustained and severe distress they have experienced perhaps demonstrates the ability of cities to evolve, adapt, and reinvent themselves over time. In its entirety, this book poses these questions: What are the legacies of legacy cities? How do these legacies drive contemporary urban policy, planning, and decision-making? What are the prospects for the future of these cities?

We have organized the contributions into three broad categories, beginning with chapters that provide an overview of conditions and prospects across multiple US legacy cities. The remaining two sections specifically focus on the legacy of decline in Cleveland and associated local, regional, state, and federal policy responses.

THE RISE AND FALL OF US LEGACY CITIES

As powerhouses of industrial production, legacy cities such as Cleveland, Pittsburgh, St. Louis, and Buffalo boomed in the late nineteenth and early twentieth centuries. Cleveland, situated on the south shore of Lake Erie, rose to prominence as an industrial center first associated with oil and gas production via John D. Rockefeller's Standard Oil Company and later as a center of steel and auto production. Waves of immigration and migration further fueled its rapid growth (Souther 2017a). In 1840 Cleveland had a mere 6,071 residents, making it the forty-fifth-largest city in the United States. By 1920 the city had grown to 796,841 residents and claimed a spot in the top ten largest cities in the United States—staying there for the ensuing five decades. During the first half of the twentieth century, legacy cities grew rapidly—developing manufacturing districts, related infrastructure (roads, bridges, and rail lines), arts and cultural facilities, downtown centers, mixed-use neighborhoods of varying socioeconomic and racial/ethnic composition, inner-ring/streetcar suburbs, and all of the other common elements of early twentieth-century American cities.

Legacy cities were among the largest in the nation in 1950, when eight of the ten most populous cities saw their population peak. Since then, Baltimore, Cleveland, Detroit, St. Louis, and others have steadily declined. After reaching its peak population (914,808) in 1949, for instance, Cleveland began a decades-long slide that continues today. The forces of economic restructuring, deindustrialization, and suburbanization have resulted in Cleveland losing more than 55 percent of its population (ECH 2017). Today, Cleveland is once again the forty-fifth largest city in the nation with a population just under 400,000, and was recently named the most distressed city in the country (Holder 2017).

Decades of decline, disinvestment, population and job loss have resulted in severe urban distress that manifests physically via vacant land and buildings (Immergluck 2010; Pagano and Bowman 2000), deteriorated infrastructure and deferred maintenance (Hoornbeek and Schwartz 2009; Mallach 2011; Schilling and Logan 2008), and socially via high levels of concentrated poverty (Dewar and Thomas 2013), racially segregated neighborhoods (Tighe and Ganning 2015), and extreme jurisdictional fragmentation (Adhya 2017). In Cleveland vacancy and abandonment plague neighborhoods, homes, industrial sites, warehouses, and offices. A population decease results in an oversupply of buildings, depressing market values. The recent foreclosure crisis exacerbated the situation, and now about 20 percent of the city's housing stock is vacant (Ellen et al. 2014; Hall et al. 2014). Waves of demolition have permanently altered the city's landscape as well. During the mid-twentieth century, Cleveland had more land dedicated to federal urban-renewal projects than any other city in the nation, resulting in large swaths of demolition (Souther 2017a). In response to escalating decline, demolition continued throughout the 1980s and 1990s and escalated in response to the recent foreclosure crisis.

The social ramifications of decline are also vividly apparent in Cleveland. About 35 percent of the city's residents live in poverty, and the median household income is roughly $26,000 (US Census 2014). Concentrated poverty across many neighborhoods presents a dire need for high quality urban education, transportation connections to employment opportunities that may be spread across the region, social service provision, and assistance in reducing the health impacts of poor-quality housing and environmental threats (Keating 2010). Yet population and economic contraction have emptied municipal coffers of much-needed tax revenue, and federal assistance continues to decline (Hollander et al. 2009). Legacy cities, including Cleveland, have long histories of immigration and immigrant enclaves, but also extreme racial and class segregation. Today Cleveland is the fifth most segregated city in the United States, with a dissimilarity index of sixty-nine. As in other legacy cities, the city's African American community continues to bear the brunt of the worst aspects of urban decline (Tighe and Ganning 2015).

Yet amid this fairly dire portrait of decline, there are hopeful signs. Downtown Cleveland, as with many legacy cities' downtowns, has experienced a recent resurgence, largely spurred by tax abated housing development (Bier and Post 2014), a growing health-care industry (Lendel 2006), increasingly diverse manufacturing sectors (Austrian 2006), and adaptive reuse of former office buildings into residential and mixed-use properties (Ryberg-Webster 2013). Some neighborhoods, such as Cleveland's Ohio City, Tremont, and Detroit Shoreway, are continuing to revitalize with all the telltale markers of gentrification: newcomers moving in; housing rehabilitations; infill construction; new restaurants, retail shops, and breweries; improvements to parks and open space; bike lanes; and, of course, rising property values. At the same time, legacy cities remain stunningly affordable compared to their high-growth counterparts and housing quality presents a significantly greater immediate challenge than supply of affordable units (Silverman et al. 2016). An overlooked benefit of decline may, in fact, be the opportunity to craft a more equitable urban future for all who call legacy cities their home.

THE LEGACIES OF THE LEGACY CITY

The word *legacy* holds multiple meanings that makes it ideally suited as a framework for exploring the complex past, present, and future of cities such as Cleveland. On the one hand, legacies are positive assets that pass down from generation to generation; described in the *Oxford English Dictionary* as a "bequest, inheritance, heritage, endowment, gift." On the other hand, legacies are burdens, epitomized by legacy loans in banking or the legacy of environmental degradation as a by-product of industrialization. Following these dueling perspectives, legacy cities are places where former generations have passed down great assets and that face the heavy burden of population and economic decline (figure I.1).

The complex legacies of legacy cities manifest in multiple, sometimes conflicting, narratives based on individual and collective memories. Decline is not a uniform, linear process that impacts all people equitably. While cities such as Cleveland are often characterized by the conditions of decline and distress (Holder 2017), the reality on the ground is a nuanced landscape of racial segregation, industrial decline, vacancy and abandonment, revitalized neighborhoods, vibrant downtowns, and so forth. In recent years decline has, at times, been rebranded as locals attempt to transform negative legacies into positive assets. For instance, one of the most notorious negative aspects of Cleveland's late-twentieth-century history was the 1969 Cuyahoga River fire. Now, though, one can find locally brewed Burning River Pale Ale or attend the annual Great Lakes Burning River Fest. This is just one example of owning and embracing the manifestations of decline that contribute to the transformation of meaning and shifts in the collective memory associated with decline (Souther 2017b).

The legacies of legacy cities manifest in the physical and social fabric of

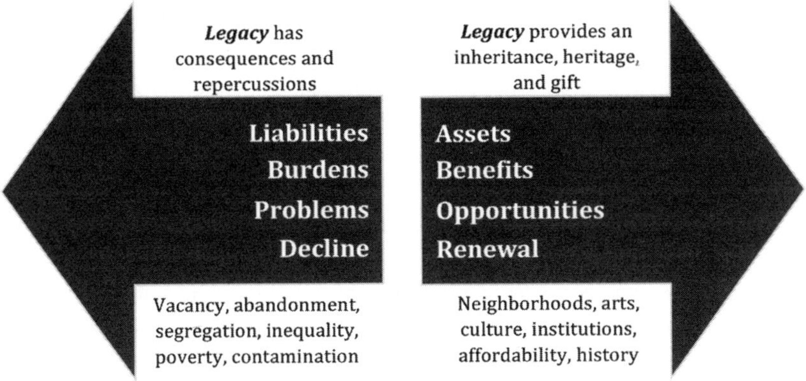

FIGURE I.1: The dueling forces of legacy cities' legacies

the city and the duality of the legacies are ever present. Cleveland retains neighborhoods of working-class housing, grand mansions of industrial magnates, manufacturing facilities, cultural institutions, natural resources, roads, bridges, railroads, commercial centers, and so forth. These tangible elements of the urban fabric harken to the city's heyday, while their deterioration and oversupply speaks to the ongoing dilemma of urban contraction. Racial and class segregation, job loss, regional fragmentation, and recent revitalization create a complex social landscape with deep roots in the processes of urban and regional development. Vacant industrial facilities reflect economic loss and possible environmental contamination, while also providing potentially affordable and unique spaces for adaptive reuse or entrepreneurial business incubation. Population decline has exacerbated segregation, depressed market values, and stressed municipal coffers, yet the result is an affordable housing market with potential for new approaches to future equitable development.

The contributions to this volume touch upon multiple, intersecting legacies, including: (1) population decline and economic restructuring, (2) the production of urban space, (3) arts and culture, (4) environmental conditions, (5) regional fragmentation and governance, and (6) racial segregation and discrimination. We believe that these are six of the fundamental legacies for legacy cities. In this volume we argue that through greater understanding of these legacies, planners and policymakers can craft a more just, sustainable, and vibrant future. With that aim in mind, we pay particular attention to communities traditionally neglected or excluded from growth-oriented urban development perspectives. The issues of racial inequality, segregation, and discrimination are, in our view, fundamental to understanding legacy cities and placing these at the forefront of scholarship on legacy cities is one way to ensure their primacy in ongoing planning and policymaking.

POPULATION DECLINE AND ECONOMIC RESTRUCTURING

The most oft-discussed legacy for legacy cities is economic restructuring, along with associated processes of industrial change and population decline. While each of these factors individually contributes to the on-the-ground realities in legacy cities, they are also deeply intertwined. Among the ten most populous cities in the nation in 1950, Cleveland, Detroit, and St. Louis have since lost more than half of their peak population. While cities across the country have struggled with economic restructuring (Bluestone and Harrison 1982), the combination and severity of manufacturing job losses, globalization, and severe population out-migration compounded the economic challenges for legacy cities and limited their ability to bounce back from the crises and challenges of the late twentieth century (Cowell 2013).

Steep and continuous population decline had massive ramifications on legacy cities' fiscal health and associated urban service provision. As these cities' property, income, and sales tax bases eroded, infrastructure deteriorated and households lost access to amenities and key services (Hoornbeek and Schwartz 2009; Schilling and Logan 2008). Vacancy and abandonment escalated, yet the scale of roadways, sewer lines, and other physical infrastructure remained the same, creating an imbalance in maintenance and operating costs relative to the new reality of much-reduced populations. The cumulative result is that legacy cities struggle with neighborhood instability, blighted properties, high service demands, cash-strapped municipal budgets, and low quality schools (Immergluck 2010). Ultimately, predicting the long-term population trajectory for legacy cities is difficult. Although there are few signs of widespread turnaround in the short-term, some legacy cities have regained small percentages of residents in recent years. However, past projections (such as those in the 1940s and 1950s) certainly got it very wrong, and forces such as climate change, natural resource scarcity, and myriad other factors could undermine projections.

PRODUCTION OF URBAN SPACE AND THE BUILT ENVIRONMENT

The urban space comprising legacy cities reflects evolving urban planning and development trends from the late nineteenth through the twentieth century. Over their history, their streets, infrastructure, buildings, parks, open spaces, neighborhoods, and a multitude of other components were built, modified, demolished, rebuilt, preserved, and appropriated. As with most cities, the economic forces, basic needs, and cultural preferences of any given era drove urban development. The built environment of legacy cities is the direct result of planning, investment, settlement, and migration on the part of everyone from industrial magnates to civic leaders to immigrants from a range of places, to African American migrants who moved north in waves of early twentieth-century migrations. The result are cities that have accrued a patina of their own, sometimes rusty, that teem with memories, stories, and continued lived experiences of those who call legacy cities their home. It is impossible to accurately and completely describe the physical landscape of legacy cities in brief, but, nonetheless, they are comprised of a rich tapestry of neighborhoods with a range of vernacular building types, all connected via roads, rail lines, bus routes, utilities, and other infrastructure. This legacy results in a large collection of older and historic buildings and districts including residential fabric, neighborhood mixed-use business districts, institutional facilities (e.g., libraries, religious institutions, schools, and hospitals), arts, cultural and community centers, and downtown cores. This array of assets invites contestation over the future of legacy cities' built environment—are older buildings amenities with historic, social, cultural, and other values, or are they burdensome, outmoded spaces rife with lead paint, asbestos, outdated mechanical systems, and other issues?

In the 1970s urban planning and development were transformed by the rise of equity planning and nonprofit community development corporations. Championed by Norm Krumholz, then the director of the Cleveland Planning Commission, equity planners called for decision-making that benefits the city's poorest and most disadvantaged residents; always posing the questions: Who benefits? Who pays? (Krumholz 1982; Krumholz 2011) Around the same time, neighborhood-based community development corporations (CDCs) began to form, again with Cleveland serving as a model (Yin 1998). A reaction to federal devolution and a desire for increased local control of neighborhood futures, nonprofit CDCs had a tradition of community organizing and empowerment, with many evolving to provide a range of services, such as housing, education, safety, child and heath care, among others (O'Connor 1999).

While legacy cities struggle with the effects of population decline, they have assets and tools available to assist them in promoting equitable community development. Locally rooted philanthropic foundations such as the Cleveland Foundation (est. 1914), the Community Foundation for Greater Buffalo (est. 1919), Detroit's Kresge Foundation (est. 1924), or Pittsburgh's Heinz Endowments (est. 1941) continue to invest in the redevelopment of their host cities. Typically established by wealthy donors, these foundations are one manifestation of the complex vestige of industrialization that continues to benefit legacy cities. Their focus has evolved with changing needs, with many of them now functioning as funders and decision-makers related to community and economic development and promoting a range of priorities from social justice to the arts. As such, these philanthropic foundations have become key actors in the production of contemporary urban space.

ARTS AND CULTURE

Legacy cities have rich traditions in arts and culture, dating to their prominence as industrial powerhouses. During the boom era for legacy cities—the early twentieth century—wealthy civic leaders invested in a range of arts and cultural institutions, laying the groundwork for a renewed emphasis on these assets in the present day. For example, in the late 1800s, city leaders invested in municipal art in the nation's industrializing cities. The resulting sculptures, public artworks, and parks improved the aesthetic appeal and livability of these rapidly developing cities (Ashley 2015). Many early municipal art investments have proven to be lasting trademarks in many legacy cities, as is the case for Cincinnati's Tyler Davidson Fountain, which has served as the centerpiece of the city's Fountain Square since 1871. This aesthetic drive in urban development was reflected in the City Beautiful Movement. While not limited to legacy cities, plans by prominent early planners such as Daniel Burnham further enhanced the tradition of urban public art and aesthetic improvement (Ashley 2015). Burnham designed Cleveland's Group Plan in 1903, which included neoclassical buildings, a large public park, and the Fountain of Eternal Life.

By the 1920s civic leaders in Cleveland had invested in the city's Cultural Gardens, the Museum of Art, Severance Hall, and Playhouse Square theaters, among others. Industrialists and other wealthy urban promoters were often behind these ventures as a way to improve cities' conditions and enhance their prominence. In 1897 John D. Rockefeller donated the land that became the Cleveland Cultural Gardens—a 254-acre public park featuring works of sculpture and landscape architecture—that continues to evolve today (ECH 2017). Severance Hall, home to the Cleveland Orchestra, benefitted from the philanthropy of the city's wealthy elites, including John L. Severance, who viewed the building as "akin to the Taj Mahal" (Daling and Meiksins 2017). While dependent upon the philanthropy of industrial elites, many of these early arts and cultural investments were specifically intended to benefit cities as a whole. A prime example is the Cleveland Museum of Art, which opened in 1916. The museum, made possible due to funds bequeathed by some of the city's prominent industrial magnates, opened (and continues to operate) under the motto "for the benefit of all the people forever" (CMA 2017), as further discussed by Liggett in this volume. Public art was often included in urban infrastructure projects, as was the case with the creation of Cleveland's *Guardians of Transportation*, carved sandstone pylons along the city's Hope Memorial Bridge, spanning the Cuyahoga River and completed in 1932.

In some ways, the Great Depression marked the beginning of decline for legacy cities. Industrial production ebbed and workers—including artists and architects—found themselves unemployed. Federal New Deal programs included remedies for the widespread unemployment, including investments in municipal art and building (Ashley 2015). The legacy of these investments still remains across the United States. In Cleveland prominent examples include murals throughout the Cleveland Public Library's main library facility, funded by the Public Works of Art Project, and improvements to the Cleveland Metroparks Zoo and the Cleveland Cultural Gardens by the Works Progress Administration.

While narratives chronicling arts-based revitalization prioritize New York City (Zukin 1982), similar processes were occurring in legacy cities. The revitalization of Cleveland's Warehouse District, now a successful mixed-use downtown neighborhood, began in the 1970s with artists illegally occupying the former industrial warehouse's buildings. Similarly, artists are credited with the early transformation of Cleveland's Tremont neighborhood and later improvements to other formerly distressed parts of the city (Keating 2016).

ENVIRONMENTAL CONDITIONS

Legacy cities have long grappled with environmental issues, many of which stemmed from unregulated industrial production during their heyday. Before the rise of a modern environmental consciousness in the 1960s and 1970s, it was common (and generally legal) for manufacturing and other polluters to emit air pollution, dump waste into rivers and other waterways, and/or bury contaminants in the ground. Perhaps some of the more infamous environmental legacies are those related to legacy city waterways. The 1969 Cuyahoga River fire, an event that made the cover of *Time* magazine, is often credited as being significant catalyst for the modern environmental movement, despite the fact that this particular fire was neither the first nor the worst river fire on the Cuyahoga, which had caught fire at least thirteen times (Scott 2009). Declining industrial production, combined with increased federal legislation, has resulted in improved water quality and reduced pollution in many legacy city waterways, although the stigma of the "burning river" remains.

While not exclusive to legacy cities, physical contamination of land and the built environment are core issues in these locations. Brownfields occur when land—and/or buildings—contain harmful pollutants, which may include buried drums of industrial waste, soil contamination, asbestos, and lead paint, among others. Brownfield contamination presents a significant barrier to land reutilization and poses threats to health and safety. During the height of industrial production in legacy cities, air pollution was often so bad that neighborhoods and cities were effectively dark for much of the day. Cleveland's Slavic Village, which sits in the industrial valley, had some of the highest air pollution rates in the 1950s, with residents suffering high levels of related health impacts (Nemeth 2017); Pittsburgh began keeping street lights on twenty-four hours a day due the dense soot in the air (Byrnes 2012). In the past few decades, building restorations in downtown Pittsburgh have continued to remove the soot that blackened the facades of buildings—yet the devastating health consequences suffered by city residents breathing toxic air cannot be undone. Given their industrial past, many legacy cities have vast swaths of brownfields and not nearly enough funds for remediation.

JURISDICTIONAL FRAGMENTATION

Legacy cities, and their associated metropolitan regions, suffer from a high degree of jurisdictional fragmentation and suburban sprawl without accompanying growth. For example, there are five counties in the Cleveland-Elyria Metropolitan Statistical Area—Cuyahoga, Geauga, Lake, Lorain, and Medina. There are 57 municipalities and two townships in Cuyahoga County alone, and a total of 112 municipalities and 56 townships in the five-county region. Overlaid on top of this patchwork are various special districts (schools, utilities, water, and sewer), transportation providers, the metropolitan planning organization (Northeast Ohio Areawide Coordinating Agency), housing authorities, and other public and quasi-public entities.

In the mid-twentieth century legacy regions experienced massive suburbanization resulting from well-known forces such as the GI Bill, the construction of interstate highways, and new methods of mass-produced housing (Jackson 1987). Busing programs aimed at public school desegregation, upheld by the Supreme Court in 1971, exacerbated white flight from legacy cities to their suburbs (Baugh 2011; Orfield and Eaton 1996). Although many US cities experienced the trend of sprawl and white flight, stagnating regional populations exacerbated the outcomes in legacy cities. As employment suburbanized, moved to the Sunbelt, and eventually globalized, regional growth did not keep pace with sprawling residential, retail, and office development. This resulted in a pattern of vacant buildings and land in the core city and eventually inner-ring suburbs that continues to create financial and built environment challenges too big for municipalities to face on their own.

RACIAL SEGREGATION AND DISCRIMINATION

Racial minorities' experience of the aforementioned legacies was typically more intense and far more negative than their white counterparts. Poor and nonwhite communities bore the brunt of negative outcomes caused by sustained decline. Like other legacy cities, Cleveland's demographics changed considerably as the result of the Great Migration (Wilkerson 2011). Cleveland's African American population grew by approximately 750 percent between 1910 and 1940—by which time African Americans comprised roughly 10 percent of the city's overall population. In cities across the United States, minority communities were disproportionately located near industrial locations, and consequently faced significant challenges when those industrial tenants departed, leaving large, vacant properties behind (Maantay 2001). Lacking significant public investment, and suffering from racist restrictions on private investment, such areas—as well as their surrounding low-income neighborhoods—degraded over time.

While the effects of economic restructuring and job losses were felt across legacy cites, the depth of the effect was highly dependent upon geography and race. By 1960 Cleveland, St. Louis, Detroit, and most other Rust Belt cities were highly segregated by race. As the financial challenges of population loss and industrial decline hit these cities, neighborhoods with disproportionate numbers of racial minorities were hit hardest. By 1960 African Americans comprised a third of Cleveland's population, and by 2010 more than 50 percent. These changing demographics were the result of systemic realities present in most US cities in the decades following World War II—suburbanization, white flight, racial discrimination, mortgage redlining, desegregation, and busing—they were compounded in Cleveland and other legacy cities because all of those realities were coupled with massive losses in population as a result of manufacturing job losses and a failure on the part of these cities to respond quickly to the realities of the new American economy.

Furthermore, in most legacy cities, the communities that experienced drastic population loss were those which were predominantly nonwhite in 1970. On the whole, areas of concentrated nonwhite populations were those that experienced the most extreme populations losses as well as were hardest hit in the foreclosure crisis (St. Louis, for example—see Tighe and Ganning 2015). Moreover, in lower-income areas, where foreclosures occur at higher rates, foreclosed properties are much more likely to become vacant for extended periods of time (Bowman and Pagano 2000). In shrinking cities, where vacancy rates were already significantly higher than national averages, the compounded effects of foreclosures and vacancy have resulted in long-term blight, and these are most common in neighborhoods that have a disproportionately large nonwhite population.

BOOK ORGANIZATION

This volume brings together a set of diverse perspectives from disciplines including urban planning, city management, historic preservation, and public administration, and draws on the work of scholars, applied researchers, and practitioners. The contributions are organized in three parts: "US Legacy Cities: Conditions and Prospects," "The Legacy of Decline in Cleveland," and "Strategies for Mitigating Decline in Cleveland." Each author explores one or more core legacies, with the collection drawing connections between the past, present, and future of Cleveland and similarly situated cities.

Part 1, "US Legacy Cities: Conditions and Prospects," explores a range of issues across multiple legacy cities. Meghan Rubado addresses the legacy of jurisdictional fragmentation, which, combined with the reduced municipal capacity in legacy cities, drives a need for vertical, horizontal, and intersectional collaborations. Candi Clouse, Jinhee Yun, and Merissa C. Piazza explore the economics of legacy cities, focusing on population, employment, and fiscal factors, while also offering ideas about building a stronger economic future. Tatyana Guzman explores the legacy of population decline and economic restructuring, as it has impacted the fiscal health of legacy city municipal governments, describing a range of conditions and suggesting reasons why some have fared better than others. Kelly Kinahan explores how one vertical collaboration, federal historic rehabilitation tax credits, helps restore the built legacy across legacy city neighborhoods. Megan Hatch discusses the intersecting legacies of population decline, housing, and the built environment in an exploration of the conditions, causes, and consequences of poorly maintained rental housing. Robert Simons and Eunkyu Lee also explore the legacy of the built environment, with a focus on green building overall, and the levels of new construction versus retrofits.

Part 2, "The Legacy of Decline in Cleveland," focuses on the forces of decline and the resulting conditions in Cleveland. Norm Krumholz addresses the legacy of racial segregation, exploring its current manifestation while emphasizing for strategies to develop a more equitable future. Ronnie Dunn, Terrance Allen, and Ahmed Whitt also discuss the legacy of racial discrimination with a focus on the relationship between the police and African American communities. Kirby Date focuses on the legacy of the built environment, combined with population and economic decline, characterizing the conditions, difficulties, and possibilities for neighborhood retail.

Focusing on Cuyahoga County in the first decade of the twenty-first century, Brian Mikelbank addresses the legacy of population decline, regional sprawl, and housing market changes through an analysis of fundamental changes to the region's housing market.

Part 3, "Strategies for Mitigating Decline in Cleveland," highlights ways in which local actors are identifying and capitalizing on legacy city assets to craft a better future. Using a case study of Re-Imagining Cleveland, Helen Liggett explores the legacies of urban space, cultural production, and civic engagement, arguing for more radical approaches to valuing and, ultimately, rebuilding legacy cities. Through case studies of four Cleveland neighborhoods, Dennis Keating highlights the changing legacy of arts and culture as a driver of legacy city neighborhood revitalization. Aritree Samanta and Wendy Kellogg highlight Cleveland's environmental legacy through an analysis of the Cuyahoga River's evolution as a driver of urban development. Finally, Hunter Morrison and Mark Salling speak to the legacy of regional fragmentation, calling for new methods of scenario planning for legacy city regions.

REFERENCES

Adhya, Anirban. 2017. *Shrinking Cities and First Suburbs: The Case of Detroit and Warren, Michigan*. New York: Springer.

American Assembly. 2011. *Reinventing America's Legacy Cities: Strategies for Cities Losing Population*. http://americanassembly.org/sites/default/files/download/publication/reinventing_americas_legacy_cities.pdf.

Ashley, Amanda Johnson. 2015. "Beyond the Aesthetic: The Historical Pursuit of Local Arts Economic Development." *Journal of Planning History* 14, no. 1: 38–61.

Austrian, Ziona. 2006. "Manufacturing Brief: Trends in Manufacturing Industries in Northeast Ohio." *Urban Publications*. http://engagedscholarship.csuohio.edu/urban_facpub/240.

Baugh, Joyce A. 2011. *The Detroit School Busing Case:* Milliken v. Bradley *and the Controversy over Desegregation*. Lawrence: University Press of Kansas.

Bier, Thomas, and Charlie Post. 2014. "Cuyahoga County's Tax-Base Challenge: Renewing and Redeveloping Core Communities." *Urban Publications*. http://engagedscholarship.csuohio.edu/urban_facpub/1182.

Binelli, Mark. 2013. *Detroit City Is the Place to Be: The Afterlife of an American Metropolis*. New York: Henry Holt and Company.

Bluestone, Barry, and Bennett Harrison. 1982. *The Deindustrialization of America: Plant Closings, Community Abandonment, and the Dismantling of Basic Industry*. New York: Basic Books.

Byrnes, Mark. 2012. "What Pittsburgh Looked Like When It Decided It Had a Pollution Problem." CityLab, June 5. https://www.citylab.com/design/2012/06/what-pittsburgh-looked-when-it-decided-it-had-pollution-problem/2185/.

Cleveland Museum of Art (CMA). 2017. "For the Benefit of all the People Forever." http://www.clevelandart.org/for-the-benefit-of-all-the-people-forever.

Cowell, Margaret M. 2013. "Bounce Back or Move on: Regional Resilience and Economic Development Planning." *Cities* 30: 212–22.

Daling, Janelle, and Robin Meiksins. 2017. "Severance Hall." Cleveland Historical. https://clevelandhistorical.org/items/show/31.

Dewar, Margaret, and June Manning Thomas, eds. 2013. *The City after Abandonment.* Philadelphia: University of Pennsylvania Press.

Ellen, Ingrid Gould, Josiah Mader, and Mary Weselcouch. 2014. "The Foreclosure Crisis and Community Development: Exploring REO Dynamics in Hard-Hit Neighborhoods." *Housing Studies.* doi: 10.1080/02673037.2014.882496.

Encyclopedia of Cleveland History (ECH). 2017. "Rockefeller Park." https://case.edu/ech/articles/r/rockefeller-park/.

Farley, Reynolds. 2000. *Detroit Divided.* New York: Russell Sage Foundation.

Galster, George. 2012. Driving Detroit: The Quest for Respect in Motown. Philadelphia: University of Pennsylvania Press.

Hall, Matthew, Kyle Crowder, and Amy Spring. 2015. "Variations in Housing Foreclosures by Race and Place, 2005–2012." *ANNALS of the American Academy of Political and Social Science* 660, no. 1: 217–37.

Holder, Sarah. 2017. "America's Most and Least Distressed Cities." CityLab. https://www.citylab.com/equity/2017/09/distressed-communities/541044/.

Hollander, Justin B., Karina Pallagst, Terry Schwarz, and Frank J. Popper. 2009. "Planning Shrinking Cities." *Progress in Planning* 72, no. 4: 223–32.

Hoornbeek, John, and Terry Schwarz. 2009. "Sustainable Infrastructure in Shrinking Cities: Options for the Future." Kent State University Center for Public Administration and Public Policy, in association with the Cleveland Urban Design Collaborative, Kent, OH.

Immergluck, Daniel. 2010. "Neighborhoods in the Wake of the Debacle: Intrametropolitan Patterns of Foreclosed Properties." *Urban Affairs Review* 46, no. 1: 3–36.

Jackson, Kenneth T. 1987. *Crabgrass Frontier: The Suburbanization of the United States.* New York: Oxford University Press.

Keating, W. Dennis. 2010. "Redevelopment of Vacant Land in the Blighted Neighborhoods of Cleveland, Ohio, Resulting from the Housing Foreclosure Crisis." *Journal of Urban Regeneration and Renewal* 4, no. 1: 39–52.

Keating, W. Dennis. 2016. *A Brief History of Tremont: Cleveland's Neighborhood on a Hill.* Mount Pleasant SC: Arcadia Publishing.

Krumholz, Norman. 1982. "A Retrospective View of Equity Planning, Cleveland, 1969–1979." *Journal of the American Planning Association* 48, no. 2: 163–74.

Krumholz, Norman. 2011. *Making Equity Planning Work: Leadership in the Public Sector.* Philadelphia: Temple University Press.

LeDuff, Charlie. 2014. *Detroit: An American Autopsy.* New York: Penguin.

Lendel, Iryna. 2006. "The Healthcare Cluster in the Cleveland-Elyria-Mentor MSA, 2000–2005." *Urban Publications.* http://engagedscholarship.csuohio.edu/urban_facpub/243.

Maantay, Juliana. 2001. "Zoning, Equity, and Public Health." *American Journal of Public Health* 91, no. 7: 1033.

Mallach, Alan. 2011. "Demolition and Preservation in Shrinking US Industrial Cities." *Building Research & Information* 39, no. 4: 380–94.

Maraniss, David. 2015. *Once in a Great City: A Detroit Story.* New York: Simon & Schuster.

Nemeth, Sarah. 2017. "Republic Steel Corporation." Cleveland Historical. https://clevelandhistorical.org/items/show/790.

O'Connor, Alice. 1999. "Swimming Against the Tide: A Brief History of Federal Policy in Poor Communities." In *Urban Problems and Community Development*, edited by Ronald F. Ferguson and William T. Dickens, 77–137. Washington, DC: Brookings Institution Press.

Orfield, Gary, and Susan E. Eaton. 1996. *Dismantling Desegregation: The Quiet Reversal of* Brown v. Board of Education. New York: New Press.

Pagano, Michael A., and Ann O'M. Bowman. 2000. *Vacant Land in Cities: An Urban Resource*. Washington, DC: Brookings Institution, Center on Urban and Metropolitan Policy.

Ryan, Brent D. 2012. *Design after Decline: How America Rebuilds Shrinking Cities*. Philadelphia: University of Pennsylvania Press.

Ryberg-Webster, Stephanie. 2013. "Preserving Downtown America: Federal Rehabilitation Tax Credits and the Transformation of US Cities." *Journal of the American Planning Association* 79, no. 4: 266–79.

Ryberg-Webster, Stephanie. 2016. "Heritage Amid an Urban Crisis: Historic Preservation in Cleveland, Ohio's Slavic Village Neighborhood." *Cities* 58: 10–25.

Schilling, Joseph, and Jonathan Logan. 2008. "Greening the Rust Belt: A Green Infrastructure Model for Right Sizing America's Shrinking Cities." *Journal of the American Planning Association* 74, no. 4: 451–66.

Scott, Michael. 2009. "Cuyahoga River Fire 40 Years Ago Ignited an Ongoing Cleanup Campaign." *Plain Dealer* (Cleveland, OH), June 22, 2009. http://www.cleveland.com/science/index.ssf/2009/06/cuyahoga_river_fire_40_years_a.html.

Silverman, Robert Mark, Kelly L. Patterson, Li Yin, Molly Ranahan, and Laiyun Wu. 2016. *Affordable Housing in US Shrinking Cities: From Neighborhoods of Despair to Neighborhoods of Opportunity?* Bristol, UK: Policy Press.

Souther, J. Mark. 2017a. *Believing in Cleveland: Managing Decline in "The Best Location in the Nation."* Philadelphia: Temple University Press.

Souther, J. Mark. 2017b. "From 'The Mistake on the Lake' to 'Defend Together': The Long (and Amusing) History of Trying to Rebrand Cleveland." *Belt Magazine*, October 3. http://beltmag.com/mistake-lake-defend-together-long-amusing-history-trying-rebrand-cleveland/.

Tighe, J. Rosie, and Joanna P. Ganning. 2015. "The Divergent City: Unequal and Uneven Development in St. Louis." *Urban Geography* 36, no. 5: 654–73.

United States Census Bureau. 2014. "Summary File." *2009–2013 American Community Survey*. US Census Bureau's American Community Survey Office. http://ftp2.census.gov/.

Wilkerson, Isabel. 2011. *The Warmth of Other Suns: The Epic Story of America's Great Migration*. New York: Vintage Books.

Yin, Jordan S. 1998. "The Community Development Industry System: A Case Study of Politics and Institutions in Cleveland, 1967–1997." *Journal of Urban Affairs* 20, no. 2: 137–57.

Zukin, Sharon. 1982. "Loft Living as 'Historic Compromise' in the Urban Core: The New York Experience." *International Journal of Urban and Regional Research* 6, no. 2: 256–67.

US LEGACY CITIES

PART ONE

CONDITIONS AND PROSPECTS

1

The Role of Local Government Collaboration in Legacy Cities

MEGHAN RUBADO

In the United States' decentralized federalist system, cities are situated within complex, layered, and often highly fragmented systems of government. This creates hurdles, but also opportunities, for solving the problems faced by legacy cities and the regions they anchor. In regions throughout the country, the scale of local government boundaries often to do not match the scale of the problems they face. This mismatch of scale has been identified as "the central problem for modern public administration" (Kettl 2006, 10). The boundary mismatch is a reality faced by all local governments, but in legacy cities contributes to especially "wicked problems" (Rittel and Webber 1973) that more regularly demand collaborative strategies. For example, the population loss and sprawl associated with legacy city status creates hollowed-out central cities with dramatically reduced human and financial capital available to support policy solutions (see chapter 3). They become poorer and with more concentrated poverty as middle-class residents continue flight to the suburbs, many of which also have stagnant or declining populations (Brachman 2012; see also chapter 7). In legacy cities, the scale of decline means the city government will more often *need* to collaborate to solve problems.

To create successful policy and effectively deliver public goods and services, cities may need to coordinate with neighboring municipalities and special districts, with private companies and nonprofit organizations, and with higher levels of government, including states and the federal government. Legacy cities have long been engaged in cooperation and collaboration in their attempts to solve local and regional problems. They have done so using a variety of strategies and in a variety of contexts and, as such, have experienced a wide range of outcomes. Successful use of collaborative strategies with measureable improvement in outcomes, though, has occurred often in and around legacy cities, and this provides reason for optimism that legacy cities can use collaboration to help them thrive. Examples of such collaborations have produced successes in legacy cities such as Baltimore, Cleveland, and Cincinnati.

The emergence of legacy cities owes, in no small part, to the fragmented nature of local government, which creates intermunicipal competition for resources and strong incentives for city leaders to focus on narrow, parochial goals at the expense of the health of the region as a whole (Mallach and Brachman 2013). These competitive dynamics among local governments remain, but over time cities have learned to collaborate with one another to solve all sorts of problems, including diseconomies of scale and common property-resource problems, through self-organized collaborative networks and arrangements among localities (Feiock 2014; Feiock and Scholz 2010). Other forms of collaboration, including those that involve incentives or mandates from higher levels of government and partnerships between local governments and nongovernmental organizations also are common.

In the United States local governments and organizations have been the main players in policy solutions to decline in legacy cities. Entrepreneurial mayors and nonprofit organizations have launched or contributed to policy responses in cities such as Cleveland, Detroit, and Youngstown (Luescher and Shetty 2013). To successfully regenerate, legacy cities will need to develop, nurture, and leverage flexible partnerships to carry out policy changes that contribute to a mutually held vision for the city's future. Indeed, new governance arrangements have been identified as a critical component for legacy city regeneration (Mallach and Brachman 2013), and cities are looking to collaborative strategies to make policy and deliver goods and services under increasingly complicated and difficult conditions (Emerson and Nabatchi 2015). However, local government fragmentation remains a substantial barrier to regenerative action. Citizens and leaders in suburban municipalities and counties often see the struggling central city as a liability and fear the potential effects of intermunicipal partnerships with struggling cities or more dramatic government reorganizations, such as city-county consolidations or mergers.

This chapter introduces the concepts central to understanding the collaborative activities of cities, including three specific types of collaboration: vertical intergovernmental collaboration, horizontal intergovernmental collaboration, and cross-sector collaboration. It then synthesizes previous research on these concepts and provides evidence of use of the three types of collaboration in legacy cities in the United States.

COLLABORATION: CONTESTED CONCEPTS EXPLAINED

Scholars of policy, politics, and public administration and management have approached the collaborative activities of local governments from a variety of perspectives with myriad and often conflicting definition of concepts, such as the oft-used "collaborative governance" (O'Leary and Vij 2012; Emerson, Nabatchi, and Balogh 2012). In using this term, some scholars focus on intergovernmental collaboration, while others focus on collaborations between a public agency and nonprofits and/or private organizations. Still others focus on the role of citizen engagement in collaborative policymaking. Here, collaboration by local governments is conceptualized broadly—meaning any joint interorganizational activities, formal or informal, that involve at least one local government and at least one external organization, which may be another city, another level of government, such as a state, or a nongovernmental partner, such as a nonprofit organization, foundation, or business.

Collaboration at the local level occurs in a number of distinct forms. Three regularly studied forms of local governmental collaboration are: (1) horizontal intergovernmental collaboration, which involves joint activities among at least two localities that are the same level of government (Carr et al. 2009; Gerber and Loh 2015), such as one city contracting with another for service provision or several neighboring cities coordinating with one another to solve a specific problem; (2) vertical intergovernmental collaboration refers to a variety of interactions among different levels of government within a hierarchy, such as a city contracting with a state government for services, or the federal government providing localities with funding for projects (Carr et al. 2009; Gerber and Loh 2015); and (3) cross-sector collaboration, which involves government coordination with private and quasi-public stakeholders, including citizens, nonprofit organizations, and businesses (Agranoff and McGuire 2003; Emerson and Nabatchi 2015).

Local governments are often engaged in all three types of collaboration, sometimes simultaneously for a single purpose or project. For example, a legacy city might collaborate with neighboring localities as well as nonprofit organizations and businesses to seek state or federal funding for economic development or an infrastructure project. Cities' perspectives on intergovernmental and cross-sector collaboration vary. Some embrace collaboration as a useful strategy for problem solving, while others collaborate begrudgingly, seeing it as a "necessary evil" (Agranoff and McGuire 2003, 3). Still others elect not to collaborate at all.

TYPE 1: VERTICAL COLLABORATION

While the study of vertical collaborations between subnational governments and the US federal government became popular following the federal grants-in-aid programs of the 1930s (Agranoff 2001), there is evidence that interactive relationships existed much earlier. In *The American Partnership* (1962), Daniel Elazar found that collaboration among the various levels of government, particularly states and the federal government, existed in the nineteenth century. The design of American federalism did not produce a neat system of three stacked and separate levels of government, but rather a highly interactive "matrix" of governments that regularly cooperate and bargain with other levels of government to further their own ends (Elazar 1984). Even within a structured hierarchy, the levels of government did not create a "layer cake" system, but a "marble cake" of shared functions, resources, and power that involves regular interactions, cooperation, and coordination among the levels of government (Grodzins 1966). While the nature of the interactions between the three major levels of government has shifted over time from cooperative to coercive to contractual (Conlan 2008), the matrix of vertical layers of governments has remained, and collaboration among them continues.

The nature of collaborative interactions between levels of government in a hierarchy is unique because of the distinct types of authority held by the various levels of government, the pressures and constraints they face, and the power asymmetry among them. Vertical intergovernmental collaboration refers to interactions among at least two governments that operate at different levels within the federalist hierarchy. For example, a city may contract with a state for planning services or it may work with a federal agency to secure grant funding for an infrastructure project. Cities or higher levels of government can initiate vertical collaboration and use vertical strategies differently depending on their position in the hierarchy. Federal and state agencies can "coerce" cities to take certain actions by withholding funding—for example, by making receipt of highway funds contingent upon a city investing in a particular infrastructure upgrade. While this would not be classified as collaboration, the federal government also can use its fiscal power to incentivize particular investments, policies, or even other types of collaborative governance. For example, the federal government may provide funding to cities who agree to collaborate with other local governments or nongovernmental partners for economic development projects. The federal government may engage in this sort of collaborative activity using a variety of policy tools, including grants, information provision, and intergovernmental partnerships to target specific urban problems. While a great deal of scholarship has examined collaboration between states and federal agencies (e.g., Elazar 1962; Cho and Wright 2001), this section focuses on local government vertical partnerships, especially how local governments in shrinking regions have participated in collaborative strategies with higher levels of government, such as counties, regional governments, states, and the federal government.

Because legacy cities and their regions often lack capacity to handle complex problems, states and federal governments are in a position to initiate collaborative activities that can improve outcomes in ways local actors cannot. Additionally, collaboration costs may be higher for local political actors, who are expected by their constituents to spend their efforts on activities that directly benefit the locality (Mullin and Daley 2010). Moreover, higher levels of government have strong incentives to ensure that the economic hubs within them thrive. In an analysis of survey data from local public health agency bureaucrats in Wisconsin, Mullin and Daley (2010) find that state agencies may be able to prod along vertical collaboration through incentives that reward local agencies that collaborate with their state-level counterparts. The authors find evidence that this incentive structure may be even more important in urban settings, where local public health agencies had significantly reduced rates of collaborative activity with state agencies. Urban areas, particularly those around legacy cities, typically have relatively complex, fragmented governments, as compared to more rural regions. For instance, in Wisconsin's urban areas, cities and counties typically have health departments, while outside of these areas, counties alone have health departments (Mullin and Daley 2010). In this more vertically complex environment, collaboration becomes an activity with higher transaction costs. States could help reduce those costs with incentives for local agency collaboration.

States have a fairly diverse toolkit of strategies that can be used to support and incentivize vertical collaboration, as well as other types of local government collaboration. States can focus their efforts on providing financial support through grants, loans, and other funding streams; they can make regulatory and institutional changes that allow for local innovation and collaboration; and they can build capacity of local institutions and actors, for instance, by providing technical assistance and training (Brachman 2012). The specific tools used by a state to collaborate with local governments may depend on the degree of autonomy granted to local governments in that state, a concept known as *home rule*, which varies dramatically from state to state and even among different types of local governments within states.

Unfortunately, states have often created policies that undercut legacy cities. For example, many states have policies that encourage suburbs to compete with central cities and with one another for economic development. These sorts of policies encourage localities to view economic development as zero-sum games in which one city will win while its neighbors will lose, when in reality, economic development is most beneficial when it is approached through coordinated action at the regional scale. States could be more instrumental in creating incentives or regional institutions that encourage collaboration in economic development (Brachman 2012), while respecting local autonomy. For example, in 2016 the state of New York launched a downtown revitalization initiative that provides $10 million to ten small cities after a competitive process that seeks local strategies. The grants provide funding for detailed planning, as well as flexible funding to execute the plans. To evaluate the cities' proposals and select winners, the state enlisted the expertise of its regional economic development councils, which were created in 2011 to coordinate economic development efforts (Mallach 2017).

The federal government, too, has opportunities to promote legacy city revitalization through vertical collaboration. Metropolitan planning organizations (MPOs) are federally required regional institutions that carry out transportation planning, and sometimes other functions. While they have been around since the 1960s, MPOs gained more power in the early 1990s when the Intermodal Surface Transportation Efficiency Act granted them power to make decisions about distribution of federal funding (Weir, Rongerude, and Ansell 2009). In their case studies of Chicago and Los Angeles, Weir, Rongerude, and Ansell found that the federal policy attempted to prompt more effective transportation planning collaboration through a stronger institution with more public involvement, but that this only produced sustained regional governance capacity building in Chicago, where existing relationships among actors in business and local government allowed for horizontal *and* vertical collaboration that strengthened the MPO (2009). Top-down vertical collaboration efforts for improved urban outcomes, then, may be more or less successful depending on how they are designed and on the way local and state actors are able to respond to and leverage them.

This lesson of the variable outcomes of vertical collaboration has been echoed in other research, including Michael Rich and Robert Stoker's (2014) study of the federal Empowerment Zone (EZ) Initiative. In 1995 the federal government granted $100 million each and a package of market-oriented policy tools to the six original urban Empowerment Zones, which included three legacy cities: Baltimore, Detroit, and Philadelphia. The other original EZ cities were Atlanta, Chicago, and New York. Rich and Stoker compare outcomes in census tracts within these zones to determine how well the program worked for each city. They argue that the cities that performed better under the EZ program, including Baltimore and Philadelphia, did so because of better quality of local governance. Where Empowerment Zone programming had the greatest impact, they find, local actors were able to build new local capacity or leverage existing organizational capacity to solve collective problems. They also involved high quality, meaningful community participation in the decision-making and implementation processes. Finally, the more successful cities demonstrated better local governance by effectively matching scarce resources to holistic, coordinated programming that empowered citizens and other local actors across sectors. The federal initiative provided a toolkit of policy tools from which cities selected and customized their packages of EZ programming.

Federal and state governments can structure regulations, institutions, and policies to encourage revitalization in legacy cities. This may mean creating funding opportunities and providing other resources to help legacy cities achieve specific goals, such as improved public education or stronger city leadership. However, funding relationships between federal and local governments, and state and local governments can become adversarial when the higher level of government tries to impose too much control over the local government. Since local governments are in a better position to understand and appreciate the details and contexts of the problems they face, allowing for local autonomy to tailor programming to fit local needs is important. Other times, higher levels of government may create opportunities and incentives for horizontal collaboration among local governments, nonprofits, and businesses in order to facilitate solutions to regional problems. In these cases, the local context again is important and outcomes may depend on local factors, such as the power and resources of organizations involved and existing ties among local governments and organizations in a region.

TYPE 2: HORIZONTAL INTERGOVERNMENTAL COLLABORATION

Local governments have long worked together to solve problems through formal and informal cross-boundary arrangements. They may share equipment and staff or combine purchasing power to realize economies of scale. They might contract with one another to provide local services, such as police, fire, or planning. They may coordinate to seek grant funding for a revitalization project, to protect natural resources, or to attract a developer to a mutually beneficial site. While collaboration among local governments may involve some vertical relationships—for example, a city collaborating with the county within which it is located—this section discusses all collaboration among local governments, including cities, counties, school districts, and special districts, such as water and sewer districts, and/or metropolitan planning organizations.

Interlocal collaboration in the United States involves coordination in a context that is highly fragmented. A multitude of neighboring general-purpose governments provide tax-and-spend packages within their borders. Meanwhile, special districts serve specific functions in jurisdictions that overlap municipal borders in complicated and messy ways. This fragmented system of government means that the most efficient and effective solutions, which often involve collaboration, remain elusive due to collective action dilemmas, externalities, and common pool-resource problems. While collaboration may often provide potential gains, local governments seeking those gains may face significant hurdles, especially defection of partners, domination by a single partner, and conflict among participants (Feiock and Scholz 2010; Ostrom 1990, 2005).

Horizontal collaboration played a role in Cleveland's late 1990s and early 2000s approach to coping with its status as a shrinking city (Zingale and Riemann 2013). Local and regional governments frequently partnered with one another to advance specific projects aimed at spurring growth. At times, these local-level intergovernmental partnerships involved collaboration with higher levels of government as well. For example, the regional metropolitan planning organization partnered with local communities and public agencies through its Transportation for Livable Communities Initiative to direct federal transportation funding to Cleveland-area projects that strengthened community livability and regional economic competitiveness (Zingale and Riemann 2013). This partnership continues.

This sort of intergovernmental collaboration among local governments would not always have been expected. Local governments have, in the past, been seen as holding monopolies on local policymaking and service delivery. However, with complex problems that often do not match the scale of local jurisdictions, collaboration among local governments is seen as an increasingly important strategy (Zeemering and Romero 2011; Agranoff and McGuire 2003; Miller 2002). In legacy regions the increasing complexity and wickedness of problems—for example, overbuilt and aging infrastructure—may create particular demand for horizontal interlocal collaboration as resource problems are especially severe due to population decreases and job losses. Legacy cities and their surrounding suburbs continue to suffer under these conditions in ways other regions do not. Legacy cities operating in an era of devolution, reduced state and federal aid, and increased mandates are at an extreme disadvantage as compared to growing cities that can leverage burgeoning local resources (see chapter 3). Local governments in and around legacy cities that seek to solve problems, create efficiencies, and provide more effective services will more often *need* to seek out partners to do so.

The Institutional Collective Action (ICA) framework provides a comprehensive lens through which to understand collaboration among local governments. The framework extends theories of contracting and individual collective action problems to groups and organizations, including local governments (Carr et al. 2009; Feiock 2007, 2013). The ICA framework conceptualizes interlocal collaboration as a product of cost-benefit assessments. Legacy cities may face ICA dilemmas in policy areas from natural resource management, to air pollution control, to provision of basic services, such as sewerage and road maintenance. Local governments might often be able to achieve better outcomes through collaboration with other jurisdictions, but must overcome transaction costs.

ICA dilemmas may be mitigated using a number of strategies that require varying levels of formal action from local or higher levels of government. Among these are "self-organized" mechanisms such as informal networks, intergovernmental contracts, and partnerships that retain local autonomy, as well as imposed mechanisms that involve local government reorganization, such as creation of new special districts or consolidation of local governments (Feiock and Scholz 2010). With more complex and controversial policy problems, such as many of those faced in legacy regions, self-organizing mechanisms may be unlikely to emerge. In these cases, higher levels of government, such as states, may need to coordinate or incentivize horizontal collaboration (Feiock and Scholz 2010).

ICA theory predicts that those government actors that have cooperated previously will develop norms of reciprocity that reduce transaction costs and build social capital. Social and professional connections among decision-makers in different localities also can make these localities more likely to overcome the transaction costs associated with collaboration (Gerber and Loh 2014; Kwon and Feiock 2010). Scholars have found local governments are more likely to collaborate with one another when there is a greater availability of potential partners (Post 2002), when leaders have more trust and connections with leaders in neighboring jurisdictions (LeRoux et al. 2010; Kwon and Feiock 2010), when collaboration is sought by entrepreneurs in city governments (Zeemering 2008), and when the service to be provided is uncontroversial and associated with uniform citizen preferences (LeRoux and Carr 2010). Others have found that horizontal interlocal collaboration is driven by diffusion mechanisms among local governments who learn from one another's past collaborative agreements (Rubado 2016), by federal grant opportunities (Bickers and Stein 2004), and by heightened incentives caused by increased externalities over time (Scholz and Stiftel 2005).

While a large body of past and ongoing scholarly work investigates how and why interlocal collaboration occurs, there is less evidence about the outcomes of horizontal collaboration. Some recent research questions the feasibility and success rates of voluntary collaboration among local governments. New regionalists, such as Katz and Bradley (2013), argue that complex networks of cooperation will necessarily improve policy outcomes and enhance equity for people living in metropolitan areas. However, Kantor (2015) argues that the ability of local governments to successfully collaborate on their own has been remarkably variable, with many instances of failure. Successes have tended to occur within limited functional scopes or under exceptional circumstances. Kantor notes that state and federal intervention may be key to producing the kinds of interlocal collaboration required for improving social equity in urban areas.

In another study focused on horizontal collaboration outcomes, Hoornbeek, Beechey, and Pascarella (2015) examine eight collaborative proposals in northeast Ohio over a four-year period to identify predictors of success, measured as goal attainment. The authors find that some of the same predictors of collaboration extend to prediction of success of the collaborative endeavor. Trust among collaborating governments, as measured by previous collaborative experiences with proposal partners, was associated with goal attainment. The single most consistent predictor of collaborative success, however, is a factor that may be especially critical in legacy regions: external influences in the form of a mandate or grant from a higher level of government. In fiscally strapped localities, collaboration may be particularly challenging without external encouragement. Collaboration comes with high costs. Information must be gathered and shared, technical and administrative capacity must be present, and partners must negotiate agreements that produce equitable costs and benefits for all parties. Moreover, these transactions occur largely among municipal governments that also must compete with one another for development and taxpayers, which are often scarce in legacy regions. In legacy cities, then, successful horizontal local government collaboration may more often require inducements from state and federal government.

TYPE 3: CROSS-SECTOR COLLABORATION

A large body of literature on local collaboration for public policy and management focuses on the role of nongovernmental actors in *collaborative networks* that also include local governments, and often state and federal agencies. Scholarship has increasingly recognized that governments are not alone in the process of governance. They are networked with a multitude of diverse actors, including interest groups, nonprofit organizations, businesses, and citizens (Arnoff and McGuire 2003). The roles of nongovernmental actors in collaborative efforts operate amidst existing vertical and horizontal intergovernmental relations, creating a complex network of governance. The role of such actors is often seen as definitional to the term *collaborative governance*, a topic of intense recent study by scholars of public administration and management (Ansell and Gash 2008). However, there is disagreement about whether non-state actors, such as nonprofit organizations, must be involved in governance for it to qualify as "collaborative" (Kettl 2006; Emerson and Nabatchi 2015).

Legacy cities, as their moniker suggests, were once powerhouses of industry and culture, and still often retain the majority of their region's most important private and nonprofit institutions (see Ryberg-Webster and Tighe's introduction to this volume). This makes cross-sector collaboration an especially promising avenue for legacy cities. Moreover, other options for revitalization are unlikely to be successful, on their own, in legacy cities due to poor economic conditions. Private markets are unlikely to reinvigorate legacy cities without intervention given the cities' long trajectory of economic decline, and horizontal, self-organizing collaboration may be particularly challenging for legacy cities because their fiscal conditions make them undesirable partners (Mallach 2017). Citizens and leaders in suburban municipalities and counties often see the struggling central city as a liability and fear the effects of intermunicipal partnerships or more dramatic government reorganizations, such as city-county consolidations or mergers (Mallach and Brachman 2013). Given this more challenging path for horizontal intergovernmental collaboration, the role of the private and nonprofit sectors in collaborative policymaking and management will likely be important for legacy cities.

In a typology of collaborative management approaches, Agranoff and McGuire (2003) distinguish between two dimensions: activity (inactive to active) and strategy (passive to opportunistic). The most opportunistic and active cities are identified as *jurisdiction-based* cities. In these cities, public managers take part in a high level of strategic action with actors from various agencies, governments, and sectors for the benefit of the jurisdiction. In their case studies of six cities, Agranoff and McGuire identify Cincinnati, the only large central city in the case study, as the prototypical jurisdiction-based city. They found that Cincinnati had actively developed intergovernmental programs with both horizontal and vertical linkages with hundreds of collaborators—public, private, and nonprofit. They had strategic and project partnerships with the chamber of commerce and Downtown Cincinnati Inc. (a local development corporation) to work toward redevelopment of the central business district and entertainment core. In jurisdiction-based cities, public managers actively and strategically seek linkages for collaboration, using a flexible network of partners to match resources to needs for a host of policies and programs (Agranoff and McGuire 2003).

Cleveland, a city with a large nonprofit sector, too has engaged in cross-sector collaboration. Public-private partnerships during economic turmoil provide examples of the linkages among the city government, private businesses, nonprofits, and foundations. In a study of public-private partnerships under Mayor George Voinovich and Mayor Frank Jackson, leverage of cross-sector relationships for a common cause were found to produce transformative administrative change and allowed the city to adjust to challenges of declining population and resources while meeting demands for increased transparency and good government (Vogelsang-Coombs et al. 2016).

Federal and state governments are in a position to make cross-sector collaborations easier for cities, as these higher levels of government often set the rules of collaboration—for example, by allowing a nongovernmental organization to take a central role in managing grant projects for local communities. They can allow cities autonomy to decide how to structure federal- or state-funded projects in ways that actively engage private actors, nonprofits, and citizens. For example, due to federal deference to cities in the Empowerment Zone program, Baltimore's EZ initiative included a well-coordinated set of strategies that allowed for workforce development and effective use by local businesses of tax incentives and loan programs (Rich and Stoker 2014). There, vertical collaboration combined with cross-sector collaboration to produce the most positive outcome of the original EZ cities.

CONCLUSION

Collaborative strategies for legacy city revitalization abound, and many have been used to achieve significant success in these cities and their regions. Collaboration, in its various forms, has long been used by cities to solve problems and effectively provide services to citizens. In and around legacy cities, it is likely that the wickedness and scale of problems will more regularly demand collaborative strategies. Moreover, many legacy regions are situated in intensely fragmented settings, with dozens or even hundreds of distinct jurisdictions, creating greater likelihood of mismatch between scales of government and scales of problems.

Collaborative strategies differ in important ways, and some may be more feasible and more likely to succeed than others in various contexts. Self-organizing horizontal collaboration among local governments, for example, may exclude local governments that are in the most desperate of conditions, since these cities are likely to be unattractive partners to other local governments. Because more attractive partners in particular policy areas may be selected by their peers for collaboration that provides benefits, those involved in partnerships may continue to gain while others lose. There is potential for this sort of collaboration to exacerbate existing inequalities among local governments within regions (Feiock 2015). Given that legacy cities are already prone to intense inequality between the city and its suburbs, horizontal collaborations may require coordination by a regional institution, state, or federal government to ensure that legacy cities are not left behind.

Vertical collaboration among cities, states, and the federal government can provide for legacy city improvements, as central cities like Cincinnati engage in interactive relationships with state and federal agencies and secure state and federal funding for projects (Agranoff and McGuire 2003). While devolution, mandates, and a more coercive style of federalism have produced difficult conditions for cities, vertical collaboration provides a key opportunity for cities in desperate need of resources. States and federal agencies, too, have incentives to target their vertical collaborative efforts in ways that specifically benefit legacy cities, which are the economic drivers of their regions and likely need more help than other local governments. Metropolitan region prosperity correlates with central city prosperity (Vey 2007), suggesting that higher levels of government will benefit from stronger regional economies if legacy cities make gains.

In legacy cities, which tend to have a large share of their regions' major non-state institutions, including nonprofit organizations, foundations, and major corporations, cross-sector collaboration has particular promise in driving legacy city revival. Cities often begin seeking out cross-sector collaboration as a result of failure—when, after failed attempts, they realize they cannot solve particular problems on their own (Bryson et al. 2006). In legacy cities the opportunities to collaborate with other local governments or even state governments may be severely limited due to the disadvantaged position of the city and potential adversarial relations with state government. For example, legacy cities that struggle to find willing partners among neighboring cities and state agencies will likely benefit from seeking out nonprofit partners. Under these conditions, cross-sector partnerships may be essential to achieving goals.

REFERENCES

Ansell, Chris, and Alison Gash. 2008. "Collaborative Governance in Theory and Practice." *Journal of Public Administration Research and Theory* 18, no. 4: 543–71.

Agranoff, Robert. 2001. "Managing Within the Matrix: Do Collaborative Intergovernmental Relations Exist?" *Publius: The Journal of Federalism* 31, no. 2: 31–56.

Agranoff, Robert, and Michael McGuire. 2003. *Collaborative Public Management: New Strategies for Local Governments*. Washington, DC: Georgetown University Press.

Bickers, K. N., and R. M. Stein. 2004. "Interlocal Cooperation and the Distribution of Federal Grant Awards." *Journal of Politics* 66, no. 3: 800–822.

Brachman, Lavea. 2012. "New State and Federal Policy Agendas: Realizing the Potential of America's Legacy Cities and Their Regions." In *Rebuilding America's Legacy Cities: New Directions for the Industrial Heartland*, edited by Alan Mallach, 265–94. New York: American Assembly.

Bryson, John. M., Barbara C. Crosby, and Melissa Middleton Stone. 2006. "The Design and Implementation of Cross-Sector Collaboration: Propositions from the Literature." *Public Administrative Review* 66, no. 1: 44–55.

Carr, Jered B., Elisabeth R. Gerber, and Eric W. Lupher. 2009. "Explaining Horizontal and Vertical Cooperation on Public Services in Michigan: The Role of Local Fiscal Capacity." In *Metropolitan Affairs in Michigan: Case Studies and Best Practices*, edited by G. Sands and R. Jelier, 207–36. East Lansing: Michigan State University Press.

Chen, Yu-Che, and Kurt Thurmaier. 2009. "Interlocal Agreements as Collaborations: An Empirical Investigation of Impetuses, Norms, and Success." *American Review of Public Administration* 39, no. 5: 536–52.

Cho, Chung-Lae, and Deil S. Wright. 2001. "Managing Carrots and Sticks: Changes in State Administrators' Perceptions of Cooperative and Coercive Federalism during the 1990s." *Publius: The Journal of Federalism* 31, no. 2: 57–80.

Conlan, Timothy J. 2008. "Between a Rock and a Hard Place: The Evolution of American Federalism." In *Intergovernmental Management for the 21st Century*, edited by Timothy J. Conlan and Paul L. Posner, 26–41. Washington, DC: Brookings Institution.

Elazar, Daniel J. 1962. *The American Partnership: Intergovernmental Co-Operation in the Nineteenth-Century United States*. Chicago: University of Chicago Press.

Elazar, Daniel J. 1984. *American Federalism: A View from the States*. 3rd ed. New York: Harper and Row.

Emerson, Kirk, and Tina Nabatchi. 2015. *Collaborative Governance Regimes*. Washington, DC: Georgetown University Press.

Emerson, Kirk, Tina Nabatchi, and Stephen Balogh. 2012. "An Integrative Framework for Collaborative Governance." *Journal of Public Administration Research and Theory* 22, no. 1: 1–29.

Feiock, Richard C. 2007. "Rational Choice and Regional Governance." *Journal of Urban Affairs* 29, no. 1: 47–63.

Feiock, Richard C. 2013. "The Institutional Collective Action Framework." *Policy Studies Journal* 41, no. 3: 397–425.

Feiock, Richard C. 2014. "How Cities Collaborate While Competing in the New Economy." In *Metropolitan Resilience in a Time of Economic Turmoil*, edited by Michael A. Pagano, 89–112. Urbana: University of Illinois Press.

Feiock, Richard C., and John T. Scholz. 2010. *Self-Organizing Federalism: Collaborative Mechanisms to Mitigate Institutional Collective Action Dilemmas*. New York: Cambridge University Press.

Gerber, Elisabeth R., and Carolyn H. Loh. 2015. "Spatial Dynamics of Vertical and

Horizontal Intergovernmental Collaboration." *Journal of Urban Affairs* 37, no. 3: 270–88.

Grodzins, Morton. 1966. *The American System: A New View of Government in the United States*. Edited by Daniel J. Elazar. Chicago: Rand McNally.

Hoornbeek, John, Tegan Beechey, and Thomas Pascarella. "Fostering Government Collaboration: An Empirical Analysis of Case Studies in Ohio." *Journal of Urban Affairs* 38, no. 2: 252–79.

Kantor, Paul. 2015. "The End of American Urban Policy: Or a Beginning." *Urban Affairs Review*, December 13, 2015.

Katz, Bruce, and Jennifer Bradley. 2013. *The Metropolitan Revolution*. Washington, DC: Brookings Institution Press.

Kettl, Donald F. 2006. "Managing Boundaries in American Administration: The Collaboration Imperative." *Public Administration Review* 66, no. 1: 10–19.

Kwon, Sung-Wook, and Richard C. Feiock. 2010. "Overcoming the Barriers to Cooperation: Intergovernmental Service Agreements." *Public Administration Review* 70, no. 6: 876–84.

LeRoux, K., Paul W. Brandenburger, and Sanjay K. Pandey. 2010. "Interlocal Service Cooperation in U.S. Cities: A Social Network Explanation." *Public Administration Review* 70, no. 2: 268–78.

LeRoux, Kelly, and Jered B. Carr. 2010. "Prospects for Centralizing Services in an Urban County: Evidence from Eight Self-Organized Networks of Local Public Services." *Journal of Urban Affairs* 32, no. 4: 449–70.

Luescher, Andreas, and Sujata Shetty. 2013. "Introductory Review to the Special Issue: Shrinking Cities and Towns: Challenge and Responses." *Urban Design International* 18, no. 1: 1–5.

Mallach, Alan. 2017. "State Government and Urban Revitalization: How States Can Foster Stronger, More Inclusive Cities." Working paper WP17AM1. Cambridge, MA: Lincoln Institute of Land Policy.

Mallach, Alan, and Lavea Brachman. 2013. *Regenerating America's Legacy Cities*. Cambridge, MA: Lincoln Institute of Land Policy.

Miller, David Y. 2002. *The Regional Governing of Metropolitan America*. Boulder, CO: Westview Press.

Mullin, Megan, and Dorothy M. Daley. 2010. "Working with the State: Exploring Interagency Collaboration within a Federalist System." *Journal of Public Administration Research and Theory* 20, no. 4: 757–78.

O'Leary, Rosemary, and Nidhi Vij. 2012 "Collaborative Public Management: Where Have We Been and Where Are We Going?" *American Review of Public Administration* 42, no. 5: 507–22.

Ostrom, Elinor. 1990. *Governing the Commons: The Evolution of Institutions for Collective Action*. New York: Cambridge University Press.

Ostrom, Elinor. 2005. *Understanding Institutional Diversity*. Princeton, NJ: Princeton University Press.

Post, Stephanie S. 2002. "Local Government Cooperation: The Relationship between Metropolitan Area Government Geography and Service Provision." Paper presented at the annual meeting of the American Political Science Association, Boston, MA, August 29–September 1, 2002.

Rich, Michael J., and Robert P. Stoker. 2014. *Collaborative Governance for Urban Revitalization: Lessons from Empowerment Zones*. Ithaca, NY: Cornell University Press.

Rittel, Horst W. J., and Melvin M. Webber. 1973. "Dilemmas in a General Theory of Planning." *Policy Sciences* 4, no. 2: 155–69.

Rubado, Meghan E. 2016. "From Neighbors to Partners: The Spread of Interlocal Government Cooperation in the United States." PhD diss., Temple University.

Scholz, John T., and Bruce Stiftel, eds. 2005. *Adaptive Governance and Water Conflict: New Institutions for Collaborative Planning.* Washington, DC: Resources for the Future Press.

Vey, Jennifer. 2007. *Restoring Prosperity: The State Role in Revitalizing America's Older Industrial Cities.* Washington, DC: Brookings Institution.

Vogelsang-Coombs, Vera D., William M. Denihan, and Melanie F. Baur. 2016. "The Transformative Effects of Public-Private Partnerships in Cleveland: An Inside View of Good Government under Mayors Voinovich and Jackson." *Journal of Public and Nonprofit Affairs* 2, no. 2: 101–26.

Weir, Margaret, Jane Rongerude, and Christopher K. Ansell. 2009. "Collaboration Is Not Enough: Virtuous Cycles of Reform in Transportation Policy." *Urban Affairs Review* 44, no. 4: 455–89.

Zeemering, Eric S. 2008. "Governing Interlocal Cooperation: City Council Interests and the Implications for Public Management." *Public Administration Review* 68, no. 4: 731–41.

Zeemering, Eric S., and Juan M. Romero. 2011. "The Evolution of Sustainable Cities as a Metropolitan Policy Change." In *Networked Governance: The Future of Intergovernmental Management*, edited by Jack W. Meek and Kurt Thurmaier, 281–302. Washington, DC: CQ Press.

Zingale, Nicholas C., and Deborah Riemann. 2013. "Coping with Shrinkage in Germany and the United States: A Cross-Cultural Comparative Approach toward Sustainable Cities." *Urban Design International* 18, no. 1: 90–98.

2

The Economics of Legacy Cities

CANDI CLOUSE, JINHEE YUN, AND MERISSA C. PIAZZA

Academics and practitioners have traditionally characterized midwestern cities as ugly and dirty places reminiscent of the heyday of heavy manufacturing. Lopez (2004) recalled the city of Pittsburgh through a childhood train trip from New York to St. Louis in the late 1970s and described it as a place "polluted and stained with soot" with "a gray vista of dirty brick buildings" with "the faint smell sulfur" (10). This pollution, like so many other indicators of a growing economy, was one outward symbol of working industry and regional prosperity when Pittsburgh was the epicenter of US steel manufacturing. In the Pittsburgh case, big steel companies and their high-wage manufacturing jobs both died, and since the economy was not diversified in other industries, so too did the regional economy (Lopez 2004). The factory smoke that once covered entire cities had mostly abated, and factories that used to underpin regional prosperity had rusted. The cities are now filled with vacant shells of industry and housing. These cities were often referred to with the unfortunate moniker *Rust Belt* until the current literature adopted the term *legacy cities* in 2011.[1]

The economic changes that have happened in midwestern economies from the 1980s to the 2000s partially resulted from changes in trade policies, offshoring, and a decrease in defense spending that caused structural economic changes in the US economy and deindustrialization (Bartik, 1990; Malecki, 1984; Markusen and Carlson, 1989). In the early part of the 2000s, the economic prospects of legacy cities were not bright. These cities that were once industrial powerhouses across the Midwest and Northeast faced drastic declines in manufacturing, coupled with suburban flight and southward migration leading to biting population losses. The subprime lending boom and ensuing foreclosure crisis, compounded the crises these cities were already experiencing because of manufacturing decline and population loss. Following the great recession, bankruptcy in the automotive industry, the credit crunch, and an overall decrease in consumer spending have continued to hamper conditions in more recent years. These economic and population declines have created further problems related to the infrastructure and built environment in legacy cities as property abandonment, lower municipal revenues, and an infrastructure that is too large for the remaining residents impede progress (Grodach and Ehrenfeucht 2016).

Many, however, view legacy cities as not a lost cause, but places of considerable opportunity. These cities are now ground zero for individuals, nonprofits, the public sector, and corporations to try new ideas and policies to remake urbanism in these new post–industrial cities. Mallach (2011) notes that 15 percent of the US population lives in legacy cities throughout Pennsylvania, Ohio, Michigan, and New York. He argues that these cities have inherent value, mostly from their still-intact historical buildings, affordability, access to transit hubs, and educational institutions, all of which can be tapped into for future growth and prosperity.

In this chapter we examine the economics of legacy cities and explore their paths forward. We discuss this issue in two major sections. First, we examine the economics of legacy cities through a lens of population decline, employment and output loss, and fiscal factors that plague these cities' growth. Second, we outline new and innovative initiatives legacy cities have been conducting and investing in to find a new path for them in the twenty-first century.

DEMONSTRATED DOWNTURN

Mallach and Brachman (2013) describe archetypical legacy cities such as Detroit, Pittsburgh, Buffalo, Cleveland, St. Louis, and Newark as cities that shared the glory of the United States' manufacturing history together. These cities led global industries and provided the nation's working class, including immigrants, upward social mobility until the 1970s and 1980s. At their zenith, these cities symbolized social change and prosperity. However, as legacy cities faced sharp decreases in population, manufacturing, employment, and gross domestic product, their previous glory faded. In 1970 the Cleveland Metropolitan Statistical Area (MSA) had a population of 2.3 million people. That number decreased 10 percent by the 2010 Census to just under 2.1 million, while the nation saw a 52 percent population increase. The city of Cleveland proper had just under 400,000 residents in 2010, down from a record high in 1950 of 914,000 (US Census 2018).

Between 1980 and 1990 Pittsburgh lost 39 percent of its manufacturing

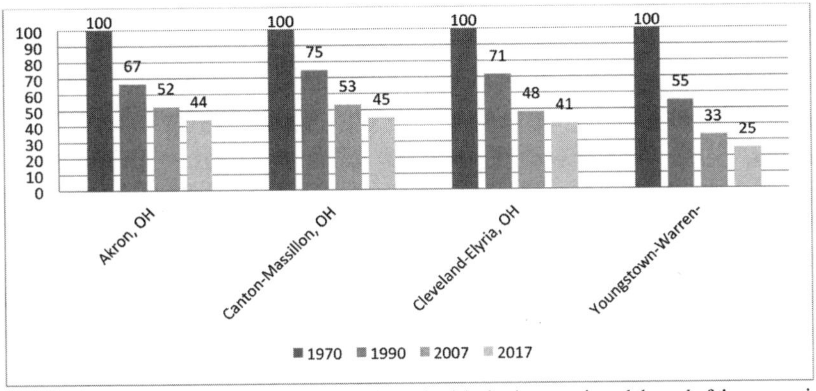

Source: Moody's Analytics. Note: 2007 marks the peak of the business cycle and the end of the economic expansion (National Bureau of Economic Research, 2010).

FIGURE 2.1: Manufacturing employment index in the dour MSAs, 1970–2017 (1970 = 100 percent)

jobs (roughly 83,000 jobs), while the United States lost 6 percent in manufacturing employment. Northeast Ohio—which contains eighteen counties and is home to four metropolitan statistical areas that were once manufacturing hubs—lost 18.7 percent of its manufacturing jobs between 1980 and 1990 as well, and one of the four MSAs, Youngstown, lost 34 percent of its manufacturing employment.[2]

In northeast Ohio total employment only grew by 19 percent between 1970 and 2017, while in the United States it grew by 96 percent. In that same time, however, manufacturing jobs decreased 27 percent nationally and 56 percent in northeast Ohio (341,180 manufacturing jobs were lost in northeast Ohio). Figure 2.1 shows a manufacturing employment index for the Akron MSA, Canton MSA, Cleveland MSA, and Youngstown MSA. The base year of the index is 1970, shown at a base rate of 100. All four MSAs in northeast Ohio experienced manufacturing job decline of at least 55 percent between 1970 and 2017; the Youngstown MSA saw the largest percent of employment decline with -75 percent, and the Cleveland MSA lost the largest absolute number of jobs (176,850 jobs, or a loss of 59 percent) from 1970 to 2017. The Youngstown MSA experienced a huge decrease in manufacturing jobs at -45 percent between 1970 and 1990. Youngstown is still well-known for Black Monday, which occurred on September 19, 1977, when the Youngstown Sheet and Tube Company was closed (Mallach and Brachman 2013).

Examining how local economies compared to the national economy can help explore local competitive advantage. Location quotients are a tool used for analyzing industry concentration to identify specializations in the local economy, comparing the local share of an industry to the national share of the same industry.[3] The gross metropolitan product (GMP) from 1978 indicates that the Canton and Youngstown MSAs both had location quotients of 2.1 in manufacturing, the Akron MSA had a manufacturing location quotient of 1.8, while the Cleveland MSA's was 1.6 (figure 2.2).[4] By 2017 the Canton MSA declined to 1.9, indicating a decline in local competitive advantage in manufacturing compared to the nation. The Youngstown MSA plummeted to 1.8, and the Akron and Cleveland MSAs to 1.3, showing the loss of industrial might in northeast Ohio relative to the United States.

Furthermore, in terms of gross domestic product (GDP), the United States saw a total increase of 120 percent between 1978 and 2017, while northeast Ohio saw only a 25 percent increase. In the manufacturing industries, the United States experienced an 11 percent growth between 1978 and 2017, while northeast Ohio's manufacturing industries declined 45 percent. Average wages also have not rebounded. Northeast Ohio's total average wage was 110 percent of the average US wage in 1975. While the United States experienced a 25 percent growth rate in total average wages between 1975 and 2017, northeast Ohio had just a 1 percent increase. The Akron and Cleveland MSAs saw 3 percent growth in total average wage, the Canton MSA experienced an 8 percent decline, and the Youngstown MSA a 15 percent decline. This shows that the problem facing legacy cities is not only a shortage of jobs but also a shortage of former high-wage jobs.

There has been considerable research into why regions develop differently from each other. Regions develop a distinctive mix of industrial structures as they mature and age. Most of the time, the market works at balancing the mix of industries—through the exit of the old and entrance of the new in the process of creative destruction (Schumpeter 1942). Sometimes, however, the market fails, and old firms stay in the market longer than expected, which can change the industrial mix. Booth (1986) analyzed how certain regions experienced uneven economic growth and found that in older industrial regions, there was not an adequate mix of new to old firms. He found that regions were facing the inherited costs of many firms in the later stage of their life cycle.[5] In the end, Booth showed older firms are mature and have achieved economies of scale, and instead of innovating with new products, they instead became managerial epicenters. These firms then attract and promote inefficiencies, which is extremely unhealthy for the business and the larger economy of the city, especially in older industrial regions. Legacy cities, in particular, suffer from this trend. Austrian and Piazza (2014) show that in the Cleveland region, there was a disproportionate amount of large manufacturers, which created a risk-adverse culture and discouraged entrepreneurship.

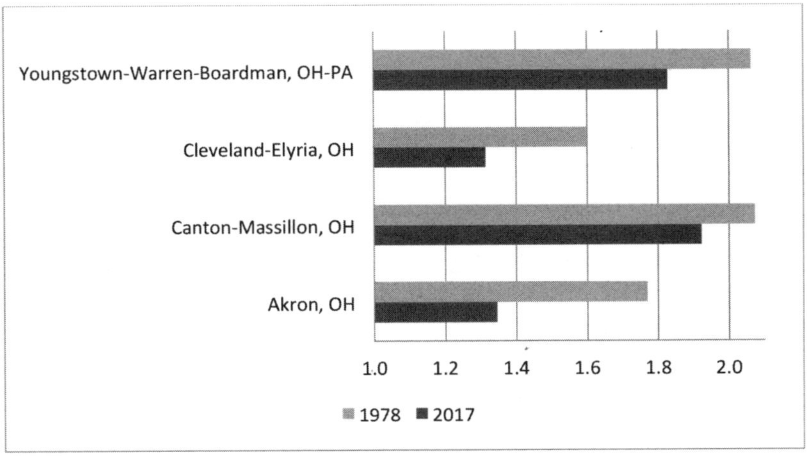

FIGURE 2.2: Location quotient of manufacturing industry in the four MSAs in 1978 and 2017

The decline in these cities was not only the effect of regional deindustrialization. Macroeconomic changes including advances in technology, globalization, and ever-changing regional economic development incentives also affected the job losses (Bowen and Song 2014; Kodras 1997; Ploger 2012). These patterns occur over the course of several business cycles, more along the lines of what Kondratieff (1935) would consider a long wage (approximately sixty years). Also, many economies become path dependent upon these industries (Martin and Sunley 2006). Path dependence can take one of three forms: as a technological "lock-in," whereby a firm or region is set in a particular technology trajectory (even if the alternative is more efficient), as dynamic increasing returns and externalities always produce positive feedback loops, and as "institutional hysteresis," where the institution is ground to a halt because of its legacy (400).[6] The major key that Martin and Sunley (2006) point to is that to break free from this path dependence, "major and radical change must always originate from outside" (407).[7]

Legacy cities have been plagued not only by this demonstrated population and economic decline but also a poor reputation. For decades, media coverage of Cleveland as the "mistake on the lake" or Detroit as a "war zone" (Clouse 2017b) have created a stereotype that the quality of life in the Rust Belt must be terrible. However, a snapshot of the midwestern economy according to Austrian and Piazza (2014) tells a different story—large manufacturing companies provided jobs when social norms did not encourage individuals to pursue entrepreneurial abilities. Over the years, with the decline in manufacturing, many companies shut their doors, and the economy declined while maintaining the same culture of working for a large firm.

The midwestern experience is much different than that of the evolution of the Silicon Valley economy and its culture of a network of smaller firms collocated along a corridor (Saxenian 1994).

At this point the economic markets in legacy cities are operating inefficiently because they are fixed within their path dependency either through their technological lock-in or their institutional legacy, and their economy needs an external shock to counter the status quo. Their reputation as communities fraught with social, environmental, and economic problems has not helped their recovery. Since the market has failed to correct itself, it needs external government intervention to shock the system.

IMMINENT SHIFT: ECONOMIC POLICY INTERVENTIONS TO REVITALIZE LEGACY CITIES

In the 1990s Cleveland embarked on a massive downtown revitalization campaign, building the Rock and Roll Hall of Fame and Museum, the Great Lakes Science Center, new baseball and basketball stadiums, new shopping malls, and improved streetscaping and signage. Despite these significant investments, the local economy was still in crisis (Katz and Bradley 2013). Manufacturing and overall employment numbers were even lower than the national average, and industry mergers and relocations worsened the landscape. Cleveland lacked the entrepreneurial infrastructure to absorb knowledge spillovers and therefore lagged larger markets (Mayer 2011). City and regional anchor institutions were also focused inward, rather than toward their neighborhoods and cities (Katz and Bradley 2013). And while these large-scale infrastructure improvements and investments may lead to an improved reputation and increased tourism dollars, these are not enough to dramatically transform an area (Mallach and Brachman 2013). That was the case in Cleveland. Places need to find ways to sustain and grow, while also preventing unmanaged change or further decay (Kotler, Haider, and Rein 1993). Legacy cities have been working on writing their next chapters for decades. Some argue that cities must hit rock bottom before embarking on any real change (Hollingsworth and Goebel 2017); however, that approach ignores the deep costs of disinvestment and decline to neighborhoods, communities, and individuals. Thus, there is a need to focus on more resilient strategies to stall, and hopefully reverse, some of the decline (Brachman and Hollingsworth 2016).

Legacy cities need to build a framework for change that focuses on elements of both shrinkage and growth (Grodach and Ehrenfeucht 2016; Mallach 2012). Popular strategies emphasize rebuilding people-oriented places to attract millennials and other residents to central cities (Grodach and Ehrenfeucht 2016; Mallach and Brachman 2013). Legacy cities have assets stemming from their former industrial might that can be capitalized upon for the future including historic downtowns and neighborhoods, transportation networks, cultural amenities, and universities and medical centers (Mallach and Brachman 2013). These amenities are an important draw for people moving into downtowns and central cities.

Scholars have suggested numerous areas to focus on when regenerating legacy cities. These can be distilled into five major themes:

1. Creating a shared vision by building civic capacity with government, nonprofits, and philanthropy
2. Leveraging current government capacity and forging new opportunities
3. Strengthening local businesses and entrepreneurs
4. Stabilizing neighborhoods—especially downtowns
5. Expanding opportunities for all workers—especially low-income and minority residents (Brachman and Hollingswoth 2016; Hollingsworth and Goebel 2017; Mallach 2012; Mallach and Brachman 2013; McGahey 2014; Ploger 2012)

These components have the potential to generate jobs and wealth in legacy cities and, ultimately, stimulate their long-term revitalization.

SHARED VISION

The first item that must be tackled is creating a shared vision for what the future holds for a legacy region. This shared vision begins by looking honestly at the conditions in the city and suburbs, comparing it to other places, and focusing on building up local strengths and capacities (Kotler et al. 1993; Mallach and Brachman 2013; McGahey 2014; Ploger 2012). This process must be a collaborative effort including all relevant stakeholders—city leaders, government, institutional, nonprofit, business representatives (both large and small), and citizens and employees. Local and regional cooperation is paramount.

Key challenges to revitalizing legacy cities include improving the nature and image of the entire place's history and culture as well as finding a new place in the global economic market (Jensen 2005). Legacy cities must find new ways of doing business as well as organizing institutions, policy, and networks (Jensen 2005). This can be accomplished by leveraging current capacity and creating new opportunities for business growth and development. As unemployment in Cleveland is above the national average, locals are focusing on how to create more jobs and attract new workers (Bureau of Labor Statistics 2018). The region's Fund for Our Economic Future (FFEF 2018) notes, "we must understand the issues holding us back from inclusive transformation and align our regional priorities accordingly." Their plan focuses on three initiatives all around employment—job creation, job preparation, and job access—in the hopes that these will lead to a stronger and sustainable economy for Greater Cleveland.

Positive promotion showcasing new assets can change perceptions of a place and serve to pique new interest about places that people may have been indifferent to or had a negative opinion of previously. However, changing the way a place is seen does not happen suddenly. Pittsburgh, for example, has spent decades honing its image and attempting to put its negative reputation behind it—and it has found substantial success. Pittsburgh's previously dominant steel industry had all but died by 1983, and the city's transformation did not begin in earnest until 2005. Pittsburgh made major strides to improve their downtown and focused on the great contributions of their institutions of higher learning. Dewitt Peart of the Allegheny Conference in Pittsburgh noted, "A lot of Pittsburgh's transformation was very place-based and focused—improving the appearance and the land use" (personal communication, September 19, 2011). Visible improvements are essential to improve a place's image as they show growth and development, but they alone cannot change a city's future.

LEVERAGING CAPACITY

Legacy cities must build their capacity and find new ways of doing business. This can be accomplished through building stronger local governance capacity and partnerships, increasing ties between cities and their regions, and examining and potentially revamping local, state, and federal policies (Mallach and Brachman 2013). In Cleveland the Department of Economic Development adopted the moniker "built by industry, inspired by innovation" as their mantra—even renaming the department's web address www.rethinkcleveland.org as they look to expand their capacity to serve current businesses and start-ups (Cleveland 2018). The regional economic development organization, Team NEO, sets the table for conversations across northeast Ohio where "challenges regarding economic competitiveness are identified, prioritized and advanced" (Team NEO 2018).

ENTREPRENEURSHIP

Levine (2002) makes a point that places should not bet on the next big "silicon chip" but instead build on their existing businesses; noting that places cannot afford to lose what they have just to chase the next big thing. Entrepreneurship and innovation are also required for revitalizing regions as they are correlated with economic growth (Austrian and Piazza 2014). A region needs to innovate and create a vibrant and inclusive economic development ecosystem; growing regions abound with research and development, patents, start-ups, and venture capital. JumpStart Inc. in Cleveland, an economic development intermediary, has worked for sixteen years to develop the local entrepreneurial ecosystem and has only recently started seeing large-scale returns to the region regarding employment and wealth (Clouse 2017a).

Using a human capital approach to frame economic development can encourage entrepreneurship and an entrepreneurial mind-set (Davis, Hall, and Mayer 2016; Rauch and Frese 2007). The encouragement of entrepreneurship can teach individuals to be more tolerant of risk, an agent of economic change, increasing prosperity and productivity. This strategy is a proactive economic development approach that examines the entire economy, rather than dictating winners and losers. This strategy, however, is a risky one for cities to pursue since their main determinates of success are job creation and high income in the short run. The human-capital strategy is a long-term growth strategy that looks to create more entrepreneurs, increase the knowledge stock of the population, and increase prosperity overall. In the end, teaching individuals to become entrepreneurs and to foster an entrepreneurial mind-set is key to creating more firms, in the hope that these will remain in the region and become high growth.

STABILIZING NEIGHBORHOODS

Cities should build and remake places where public life can exist, including public spaces such as parks and lakefronts (Grodach and Ehrenfeucht 2016). Welcoming people, coupled with historic and interesting architecture, were rated among the best assets of downtowns (Robertson 1999). Historic downtowns are assets worthy of investment and can be restored to the center of economic activity (Mallach and Brachman 2013). Attention should also be focused on creating neighborhoods of choice for residents by investing in repurposing vacant land and managing abandoned property that is scattered throughout cities (Mallach and Brachman 2013; Grodach and Ehrenfeucht 2016). This is particularly vital in a legacy context.

The overall vision for legacy cities must work for all constituents and sometimes the hardest to help are the ones that need it the most. In 2005 the Cleveland Foundation embarked on a strategic process seeking to connect the poverty-stricken neighborhoods surrounding the Greater University Circle to the three large anchor institutions in their midst: Case Western Reserve University, the Cleveland Clinic, and University Hospitals Health System. These three institutions employ more than sixty thousand people and spend almost three billion dollars annually on goods and services (Hexter, Clouse, Downer, and Robinson 2017; Wright, Hexter, and Downer 2016). The goal of what is now known as the Greater University Circle Initiative is to harness the power of the anchor institutions to further economic development in the neighborhoods and to improve the lives of those living there.

The anchor institutions in University Circle focus on one or more of the following four basic pillars: (1) buying from local businesses and encouraging local business development; (2) hiring residents and helping them succeed and grow in their positions; (3) encouraging staff to live in the neighborhoods and supporting new housing development; and (4) using their investment portfolio to create positive change in the neighborhoods (CSU n.d.; Hexter et al. 2017). In Cleveland national attention has focused on projects like the worker-owned business model, the Evergreen Cooperatives, which both hired locals and located their businesses in the neighborhood. The anchors have not only supported the creation of the cooperatives but also awarded significant contracts to them.

In Toledo, Ohio, ProMedica is not only working on downtown development but also on making financial investments that benefit the neighborhoods instead of just their bottom line. These "impact investments" are made in the hopes of generating long-term social, environmental, and financial returns (Oostra 2018). They have partnered with the Local Initiative Support Corporation (LISC) to create a community development financial institution (CDFI) valued at $25 million, which will assemble a loan pool supporting and minority- and women-owned business in distressed communities (Oostra 2018). ProMedica opened a grocery store in a food desert and purchased a failing downtown hotel and flipped it to an investor who was able to renovate it, creating an attractive building employing more than one hundred residents (Oostra 2018). By switching their thinking from only health-related outcomes, ProMedica has made significant improvements in their neighborhood for their neighbors.

RACIAL EQUITY

Initiatives like the Greater University Circle Initiative encourage anchor institutions to take a stake in the future of their surroundings, which are often places that have been historically neglected by these very institutions. Declining neighborhoods are not currently suited for business, employees, clients, or residents, so investing in a rebirth of these areas makes smart business sense for anchoring institutions. However, current residents must be able to enjoy the benefits associated with redevelopment without being marginalized or displaced. (Oostra 2018; Sladek 2017). Traditionally, healthcare institutions tend to focus only on clinical and financial bottom lines (Oostra 2018). Nevertheless, they are starting to see the value in broadening their scope of services to foster positive change in their neighborhood.

Equity and inclusion must play a significant part in the redevelopment of low-income neighborhoods as racist economic conditions including education, employment, criminal justice, real estate practices, and the foreclosure crisis played a major role in the creation of them (Alexander 2010; CSU n.d.; Grodach and Ehrenfeucht 2016; Tighe and Ganning 2016). In Cleveland racial equity is being added to the Greater University Circle Initiative to keep these issues at the forefront of the work and to recognize the systematic barriers that have been built isolating the predominately African American neighborhoods from the economic powerhouses of the anchor institutions.

Ultimately, there is an uphill economic battle facing legacy cities as they strive to return to their former prosperity and stature in the economic market. Public policies have sought to rebuild and harness the capacity of these areas to foster growth and prosperity. The five themes discussed in this chapter suggest a way of moving forward in an equitable and inclusive manner. However, change does not happen instantly. A shared vision must be anchored in a collaborative process to include all stakeholders in the region, and that is neither quick nor easy. However, legacy cities have a rich history, high-capacity infrastructure, and engaged anchor institutions that can be used to leverage future growth. Nevertheless, they must use all the policy and innovation tools available to them to regain the prosperity they once enjoyed in the current global economic environment.

NOTES

1. This name was coined at the 110th American Assembly of Columbia University, a gathering of eighty experts, which took place in Detroit (Mallach 2011). The goal of this assembly was to discuss economic issues that face these cities like deindustrialization and how to move forward on economic, social, and environmental development strategies in places like Cleveland, Detroit, St. Louis, and Pittsburgh (Dymi 2011). The focus was turning these industrial "legacies" into what they called "assets to the nation" (Mallach 2011).

2. The four Metropolitan Statistical Areas (MSAs) are as follows: the Akron MSA, Canton-Massillon MSA, Cleveland-Elyria MSA, and Youngstown-Warren-Boardman MSA.

3. Location Quotient = (Regional Manufacturing Employment/Regional Total Employment) / (National Manufacturing Employment/National Total Employment). A level above 1.2 indicates a regional specialization.

4. The manufacturing sector consists of three major industry classification codes, or NAICS codes. Manufacturing is comprised of NAICS 31–33, and these NAICS codes are made up of several subsectors that engage in the mechanical, physical, or chemical transformation of materials, substance, or components into new products. See www.bls.gov/iag/tgs/iag31–33.htm#about.

5. Remembering Markusen's (1985) profit cycle stages, having a large portion of a region's firms in normal plus (oligopolies boost profits) or normal minus (excessive

competition crowds out profits) is essentially having most of their firms on death's door.

6. These are positive feedback loops that are coming from inside the organization.

7. Recently, Martin (2010) discussed that some industries may be able unlock themselves from an industrial path endogenously, because of "onset of agglomeration diseconomies," "exhaustion of innovation" and/or switch industries (6–7). These are benefits from the government intervening in the market from other market failures and therefore, it would not be unlocking, but instead it would be taking advantage of the economy.

REFERENCES

Alexander, M. 2010. *The New Jim Crow*. New York: New Press.

American Assembly, and the J. Max Bond Center on Design for the Just City. 2013. "What Are Legacy Cities?" http://legacycities.americanassembly.org/what-are-legacy-cities.

Austrian, Z., and M. C. Piazza. 2014. "Barriers and Opportunities for Entrepreneurship in Older Industrial Regions." In *The Road through the Rust Belt*, edited by W. Bowen, 215–43. Kalamazoo, MI: W. E. Upjohn Institute for Employment Research.

Bartik, T. 1985. "Business Location Decisions in the United States: Estimates of the Effects of Unionization, Taxes, and Other Characteristics of States." *Journal of Business and Economic Studies* 3, no. 1: 14–22.

Bartik, T. 1990. "The Market Failure Approach to Regional Economic Development Policy." *Economic Development Quarterly* 4, no. 4: 361–70.

Bluestone, B., and B. Harrison. 1982. *The Deindustrialization of America*. New York: Basic Books.

Bowen, W. M., and C. Song. 2014. "Reasons for Misgivings about Local Economic Development Initiatives." In *The Road through the Rust Belt*, edited by W. Bowen, 245–76. Kalamazoo, MI: W. E. Upjohn Institute for Employment Research.

Brachman, L., and T. Hollingsworth. 2016. *Revitalizing America's Small and Medium-Sized Legacy Cities*. Boston Fed. https://www.bostonfed.org/publications/communities-and-banking/2016/summer/revitalizing-americas-small-and-medium-sized-legacy-cities.aspx.

Booth, D. E. 1986. "Long Wages of Uneven Regional Growth." *Southern Economic Journal* 53, no. 2: 448–60.

Bureau of Labor Statistics. 2018. https://www.bls.gov/.

City of Cleveland. 2018. "Economic Development." http://www.rethinkcleveland.org/home.aspx

Cleveland State University, Anchor Institution (CSU). n.d. http://www.csuohio.edu/engagement/anchor-institution

Clouse, C. 2017a. "2016 Economic Impact of Companies Funded and/or Assisted by the Northeast Ohio Entrepreneurial Service Provider Program." https://engagedscholarship.csuohio.edu/urban_facpub/1501/.

Clouse, C. 2017b. "The Role of Place Image in the Business Site Selection Decision." PhD diss., Cleveland State University.

Comunian, R., C. Chapain, and N. Clifton. 2010. "Location, Location, Location: Exploring the Complex Relationship between Creative Industries and Place. *Creative Industries Journal* 3, no. 1: 5–10.

Davis, M. H., J. A. Hall, and P. S. Mayer. 2016. "Developing a New Measure of Entrepreneurial Mindset: Reliability, Validity, and Implications for Practitioners." *Consulting Psychology Journal: Practice and Research* 68, no. 1: 21–48.

Dymi, A. 2011. "Municipalities Join Experts to Save 'Legacy Cities.'" *Mortgage Servicing News*, August 2011, 13–16.

Fund for Our Economic Future (FFEF). 2018. "Two Tomorrows." http://www.the2tomorrows.org/.

Grodach, C., and R. Ehrenfeucht. 2016. *Urban Revitalization: Remaking Cities in a Changing World*. London: Routledge.

Hexter, K., C. Clouse, N. Downer, and L. Robinson. 2017. "Greater University Circle Initiative: Year 6 Evaluation Report." https://engagedscholarship.csuohio.edu/urban_facpub/1497/.

Hollingsworth, T., and A. Goebel. 2017. "Revitalizing America's Smaller Legacy Cities." https://www.lincolninst.edu/sites/default/files/pubfiles/revitalizing-smaller-legacy-cities-lla170702.pdf.

Katz, B., and J. Bradley. 2013. *The Metropolitan Revolution: How Cities and Metros Are Fixing Our Broken Politics and Fragile Economy*. Washington, DC: Brookings Institution.

Jenson, O. B. 2005. "Branding the Contemporary City: Urban Branding as Regional Growth Agenda?" Paper presented at the Regional Studies Association Conference, Aalborg, Denmark, May 28–31, 2005.

Kodras, J. E. 1997. "The Changing Map of American Poverty in an Era of Economic Restructuring and Political Realignment." *Economic Geography* 73, no. 1: 67–93.

Kondratieff, N., and W. F. Stolper. 1935. "The Long Waves in Economic Life." *Review of Economic Statistics* 17, no. 6: 105–15.

Kotler, P., D. Haider, and I. Rein. 1993. *Marketing Places: Attracting Investment, Industry, and Tourism to Cities, States, and Nations*. New York: Free Press.

Levine, T. M. 2002. "Six Revolutions in Economic Development Marketing." *Economic Development Journal* 1, no. 1 (Winter): 5–12.

Lopez, S. H. 2004. *Reorganizing the Rust Belt: An Inside Study of the American Labor Movement*. Berkeley: University of California Press.

Malecki, E. 1984. "High Technology and Local Economic Development." *Journal of the American Planning Association* 50, no. 3: 262–69.

Mallach, A., ed. 2011. *Reinventing America's Legacy Cities: Strategies for Cities Losing Population*. New York: American Assembly.

Mallach, A., ed. 2012. *Rebuilding America's Legacy Cities: New Directions for the Industrial Heartland*. New York: American Assembly.

Mallach, A., and L. Brachman. 2013. *Regenerating America's Legacy Cities*. Cambridge, MA: Lincoln Institute of Land Policy.

Markusen, A., and V. Carlson. 1989. *Deindustrialization in the American Midwest: Causes and Responses*. In *Deindustrialization and Economic Transformation*, edited by L. Rodwin and H. Sazanami, 29–59. Winchester, MA: Unwin Hyman.

Markusen, A. 1985. *Profit Cycles, Oligopoly, and Regional Development*. Cambridge, MA: MIT Press.

Martin, R. 2010. "Rethinking Regional Path Dependence: Beyond Lock-In to Evolution." *Economic Geography* 86, no. 1: 1–28.

Martin, R., and P. Sunley. 2006. "Path Dependence and Regional Economic Evolution." *Journal of Economic Geography* 6, no. 4: 395–437.

Mayer, H. 2011. *Entrepreneurship and Innovation in Second-Tier Regions*. Cheltenham, UK: Edward Elgar Publishing.

McGahey, R. 2014. *Regional Economic Development in Theory and Practice*. Washington, DC: Brookings Institution.

National Bureau of Economic Research (NBER). 2010. "Determination of the December 2007 Peak in Economic Activity." http://www.nber.org/cycles/dec2008.pdf.

Oostra, R. 2018. *Embracing an Anchor Mission: ProMedica's All-In Strategy*. Washington, DC: Democracy Collaborative.

Peirce, N. 2012. "'Rustbelt' to 'Legacy': Rethinking Old Cities' Potential." *Nation's Cities Weekly*, February 6, 2012, 7.

Ploger, J. 2012. "Learning from Abroad: Lessons from European Shrinking Cities." In *Rebuilding America's Legacy Cities: New Directions for the Industrial Heartland*, edited by A. Mallach, 295–322. New York: American Assembly.

Rauch, A., and M. Frese. 2007. "Let's Put the Person Back into Entrepreneurship Research: A Meta-Analysis on the Relationship between Business Owners' Personality Traits, Business Creation, and Success. *European Journal of Work and Organizational Psychology* 16, no. 4: 353–85.

Robertson, K. A. 1999. "Can Small-City Downtowns Remain Viable? A National Study of Development Issues and Strategies." *Journal of the American Planning Association* 65, no. 3: 270–83.

Saxenian, A. 1994. *Regional Advantage: Culture and Competition in Silicon Valley and Route 128*. Cambridge, MA: Harvard University Press.

Schumpeter, J. A. 1942. *Capitalism, Socialism, and Democracy*. New York: Harper & Brothers.

Short, J. R., L. M. Benton, W. B. Luce, and J. Walton. 1993. "Reconstructing the Image of an Industrial City." *Annals of the Association of American Geographers* 83, no. 2: 207–24.

Sladek, E. 2017. *Higher Education's Anchor Mission: Measuring Place-Based Engagement*. Washington, DC: Democracy Collaborative.

Team NEO. 2018. "About Us." https://www.clevelandplus.com/teamneo/about-us/.

Tighe, J. R., and J. Ganning. 2016. "Do Shrinking Cities Allow Redevelopment without Displacement? An Analysis of Affordability Based on Housing and Transportation Costs for Redeveloping, Declining, and Stable Neighborhoods." *Housing Policy Debate* 26, no. 4/5: 1–16.

US Census Bureau. 2018. "Population American Fact Finder." https://factfinder.census.gov/faces/tableservices/jsf/pages/productview.xhtml?pid=DEC_10_SF1_P1&prodType=table.

Wright, W., K. W. Hexter, and N. Downer. 2016. *Cleveland's Greater University Circle Initiative: An Anchor-Based Strategy for Change*. Washington, DC: Democracy Collaborative.

3

Fiscal Conditions of the Largest Legacy Cities

TATYANA GUZMAN

A study of fiscal conditions sheds a light on what services governments provide, which financial, human, and capital resources are appropriated to provide these services, and how well these resources are utilized. This knowledge informs residents, policymakers, and researchers about what government does and how well it functions. It can tell which practices are successful and can be employed in future and what went wrong and should be changed or avoided.

Fiscal study of legacy cities is the story of demographic, economic, political, and financial hurdles and successes that these cities have endured. Legacy cities, once highly prosperous industrial centers, have in the past several decades lost significant portions of their industrial bases, resulting in lost jobs and decreasing populations and, consequently, the tax base. Some of these cities, like Minneapolis, Minnesota, or Cincinnati, Ohio, have done remarkably well despite all the struggles, while others, such as Detroit and Flint, Michigan, have found themselves in a rather deplorable condition when the cities were unable to provide even basic services or pay their employees. What made some legacy cities prosper and brought others to crisis? What are the main sources of revenue that legacy cities rely on and how and why are they different from non-legacy cities? What is the credit quality of legacy compared to non-legacy cities and why are there differences? How do these differences, or lack thereof, affect legacy cities' fiscal conditions? What are the lessons learned and what can policymakers do to improve the legacy cities' fiscal situation? These are some of the major questions addressed in this chapter.

This chapter provides a descriptive, longitudinal analysis of the financial situation of the twenty-eight most largely populated central US legacy cities representing seventeen states over the twenty-year span from 1995 to 2014. During the studied years, these cities experienced a major population and financial decline. This is also the period of at least two national economic cycles, including a booming national economy in the late 1990s, mid-2000s, and early 2010s, and recessions in the early and late 2000s. This chapter analyzes the main sources and trends in revenues, expenditures, debt, and creditworthiness of the twenty-eight cities and discusses challenges of the most fiscally disadvantaged cities in the sample, including the causes of their misfortunes and the actions taken to stabilize the situation.

DATA

The analysis in this chapter is based on forty-eight cities identified as legacy by the Legacy Cities Partnership (LCP). The data mainly come from the Lincoln Land Institute's Fiscally Standardized Cities (FiSC) database. Credit ratings are from the Moody's and Standard and Poor's (S&P's) credit ratings agencies (ratings are generally not available before 1995). Other miscellaneous financial data come from cities' comprehensive annual financial reports (CAFRs). Since the FiSC collects data only for the largest central US cities, only twenty-nine of the LCP-defined legacy cities are included. Twenty-eight of these twenty-nine cities are included in this analysis.[1] The excluded city is Washington, DC. The nation's capital is a home to the federal government and the only city in the country that is not a part of any state. As such, compared to any other US cities, Washington, DC, receives a very high share of revenues directly from the federal government. It also provides both state- and city-level services and, consequently, incurs both state- and city-level expenses. The uniqueness of this city in these terms makes it problematic to include it in this sample—thus it has been removed.

The FiSC was selected because it allows a comparative fiscal analysis of multiple cities. The fiscal structure of US cities is very different, and it is hard to disentangle the true expenditures and revenues for each city and compare them between each other since some city services may be provided by a state (pension plans are often managed by the states), county (like libraries), or the neighboring cities (cities may share a school district, fire, or police departments). The FiSC attempts to address these challenges by adding revenues and expenditures not only incurred by the cities themselves but also an "appropriate share from overlying counties, school districts, and special districts" (FiSC). Unfortunately, the FiSC does not include New Jersey or Hawaii due to technical issues with fiscal estimates in these states. Therefore, Newark, New Jersey—a highly populous legacy city—is not included in the analysis.

Figures 3.1 and 3.2 and table 3.1 provide mean estimates of the main fiscal variables analyzed in this chapter for 28 legacy and 121 non-legacy cities in the FiSC sample (Washington, DC, is excluded from the list). The table additionally offers the t-statistics of the mean differences between legacy and non-legacy cities.

LEGACY CITIES' EXPENDITURES

For thirty-seven years, from 1977 to 2014, currently included in the FiSC, legacy cities lost on average 20 percent of their population, while non-legacy cities gained over 41 percent. The population decline slowed down in the 2000s, but remains very problematic for legacy cities. Cities built to accommodate a much higher number of residents, commuters, and businesses spend a lot to support larger-than-needed infrastructure, fire and police protection, and other basic services. Abandoned and underutilized properties, and overbuilt infrastructure not only generate little to no property tax revenues—they are also costly to maintain or demolish (see chapter 5). On average per capita expenditures in legacy cities were about $954 higher than in non-legacy cities during the considered twenty years (table 3.1). From 1977 on the expenditures in these twenty-eight legacy cities grew by 55 percent, to $6,490 in 2014. In 121 non-legacy cities, the expenditures increased by 48 percent over the same time, to $5,792 in 2014. Expectedly, legacy and non-legacy cities' expenses were higher during the recession of 2008–2009, but evened out to their pre-recession level around 2013 (FiSC).

The main local government expenditures, both operating and capital, in the United States are by far the expenses for elementary and secondary education (US Census Bureau 2014; FiSC; Mikesell 2013). Legacy cities are no exemption from the rule. On average, these cities spent almost $2,000 per capita, or over a third of all general expenditures, in this category alone during the considered twenty-year span (FiSC). The other spending in legacy cities is generally similar to those in non-legacy cities. For example, public welfare programs are managed by the states and financed mainly or entirely by the federal and state governments. The share of welfare spending in general expenditures over the studied twenty years was on average only about 3.5 percent ($196 per capita) in these twenty-eight legacy cities.

OVERVIEW OF LEGACY CITIES' REVENUES

When expenditures grow, to sustain the same level and quality of services, governments need to increase their revenues. This is exactly what has happened in legacy cities. The per capita revenues of the twenty-eight legacy cities increased by 56 percent in real terms from 1977 to 2014, imposing an even higher tax burden on their residents. For comparison, the revenues of the 121 non-legacy cities increased by 52.5 percent on average.

City revenues come from state and federal transfers and own sources, such as taxes (property, sales, and income) and nontax revenues (fees, charges, lottery proceeds, revenues from government-run utilities, and state-run liquor stores). The revenue sources also tend to indicate the fiscal health of municipalities. A diversified revenue portfolio helps municipalities earn more when the economy is strong and have stable revenue during recessions (Mikesell 2013). While fiscal structure of some states is such that the states collect the higher proportion of revenues and redistribute some of the tax collections back to localities, higher intergovernmental transfers may also be a sign of concern as localities become vulnerable to the financial conditions of the higher government levels and lose their fiscal autonomy.

FEDERAL AND STATE TRANSFERS

Mean revenues in the sample of twenty-eight legacy cities have been consistently higher than among non-legacy cities (figure 4.3). While own-source revenues were similar in legacy and non-legacy cities and followed the same trend (climbing until reaching a pick in 2007 before the Great Recession, and going slightly down since), the intergovernmental revenues (transfers from the federal and state government), on the other hand, were both statistically and substantively higher (by about $864 per capita during the considered period) in legacy compared to non-legacy cities in the FiSC sample. In the US fiscal system federal grants target mainly the states, and states target municipalities.

Legacy cities get higher per capita transfers from federal and state governments partially because of their financial struggles. Even though the federal government does not offer any major grants to equalize fiscal disparities among localities, unlike several developed countries such Canada and multiple European countries do (Mikesell 2013; Smart 1998), needy municipalities still receive more federal and state dollars compared to their wealthier neighbors.

Residents of municipalities with higher poverty and unemployment rates receive federal assistance through welfare programs like Medicaid, SNAP, energy assistance, Section 8, and social security and unemployment insurance. Distressed municipalities are more likely to have higher foreclosure and delinquency rates and be eligible for federal grants for the purchase and rehabilitation of houses through the Neighborhood Stabilization Program by the US Department of Housing and Urban Development (HUD) (see chapter 10). HUD additionally provides grants to municipalities for homeless shelters, public housing, and others. Other federal programs that may be utilized by legacy cities more than other big cities are crime-control programs (see chapter 8).

About 8 percent of general revenues among legacy cities in the FiSC sample came from the federal government in 2014. At the same time, the share of state transfers in fiscal receipts of the twenty-eight cities was almost 38 percent. The state transfers are that high because states manage and provide main financing to certain local services (like social services). But state transfers are also higher to cities in states that do not permit local sales taxes, such as Michigan, Indiana, and Connecticut (these states do not allow any local sales taxes), and Wisconsin and North Carolina (states that do not allow city, but have county sales taxes), or prohibit any local income taxes (both city and county), such as Minnesota and Wisconsin. In these cases, the taxes are collected exclusively by the states and revenues are shared with municipalities.

Similar to federal transfers, state transfers are also higher in legacy than non-legacy cities. Some legacy cities are in northeastern and midwestern states that do not permit local income or sales taxes—hence, the state transfers are high. Legacy cities also have high poverty rates. In contrast to the federal government, most states offer some sort of equalization grants to localities, especially to school districts (school districts are included in the cities' finances in FiSC) based on the number of impoverished children (and other factors).

PROPERTY TAXES

Local governments in the United States heavily rely on property taxes. Property taxes are the second largest revenue source after state transfers for the cities in this study and are by far the largest own-source tax revenue source (figures 3.1 and 3.2). Property taxes are levied and administered, and the revenues are primarily used by local governments (never by the federal government and rarely by state governments), which provides fiscal autonomy to municipalities, and visibility to how taxpayers' dollars are being used (since property taxes are spent on local schools, libraries, police and fire protection, and other local services, property taxes may serve as a good proxy to the quality of local services). The property tax collections in legacy and non-legacy cities have been very similar (table 3.1).

Over the analyzed twenty-year period, the per capita property tax revenues among the twenty-eight legacy cities were about $1,165—or over 20 percent of general revenues (FiSC). The percentage of property tax collections in general revenues of each city ranged between as little as 10 percent in Flint, Michigan, to as high as 39 percent in Providence, Rhode Island. The smaller share (and actual dollar amount) of property tax revenues is often a reflection of low assessed values and a high number of abandoned properties in cities like Flint, Detroit, or Buffalo. Detroit, for example, has the lowest median home values among all large US cities (at $41,900) and, consequently, the second largest average effective property tax rates on median-valued private homes, which are about 2.5 times higher than the US average (Lincoln Institute of Land Policy 2016). The average effective tax rate on commercial properties is also the highest in the country.

There are other potentially contributing factors as well. Michigan collects property taxes that are estimated and not based on property market value but on "acquisition value" (Mikesell 2013). The acquisition value basis for property taxation, Proposal A, was approved by Michigan voters in 1994. Acquisition-based assessment means that the taxable value of property is not equal to assessed value as it is in the other states, but is based on the value of a property at the last sale, adjusted for inflation (or 5 percent, if the inflation rate has been higher). Tax revenues are, therefore, not dependent on the growth of property values. All three studied Michigan cities experienced a 30 percent plunge in total property tax collections in 1995 compared to just a year before, as properties were reassessed for tax purposes (FiSC). Acquisition-based assessment coupled with continuing population and industrial loss (see Ryberg-Webster and Tighe's introduction to this volume), resulted in 40 percent smaller property tax collections in real dollars in 2014 compared to 1994 in Detroit, 37 percent lower collections in Warren, and alarming 72 percent loss in property tax revenues in Flint.

Some states substantively complicate cities' fiscal situations by placing legal limits on property tax revenues. One of the struggling legacy cities—Gary, Indiana—has always been heavily reliant on property taxes. Gary's ability to collect property taxes was shattered in 2008, when Indiana introduced municipal property tax caps. The city's property tax revenues dropped from $169.4 million in 2007 to under $92.6 million in 2008. In 2008 Indiana established the Distressed Unit Appeals Board (DUAB) to consider cases of municipalities that expect a decline in property tax collections of over 5 percent because of the newly established caps. The city of Gary (and multiple other taxing authorities in Gary) approached the DUAB three times between 2009 and 2011 with requests to charge higher property taxes. The city was later able to cut spending (and services) enough to deal with declined property tax revenues. However, the issue has never been resolved completely. The Gary Municipal School Corporation has appealed to the board more recently, in 2015, 2016, and 2017.

SALES TAXES

There are four types of sales taxes in the United States: (1) general retail sales taxes, RST (broad-based sales taxes); (2) use taxes (similar to RSTs, but on internet transactions); (3) selective excises (narrow-based sales taxes); and (4) gross receipts taxes, GRT (sales taxes on sellers rather than consumers).[2] Forty-five states collect general use and sales taxes on a state level. About thirty-six states permit localities to collect general retail sales taxes in addition, or instead of state sales taxes (Mikesell 2013). In this case, the consumer pays the combined tax levied by the state, county, city, and special districts. Most local governments are also permitted to levy their own selective excises. Sales tax collections are the second largest own-source revenue source for local governments. However, for legacy cities, income and sales taxes generate about the same amount of revenues (figure 3.1). The revenues generated by the sales taxes in the twenty-eight studied legacy cities are similar to those in 121 largest non-legacy cities in the FiSC sample (table 3.1).

Among legacy states, Delaware does not have either state or local general sales tax, but allows for utility and some other selective excises. Six other states—Connecticut, Kentucky, Maryland, Michigan, Indiana, and Rhode Island—collect state, but do not allow local, RST. Louisville, Detroit, Baltimore, and Akron (since 2008) collect utility revenues and some excises.

The highest combined RST among the researched twenty-eight cities are in New Orleans and Birmingham (10 percent). The per capita annual tax collections in these cities were $988 in New Orleans (20 percent of general revenue) and $803 (16 percent of general revenue) in Birmingham between 1995 and 2014 (FiSC). The per capita tax revenues in these two cities were well above the $296 average among twenty-eight legacy cities over the same period.

INCOME TAXES

There are two types of income taxes: personal and corporate. Income taxes are hugely important for the federal and state, but not local, governments. There are, however, notable exemptions, especially among legacy cities. On average, legacy cities in the FiSC sample collected both substantively and statistically much more in personal and corporate income tax revenues than non-legacy cities. In 2014, for example, non-legacy cities collected just under $48 per capita in income taxes compared to over $296 per capita in legacy cities (table 3.1). The share of revenue originating from income taxes in legacy cities that levy such taxes ranged between 2 percent (in Flint) to 21 percent of general revenues (in Louisville) in 2014 (FiSC).

Only 11 of 121 non-legacy cities, but 13 of 28 legacy cities in the FiSC sample collect personal income tax. As to corporate income tax, four legacy cities—Louisville, Philadelphia, St. Louis, and Wilmington—have been collecting the tax in the past six to twelve years. At the same time, of 121 non-legacy cities only one collected corporate income tax over the considered period, and an additional four cities collected the tax some, but not other, years.

Income taxes are popular among legacy cities mainly because many legacy cities are permitted to levy such taxes by their states in the first place. Among fourteen states that currently allow local income taxes, ten are legacy states. It is hard to say if this statistic is a coincidence, or if states intentionally permit their fiscally strained legacy cities to derive revenues from additional sources.

The title of the "worst municipal income tax system" in the nation, however, belongs to Ohio (Tax Foundation 2016a). Ohio not only has the highest combined state and municipal tax rates in the nation, but the tax rates and definitions of income differ between municipalities, which significantly complicates the tax system, making it less transparent and equitable. Ohio residents pay income taxes to both the municipalities where they work and where they live. For example, Cleveland levies the income tax rate of 2.5 percent, which is one of the highest local income tax rates in Ohio (Ohio Department of Taxation). Residents of Cleveland Heights and Shaker Heights, Cleveland's closest suburbs, who work in Cleveland, pay a combined municipal rate of 3.625 percent at the place of work and residency. In fact, 87 percent of people employed in Cleveland do not reside within city limits (Tax Foundation 2016a).

DEBT

The amount of both short-term and long-term debt outstanding was an average of $6,277 per capita for the twenty-eight legacy cities over the twenty-year period (table 3.1). On average, non-legacy cities had $6,080 in outstanding debt obligations. Statistically, though, the difference between the legacy and non-legacy cities was not significant. The amount of debt was relatively flat in the 1990s and has been steadily increasing in the 2000s.

CREDIT RATINGS

There is no uniform definition of fiscal health. Some states, like Ohio, define exactly what they consider fiscal health or the lack of thereof for their municipalities.[3] But most states don't do it. To ease the task of interpreting financial information one can simply refer to credit-rating agencies, which study a variety of fiscal, economic, demographic, and political factors to determine the credit quality of a state or municipality.

Of the 150 cities in the FiSC sample, 22 cities had the highest AAA (by Moody's) credit quality at least some years during the considered twenty-year period. Only one of these cities was legacy (Minneapolis). Of 150 cities, 54 had the second best Aa1 rating. Of them, only four were legacy cities

(Louisville, Minneapolis, Cincinnati, and Milwaukee). The credit rating of Ba1 and below is considered a non-investment grade, or a "junk" rating, meaning that the municipality is in a poor financial condition and is more likely to default on payments to its creditors. Only 8 of 150 cities in the FiSC sample had a "junk" rating at any time during the considered years. Of these eight cities, four were legacy (Washington, DC, was the fifth city with a non-investment-grade credit rating). The next section analyzes finances of three of the mentioned four cities. The fourth city, New Orleans, which never has had a particularly strong fiscal position, had its credit downgraded to "junk" following a devastation brought by Hurricane Katrina. The city's creditworthiness was restored to an investment-grade rating in about two years, once the city rebuilt its infrastructure, and residents and businesses returned to the city.

The observation of the data appears to indicate a clear correlation between population loss and credit ratings in twenty-eight legacy cities. Minneapolis' population increased about 7 percent in the past twenty years, just like Richmond, whose credit ratings stayed consistently strong. On the other side, Detroit's population dropped by 31 percent; Flint's by 26 percent; and New Orleans' by 24 percent over the past twenty years (FiSC and Moody's).

FISCAL DISTRESS AND BANKRUPTCIES

DETROIT

Detroit's creditworthiness plunged to "junk" status in 2009. On July 18, 2013, Detroit filed for Chapter 9 bankruptcy, which was the largest municipal bankruptcy ever in the United States. Detroit's population declined by 60 percent since the 1950s. The city had the highest unemployment rate in the country, at 15.1 percent in 2009 and 13.9 percent in 2010 (Bureau of Labor Statistics [BLS] Local Area Unemployment Statistics).

Detroit, heavily dependent on the automotive industry, struggled when its largest (nonpublic) employers—Chrysler, General Motors, and Ford—went through their own financial hardships as gasoline prices climbed in the 2000s, and demand for cars declined. Chrysler employed 14,282 Detroiters in 2001, but only 4,517 in 2010. General Motors also slashed employment by about 40 percent between 2001 and 2010 (Detroit CAFR 2010). Historically, Chrysler was enormously profitable for the city; it has been the city's largest taxpayer. In 2001 Chrysler's properties constituted 11.26 percent of total assessed property tax value. In 2010 this number plummeted to 6.73 percent (Detroit CAFR 2010).

Some other factors that led to bankruptcy were a high budget deficit, and general and pension debt. About $1.2 billion in pension obligations had been more than the city's general obligation debt in the 2000s and 2010s. Total (primary government) debt outstanding had been between $7.3 and $8.4 billion between 2006 and 2015, and increased from $7,723 per capita in 2006 to $11,890 per capita in 2014 (Detroit CAFR 2015). Since 2000 Detroit has consistently run a budget deficit.

Following its declaration of bankruptcy, the city restructured its debt and somewhat restored its credit ratings. Nevertheless, despite all the efforts, Detroit's finances remain in a bad shape.

FLINT

Flint, Michigan, is nicknamed a "Vehicle City" thanks to its two major employers—the Buick Motor Company and General Motors (GM). As the auto industries became more automated, the number of Flint residents employed by both companies plunged. GM employed eighty thousand in 1978 but only eight thousand in 2006. Flint's population has also declined by almost half since 1960, to under one hundred thousand in 2013 (Doidge et al. 2015).

Flint rarely invites credit-rating agencies to evaluate the city's creditworthiness. Following the population and industrial decline, and multiple issues caused by them, Moody's lowered Flint's creditworthiness to "junk" in 2001, which remained until 2006, when the rating was withdrawn, and the city hasn't been rated since.

To help alleviate the fiscal difficulties, the state of Michigan appointed an emergency fiscal manager to Flint between 2002 and 2004. The reforms undertaken during these two years lasted some time, but were not sufficient to avoid the next fiscal crisis, and Flint was placed under state control again in 2011 for four years due to its "structural deficit, increasing legacy costs, and accumulating debt" (Doidge et al. 2015, 13). In these four years about 16 percent of city employees (155 positions) were eliminated, wages and salaries were reduced across the board, and the benefit structure was changed. The mayor and council members' salary and benefits were initially eliminated and only partially restored later. The city also introduced user fees for waste collection, implemented special assessment for street lighting, increased other fees, and increased property taxes. In April 2015 control of the city was returned to the mayor and city council.

On January 5, 2016, Michigan governor Rick Snyder declared a state of emergency in Flint to deal with the city's water crisis (S&P 2016). The state then approved $28 million in emergency assistance to purchase water filters and bottled water, replace plumbing, and fund additional measures to help alleviate the crisis. The National Guard was employed to assist with water distribution. Prior to declaring a state of emergency, in October 2015 the state approved $9.39 million of additional funds to reconnect Flint to Detroit's water system. S&P notes that it would cost Flint anywhere between $700 million and $1.5 billion to replace the city's water infrastructure. Genesee County pledged to issue $220 million worth of bonds to help the city. The remainder of the funds needs to be borrowed by Flint, which will inevitably strain the city's finances even further, given Flint's current 40 percent poverty rate and high outstanding debt obligations.

PITTSBURGH

Pittsburgh, called the "Iron City" and the "Steel City," was the United States' major iron and steel producer in the nineteenth and early twentieth centuries. Facing decreasing demand for steel in the 1980s, Pittsburgh lost a lot of its industrial base and population, resulting in financial hardships. In 1995 S&P highlighted some of the poor fiscal-management decisions the city made, such as the decrease in the city's income tax rate in 1990, which led to a persisting budget deficit, and the sale of the city's water and sewer system in 1995, which was a temporary liquidity solution, but eliminated a stable income source for the city.

During the recession of 2002–2003, Pittsburgh found itself in a dire fiscal environment, facing over $90 million in deficit in 2002, 2003, and 2004 (McNulty 2003 and FiSC).[4] The city was unable to raise taxes or further cut expenses. In 2003 and 2004 credit-rating agencies lowered the city's rating to "junk"; however, that did not last long thanks to emergency measures undertaken by the state and the city.

On December 29, 2003, the Commonwealth of Pennsylvania put Pittsburgh on a distressed municipalities program and, in February 2004, created the Pittsburgh Intergovernmental Cooperation Authority (PICA), a five-member board responsible for overseeing Pittsburgh's finances. The PICA identified issues with reporting and estimating employees' compensation, unfunded pensions, health care, workers' compensation liabilities, and high debt.

In 2004 Pittsburgh increased its occupational tax from $10 to $52, created a new payroll tax, and began to phase out the business-privilege tax that allowed multiple businesses operating in the city, including twenty-four of the twenty-seven largest corporations, to avoid paying taxes (PICA 2009). The city additionally implemented cost-saving strategies, especially for emergency medical services and fire protection, and doubled the budget to demolish the city's abandoned buildings.

Despite its improved credit rating, Pittsburgh remained on the distressed municipalities program until February 2018 due to high legacy costs, especially pensions and debt.

CONCLUSIONS AND POLICY IMPLICATIONS

In the first half of the twentieth century, legacy cities were American industrial powerhouses built to accommodate growing number of residents and commuters. As manufacturing and other industries were automated, the cost of raw materials climbed and demand for them declined, plants and factories housed in legacy cities substantively downsized or even ceased to exist. This trajectory generated multiple problems, many of them discussed in this book.

From the fiscal perspective, the population and industrial decline means a shrinking tax base. Maintaining infrastructure, built to accommodate a much larger number of people, puts enormous cost pressure on local governments. Not surprisingly, legacy cities have lower credit ratings compared to non-legacy cities, and the legacy cities that experienced the largest population decline have had the lowest credit ratings, while legacy cities with the highest credit ratings gained residents.

Population and industrial decline created some of the worst cases of fiscal crisis in legacy cities. In 1978 Cleveland was the first large municipality to default on its debt obligations since the Great Depression. Detroit was the only one of the 150 largest US cities to seek Chapter 9 bankruptcy protection during the latest twenty years. Detroit bankruptcy's declaration was also the largest municipal bankruptcy in US history.

What instruments can legacy cities use to restore their fiscal base and reverse the decline? Most of the severe, yet successful, recovery actions in the past were not popular among constituents as they increased the tax rates and lowered the expenditures, hence the government's ability to provide some essential services. Voter-approved income tax increases in 1979 and 1981 contributed to Cleveland's recovery after the default. State-approved occupational tax increases, and the expansion of the tax base (by including previously tax-exempt businesses and introduction of the payroll tax) in Pittsburgh in 2004 helped to raise the city's credit rating by several notches. Cuts in expenditures (wages, benefits, pensions, and others) and the creation of independent fiscal authorities in Pittsburgh in 2004, Buffalo in 2003, and Philadelphia in 1991, were some of the extreme measures that produced positive outcomes for these cities.

Legacy cities can also employ a variety of fiscal tools to boost their population and attractiveness for business development to restore their fiscal base. Subsidized housing has proven to be successful in restoring some of the residency rates in cities like Cleveland. Property tax abatements and deferrals, corporate income tax and sales tax exemptions, the creation of tax increment financing (TIF)[5] districts, tax credits for the rehabilitation of historic buildings, and other incentives have been popularized by multiple legacy and non-legacy cities in the United States to attract new investment. Many of these incentives should, however, be used with caution as they put a further pressure on already shattered legacy cities' tax base.

NOTES

1. The twenty-eight legacy cities in the sample are AL: Birmingham; CT: Hartford, New Haven; DE: Wilmington; IN: Gary; KY: Louisville; LA: New Orleans; MD: Baltimore; MI: Detroit, Flint, Warren; MN: Minneapolis; MO: St. Louis; NY: Buffalo, Rochester, Syracuse; OH: Akron, Cincinnati, Cleveland, Dayton; PA: Philadelphia, Pittsburgh; RI: Providence; VA: Norfolk, Richmond; WI: Milwaukee; WV: Charleston, Huntington.

2. There is a lot of criticism of GRT so much so that some states even ruled them unconstitutional (see Mikesell 2013 or multiple publications by the Tax Foundation). They are, nevertheless, very popular among legacy states. Nine states currently levy GSTs; of them five are legacy states, including Alabama, Delaware, Illinois, Ohio, and Pennsylvania. Four other states repealed GRT during the twenty-year period considered in this chapter. All of these states are also legacy states. The tax was repealed in Indiana in 2002, New Jersey and Kentucky in 2006, and Michigan in 2011 (Tax Foundation 2016b). GRT are state, not city taxes and, consequently, are not discussed in this chapter.

3. See the Ohio auditor's website: https://ohioauditor.gov/fiscal/local.html#watch.

4. Pittsburgh and other Pennsylvania cities have a state balanced budget requirement and are not allowed to run budget deficits.

5. When TIF is established, the taxing jurisdiction continues to collect the property tax within the TIF area; the tax is imposed only on the base existing at a time of TIF creation, the tax on any increments of the base property value is returned to property owners (Ermasova and George 2017), which incentivizes improving existing properties.

REFERENCES

Doidge, Mary, Eric Scorsone, Traci Taylor, Josh Sapotichne, Erika Rosebrook, and Danielle Kaminski. 2015. *The Flint Fiscal Playbook: An Assessment of the Emergency Manager Years (2011–2015)*. East Lansing: Michigan State University Extension White Paper.

Ermasova, N., and George, A. 2017. "Tax Incremental Financing: Learning from Research and Municipal 'Best Practice.'" *Illinois Municipal Policy Journal* 2, no. 1: 135–46

Intergovernmental Cooperation Authority (ICA). 2009. "A Summary Report of the Intergovernmental Cooperation Authority (ICA) and its Oversight Role with the City of Pittsburgh, 2004 to Present." http://pghica.org/download/2004-2009-annual-report/?wpdmdl=1291.

Lincoln Institute of Land Policy and Minnesota Center for Fiscal Excellence. 2016. "50-State Property Tax Comparison Study: For Taxes Paid in 2015." http://www.lincolninst.edu/publications/other/50-state-property-tax-comparison-study-0.

McNulty, Timothy. 2003. "City Neighborhoods: Pittsburgh Begs State for Help with

Fiscal Crisis." *Pittsburgh Post-Gazette*, November 11, 2003. http://old.post-gazette.com/neigh_city/20031111murphy1111p1.asp.

Mikesell, John. 2013. *Fiscal Administration*. Boston: Cengage Learning.

Standard and Poor's 500 (S&P). 2016. "Credit Challenges Tied to The Flint Water Crisis Run Deep for Michigan." https://www.capitaliq.com/CIQDotNet/CreditResearch/RenderArticle.aspx?articleId=1571094&SctArtId=367568&from=CM&nsl_code=LIME&sourceObjectId=9506681&sourceRevId=1&fee_ind=N&exp_date=20260131-22:31:20.

Smart, Michael. 1998. "Taxation and Deadweight Loss in a System of Intergovernmental Transfers." *Canadian Journal of Economics* 31, no. 1: 189–206.

Tax Foundation. 2016a. "Cleveland Considers Hike to the Worst Municipal Income Tax System in the Country." https://taxfoundation.org/cleveland-considers-hike-worst-municipal-income-tax-system-country/.

Tax Foundation. 2016b. "Gross Receipts Taxes: Lessons from Previous State Experiences." https://taxfoundation.org/gross-receipts-taxes-state-experiences/.

US Census Bureau. 2014. "Annual Surveys of State and Local Government Finances." https://www.census.gov//govs/local/.

This study also relied upon:

Comprehensive Annual Financial Reports (CAFRs) for each city for various years.

Moody's Investor Service rating action press releases for a variety of years, available at www.moodys.com.

S&P Global Credit Portal rating action press releases for a variety of years, available at https://www.globalcreditportal.com/ratingsdirect.

APPENDIX

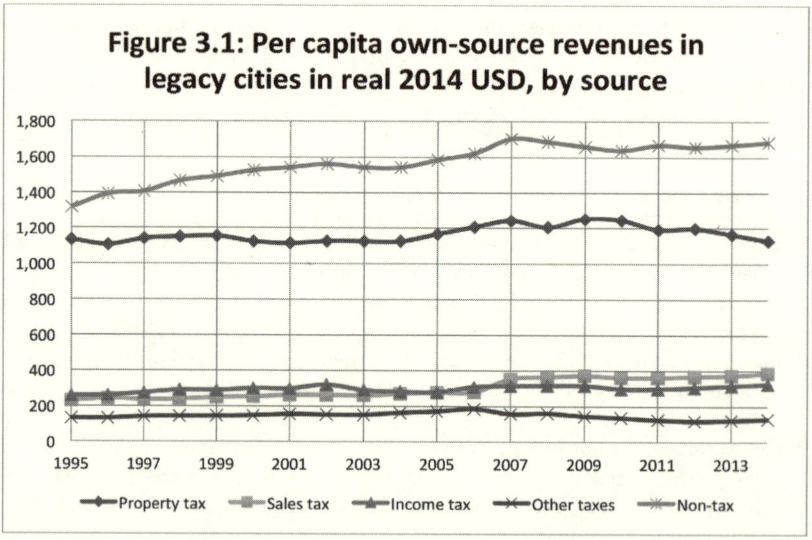

FIGURE 3.1: Per capita own-source revenues in legacy cities in real 2014 USD, by source

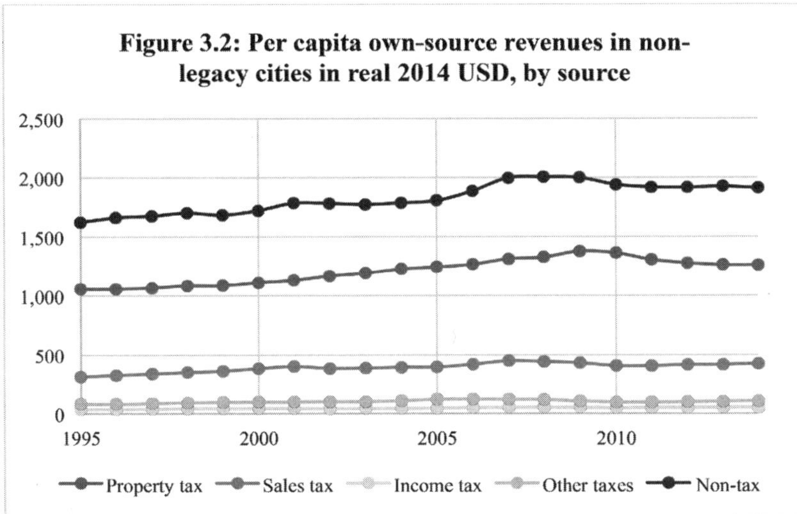

FIGURE 3.2: Per capita own-source revenues in non-legacy cities in real 2014 USD, by source

TABLE 3.1: Mean fiscal indicators in legacy and non-legacy cities between 1995 and 2014, in real 2014 USD

	Legacy	Non-Legacy	Difference
Total revenues	6,318.6	5,566.3	752.3*
Total expenditures	6,454.8	5,500.8	954*
Intergovernmental revenues	2,599.1	1,735.2	863.9***
Own-source revenues	3,099.2	2,982.5	116.7
Property tax	1,165.2	1,207.8	-42.6
Sales tax	299.2	393.0	-93.8
Income tax	296.1	47.9	248.1***
Other taxes	144.7	104.8	40*
Non tax	1,814.3	1,824.1	-9.8
Debt outstanding	6,276.7	6,079.6	197.2

Note: *** $p < 0.001$ ** $p<0.01$ * $p<0.05$

4

Legacy City Historic Preservation

NEIGHBORHOOD PATTERNS

KELLY L. KINAHAN

In the context of shrinkage and its associated challenges, concerns over history, culture, and heritage are often afterthoughts. In legacy cities, persistent depopulation and weak economic conditions translate to strategies for the built environment that often prioritize demolition. Market conditions further limit the opportunities for preserving historic buildings in legacy cities (Mallach 2011) and local historic district regulations can potentially thwart efforts focused on rightsizing and smart decline (Hollander 2010). Addressing the pressing issues of vacancy, low demand, foreclosures, and oversupply of outmoded buildings dominates the agenda of planners and policymakers focused on re-stitching legacy cities' urban fabric (Schilling and Logan 2008). For some, the memories and history embodied in these buildings are best left forgotten (Campo 2016). Because of these barriers, the tools of historic preservation are often overlooked as means of mitigating the challenges facing legacy city neighborhoods (Bertron and Rypkema 2012).

Yet historic buildings embody some of the most important legacies of legacy cities. These include the remnants of their rich industrial pasts, the settlement patterns that emerged as legacy cities grew (often in relation to their core manufacturing industries), the homes and workplaces of waves of immigrant and working-class laborers, and the investments of individuals that made their fortunes in these cities. The built environment also reflects the far less flattering histories of extensive race- and class-based segregation. Questions surrounding how to preserve historic buildings represent one of many complex challenges facing legacy cities as the historic built environment is a physical asset that supports a variety of uses including housing, commercial, and industrial, and reflects the significant heritage features of these cities including patterns of development, architectural styles, and key persons or events. On the other hand, the age, construction methods, size, and scale of these buildings mean their rehabilitation requires high costs and substantial incentives, a situation further complicated by low demand, excess supply, weak housing markets, and stressed municipal coffers in legacy cities. The duality of historic buildings, serving as both assets and burdens for legacy cities, is one example of the multiple meanings embedded in the *legacy* moniker.

One preservation tool available nationwide, but particularly well-suited to supporting reinvestment in legacy cities' historic urban fabric because it decreases the cost of preservation-based redevelopment, is the federal historic rehabilitation tax credit (RTC). This program, which has existed in various forms since 1976, provides a 20 percent income tax credit to incentivize the rehabilitation of buildings listed on or eligible for the National Register of Historic Places. An enduring (1976) and widely used program (NPS 2017), the RTC reflects a market-based approach to preservation that complements the regulatory tactics of other popular tools like historic districts (Howe 2003). In the weak-market context of legacy cities, the tax incentives attached to RTC projects provide an additional layer of financing, and have been shown to improve the economic feasibility of preservation in downtowns (Ryberg-Webster 2013) and produce market-rate and affordable housing in neighborhoods outside of downtown (Ryberg-Webster and Kinahan 2016).

The RTC represents an active investment in the physical assets of legacy cities, which makes understanding the characteristics of the places where these projects occur an important component of both rightsizing and revitalization strategies. This chapter analyzes and describes the types of neighborhoods where real estate developers are taking on preservation projects in five legacy cities: Baltimore, Cleveland, Philadelphia, Richmond, and St. Louis. The findings show that while a majority of RTC activity occurs in *low distress* neighborhoods, *high distress* areas are also benefiting from this reinvestment tool and offers insights for planners and policymakers interested in using preservation as a stabilization and revitalization strategy.

FEDERAL REHABILITATION TAX CREDITS

Starting in 1976, Congress enacted tax legislation leveling the playing field toward historic rehabilitation by encouraging investment in city centers through the federal historic tax credit program (Ryberg-Webster 2015b).[1] Over four decades, the RTC program supported more than $84 billion of investment in approximately 42,000 preservation projects (NPS 2017). The

RTC is an intergovernmental collaboration (see chapter 1), administered through the National Park Service (NPS) in coordination with State Historic Preservation Offices.[2] Program applicants are predominantly private real estate developers, although nonprofit real estate entities also participate in the program (NPS 2017).

PRESERVATION IN LEGACY CITY NEIGHBORHOODS

Nationwide, the RTC program is an important tool for creating affordable housing and mixed-use developments (Listokin, Listokin, and Lahr 1998; Cohen 1998). Rehabilitation projects are less likely to occur without the additional layer of financing provided through the tax credit (Shilling, Vandell, Koesman, and Lin 2006). In legacy cities, the "federal RTCs play an important role in the ongoing, postindustrial transformation of U.S. downtowns . . . and are a key factor in the reinvestment of declining cities" (Ryberg-Webster 2013, 266). Reinvestments in legacy city neighborhoods outside of downtowns also occur through the RTC and are spatially dispersed over time (Ryberg-Webster and Kinahan 2017). Housing is a common outcome of RTC projects nationwide with more than half (57 percent) of completed projects in fiscal year 2016 reporting this as the final primary use, followed by commercial and office uses (NPS 2017). Ryberg-Webster (2015a) declares the RTC program functions "as a de facto urban housing policy" because of the large number of rental units created by of these projects.

Alongside these positive revitalization trends are concerns over whether preservation activity results in gentrification and, specifically, the displacement of long-term, low-income, and minority residents (Smith 1998; Werwath 1998). The weak-market context of legacy cities could mute physical displacement concerns where the attraction of newcomers and the infusion of upper- and middle-income residents is a welcome departure from long-term population loss (Galster 2002).[3] Additionally, Tighe and Ganning (2016) show that transportation costs, rather than housing, are a greater budgetary constraint for families in shrinking city neighborhoods. However, as Hyra (2015) points out, there is also potential for cultural and political displacement of minority groups within the context of neighborhood change, which are relevant concerns in any market context. There is a need for greater consideration of the costs and benefits of all preservation activities, including historic tax credit investments, to understand who benefits and how low-income and other marginalized populations are affected (Minner 2016).

While legacy cities deal with a common set of issues stemming from long-term population loss and decades of economic restructuring, the neighborhoods within these cities are not monolithic. Recent research reveals that eight distinct neighborhood types populate these cities, and strong patterns of stasis within these types are evident over time (Kinahan 2016). Neighborhood strategies in legacy cities often promote the strategic, geographic targeting of investments to leverage public and philanthropic funds with those of the private sector (Accordino and Fasulo 2013; Thomson 2008, 2011, 2012). Although RTC projects are well positioned to help meet the broader goals of neighborhood stabilization and revitalization, the connections between the preservation community and rightsizing actions are limited in many legacy cities (Bertron and Rypkema 2012). The tools of historic preservation are rarely among the strategic arsenal deployed to mitigate neighborhood issues, despite a recognition that historic buildings are key physical assets in legacy cities (American Assembly 2011). Understanding the characteristics of neighborhoods where private-sector preservation activity is feasible and is occurring in legacy cities provides a foundation for better integrating RTC investments with rightsizing initiatives and supporting preservation strategies as an alternative to demolition-based approaches, which are widespread.

With the environment of oversupply and low demand that exists citywide in many legacy cities, demolition is a key component of neighborhood-stabilization strategies (Mallach 2012a). Arguments in favor of demolition cite the potential for reducing crime and blight, improving environmental sustainability, and raising property values (Dynamo Metrics 2015). However, as a stand-alone strategy, demolition is generally unsuccessful (Mallach 2012a). The finality of demolition decisions could hamper longer-term, strategic approaches focused on maintaining the "diversity, affordability, and irreplaceable urban character" embodied in legacy cities' historic built environment (PRN 2015, 1). Yet federal resources, particularly Hardest Hit Funds, often prioritize demolition over alternative strategies and can bypass existing historic preservation regulations (e.g., Section 106 review).[4] Without an up-to-date assessment of the potential preservation-related impacts of demolition, places reflecting the heritage of minority groups are particularly at risk because of disproportional lack of documentation and recognition of these resources. Historic preservation practice has often not fully embraced the role of minority cultures in terms of race, gender, ethnicity, or class (Dubrow 1998; Kaufman 2009; Ryberg-Webster 2017), despite serving as a primary means through which "public memories" and less celebrated moments of the past can be collectively understood and celebrated (Hayden 1997).

This chapter describes the types of neighborhoods where RTC activity occurs and analyzes the scale of reinvestment in terms dollars and number of projects. In light of the prioritization of demolition, the importance of the RTC for easing the financial burden of preservation-based reinvestment, and the disconnects that exist at the local policy level between historic preservation and broader urban policy issues, this analysis offers insights for planners, preservationists, and policymakers concerned with balancing preservation alongside the other acute challenges facing legacy cities.

APPROACH

To analyze the distribution of recent RTC activity (1998–2007), this chapter uses the multidimensional legacy city neighborhood typology developed by Kinahan (2016).[5] The eight neighborhood types fall into two overarching categories: high distress and low distress. High distress neighborhood types and their characteristics include:

- Black, Stressed, and Disadvantaged: Low-value housing; low-income families with little educational attainment; residents are primarily black, unemployed, and living below the poverty line;
- Black Mixed: Weak housing values, paired with low educational attainment, high rates of public assistance among low-income black and some white families;
- Collapsed Urban Core: Long-term renters, high rates of poverty and public assistance among renters; high vacancy rates, weak housing values, and low educational attainment; large share of the population is under eighteen, black, and unemployed; higher-than-average rents; some white residents; and
- White Immigrant: Very old housing stock; primarily white residents; some foreign-born and Hispanic residents.

Low distress neighborhood types and their characteristics include:

- Competitive, Educated, and Struggling: High-value housing, well-educated singles, and higher-than-average income; white residents, rents higher than city and MSA averages; high rates of poverty and public assistance among renters;
- Educated not Struggling: High housing values with well-educated, high-income singles among areas that tend to be along cities' edges;
- Established and Stable Homeowners: High levels of homeownership, low levels of poverty and public assistance, people that have lived in their homes and the neighborhood for an extended period of time, low vacancy, and little multifamily housing; and
- Highly Bifurcated: High rates of poverty and public assistance, transient renters; high-value housing occupied by well-educated singles; low-income renters.

Combining the typology with RTC data provides a framework for analyzing the patterns of preservation activity within the five legacy cities, as identified in existing literature (Brookings 2006; Hollander et al. 2009; Hill et al. 2011; LCD 2015; LCP 2015) for which data was available from the Technical Preservation Services Division of the National Park Service.[6]

RTC ACTIVITY ACROSS LEGACY CITY NEIGHBORHOOD TYPES

In 2000 the majority of legacy city neighborhoods (59 percent) in the five study cities were one of the four high distress types, characterized by weak housing values, high unemployment rates, and high poverty. On the other hand, despite the broader context of depopulation and decline, about 40 percent of neighborhoods in these five legacy cities are low distress areas with higher housing values, well-educated residents, and higher rents. These varying neighborhood contexts signify an array of market conditions. Notwithstanding, federal historic tax credit activity is present within each of the eight neighborhood types across the five-city aggregated data set (table 4.1). Overall, RTC activity is nearly as likely to occur in high distress (47 percent) versus low distress (53 percent) neighborhoods. In other words, of all the tracts with RTC activity from 1998 to 2007, about half were low distress and about half were high distress neighborhoods in 2000. Overall, approximately 20 percent of all legacy city neighborhoods experienced at least one RTC project during this time.

Between 1998 and 2007 over 1,200 federal RTC projects occurred in these five legacy cities, with low distress neighborhoods capturing 60 percent of these projects. Examining the individual types more closely shows that the competitive, educated, and struggling and highly bifurcated types are where many (58 percent) of these projects occur. Highly bifurcated areas averaged over ten projects during this period, the highest among all neighborhood types. Among the high distress neighborhoods, 32 percent of all RTC projects occurred within the black, stressed, and disadvantaged (21 percent) and collapsed urban core (11 percent) types, with the latter group experiencing the highest average projects per neighborhood (7.9) among the high distress types.

Collectively, these RTC projects accounted for more than $4.5 billion worth of investment in the five cities over the ten-year time period. The distribution of investment follows relatively similar patterns as described earlier concerning projects, with some key exceptions. RTC investments are even more concentrated in low distress areas, with 81 percent of total investment occurring within the four low distress types. The competitive, educated, and struggling and highly bifurcated types again account for the

TABLE 4.1: Distribution of RTC investments and projects by neighborhood type, all cities

	Tracts with RTC activity	Total projects	Share of RTC projects
Black, distressed, and disadvantaged	20%	255	21%
Collapsed urban core	9%	134	11%
Black mixed	9%	67	5%
White immigrants	8%	34	3%
High distressed Subtotal/avg.	47%	490	40%
Competitive, educated, and struggling	21%	280	23%
Educated not stressed	6%	20	2%
Established and stable Homeowners	4%	10	1%
Highly bifurcated	23%	436	35%
Low distress Subtotal/avg.	53%	746	60%
totals		1236	

bulk of this activity (72 percent). High distress neighborhoods capture a far smaller share of total investments (19 percent), with the majority occurring in black, stressed, and disadvantaged and collapsed urban core types. Similarly, the average investment per projects is less in high distress neighborhoods ($2.1 million), than in low distress types ($9.7 million). However, among the high distress types, white immigrant neighborhoods experienced highest average investment per project ($3.1 million), while the established and stable homeowners ($20 million) outpaced the other low distress neighborhoods.

Generally, the characteristics found in low distress neighborhoods, including higher housing values, levels of educational attainment, and incomes translate to stronger real estate markets and less risk for developers taking advantage of the RTC program. This likely supports increased preservation-based real estate activity in these parts of legacy cities. Beyond these market characteristics, the two neighborhood types with the largest shares of both projects and investment—competitive, educated, and struggling and highly bifurcated—are often within or adjacent to downtown, linking them with employment opportunities, transit, and other urban amenities and allowing developers to achieve the rents needed to make projects financially feasible. The location of these neighborhood types within the city indicates they are also likely have rich stocks of commercial and industrial historic buildings ripe for adaptive reuse projects, which convert spaces into modern housing and commercial units. The other two types of low distress neighborhoods—educated not stressed and established and

Average projects per tract	Total investment	Share of RTC investment	Average investment per project
7.3	$340,247,360	7%	$1,334,303
7.9	$328,166,976	7%	$2,449,007
3.9	$90,801,735	2%	$1,355,250
2.3	$104,478,418	2%	$3,072,895
5.8	$863,694,488	19%	$2,052,864
7.6	$1,617,883,384	35%	$5,778,155
2.0	$185,435,622	4%	$9,271,781
1.4	$219,956,316	5%	$19,996,029
10.6	$1,683,421,625	37%	$3,861,059
7.9	$3,706,696,947	81%	$9,726,756
5.7	$4,570,391,435		

stable homeowners—attract far less RTC activity, and are often along the cities' edges or away from downtown. Additionally, the building stock within established and stable homeowners neighborhoods is primarily owner-occupied housing, which is not eligible for the federal RTC.

While low distress neighborhoods are not capturing the majority of projects or investments, a substantial amount of historic preservation activity—nearly five hundred RTC projects and more than $800 million of reinvestment—occurred in high distress communities through the federal historic tax credit program. These places, characterized by lower housing values and incomes, along with high unemployment and poverty among primarily black residents, also face intense pressure for demolition (Tighe and Ganning 2015). Similar to the geographic patterns found among the low distress neighborhoods, the black, stressed, and disadvantaged and collapsed urban core types, which capture the majority of RTC activity, are often near downtown. Additionally, these high distress neighborhoods are often adjacent to low distress places, which may support the density of RTC activity taking place in these weaker market neighborhoods. This pattern could indicate that high distress neighborhoods benefit when developers exhaust the supply of historic buildings in adjacent low distress areas and shift their focus to nearby places with a ready supply of historic resources in need of renovation (Ryberg-Webster 2014a; Ryberg-Webster and Kinahan 2017). Additionally, pairing the RTC with low income housing tax credits (LIHTC), new markets tax credits (NMTC), state historic tax credit programs, or other local incentives, which is a common practice, further reduces risk and increases project feasibility in these weaker market neighborhoods.

Overall, the average investment per project in high distress neighborhoods ($2.1 million) much is smaller the investment per project in low distress ($9.7 million) areas. In addition to the previously described market conditions, the types of projects taking place within high distress neighborhoods and their physical characteristics also likely influence the lower levels of investment, including smaller buildings (e.g., neighborhood commercial buildings) or less architecturally intricate and thus less expensive rehabilitation options.

CITY-SPECIFIC TRENDS

The aforementioned patterns generally hold across the five cities with two exceptions. In Richmond high distress neighborhoods (57 percent) were more likely to experience RTC activity than low distress areas. Additionally, the shares of projects and total investment are more evenly dispersed across the two larger neighborhood groupings compared to other the cities, and Richmond's black, stressed, and disadvantaged neighborhoods have the second largest shares of total projects (34 percent) and investment (23 percent). In St. Louis high distress neighborhoods capture a larger share of projects (55 percent) than low distress types, and the city's collapsed urban core neighborhoods lead the way in terms most projects and investment among its high distress areas. In both cases, the high distress areas follow the spatial patterns previously described in that they are near low distress neighborhoods and close to downtown. There is also a clear visual pattern along the border of high distress and low distress neighborhoods, which indicates that the stronger market characteristics of the latter likely provide spillover benefits to adjacent high distress areas. The stronger presence of RTC activity in these cities' high distress neighborhoods is important to note because both Missouri and Virginia offer generous state historic tax credit programs that provide an additional 25 percent tax credit on top of the 20 percent federal credit.[7] Thus, the combination of the state and federal RTCs likely supports relatively high levels of activity in St. Louis and Richmond's high distress neighborhoods, compared to other legacy cities.

CONCLUSIONS AND POLICY IMPLICATIONS

This analysis of federal historic tax credit activity in five legacy cities offers several important insights about the characteristics of places where RTC investments occur, which can assist preservationists, planners, and policymakers. To summarize, from 1998 to 2007 RTC activity occurred in all eight neighborhood types found across these five legacy cities. However, both RTC projects (60 percent) and total investment (81 percent) were concentrated in low distress areas, and the projects that occur in low distress neighborhoods had higher average investments ($9.7 million) compared to those in high distress places ($2.1 million).

Overall, this analysis indicates that historic preservation is a potential reinvestment strategy for all legacy city neighborhoods, despite the broader narrative of low demand, weak real estate markets, and high costs of rehabilitation. In light of the current prominence of demolition-based approaches in legacy cities, this finding lends support to adding preservation to the tool kit practitioners, advocates, and policymakers consider when wrestling with the challenges of legacy cities' built environments. A wide range of neighborhoods exist across the legacy city landscape and the on-the-ground approaches used to address the specific circumstances in these places should be broad, varied, and attuned to opportunities and challenges presented by the built environment. While preservation will not always be the appropriate course of action for all neighborhoods or all buildings, it must be part of the options and frameworks for all communities in legacy cities, not just downtowns and recognized historic districts.

As these descriptive statistics show, the RTC currently functions predominantly as a reinvestment tool in legacy cities' low distress neighborhoods. Although these may not be the neighborhoods most in need of attention and resources, healthy, strong, and stable communities are vital foundations as legacy cities evolve and adapt as alternatives to their high growth and less affordable counterparts. For local planners and policymakers involved with geographic targeting and neighborhood redevelopment, greater consideration should be given to leveraging the incentives offered through state and federal RTC programs. Strategically combining historic tax credits with other resources could improve support for projects with desirable neighborhood outcomes including maintaining affordable housing options, encouraging mixed-use and mixed-income developments in stable areas, supporting a strong sense of place rooted in the preserved historic urban fabric, and densifying areas with strong transit connections. Greater integration of the RTC with local community needs and broader planning and community development goals could also help mitigate potential negative or inequitable changes, including both physical and cultural displacement, particularly as low distress neighborhoods continue to upgrade.

Although the federal RTC program functions as an intergovernmental collaboration between State Historic Preservation Offices and the National Park Service, this framework does not directly include local governments and community-based organizations, who are arguably the actors with the greatest stake in the long-term outcomes of RTC projects. Restructuring the RTC application process to allow for local comment and review would better engage residents, planners, and neighborhood organizations with the developers spearheading preservation-based redevelopments. This policy change could help ensure RTC projects are coordinated with other on-the-ground strategies, are not in conflict with neighborhood-planning goals, and would insert local actors in the RTC decision-making process to expand the focus of historic preservation toward larger community development issues. While less RTC activity occurs in high distress areas, these places are not completely devoid of reinvestment in their historic built environments. Since demolition-oriented approaches are far more likely to occur in low-income and minority neighborhoods (Tighe and Ganning 2015), characteristics that closely overlap with high distress areas, consideration of preservation-based tools including the RTC should be carefully examined before the implementation of widespread demolition plans, particularly in areas near existing low distress communities. At the same time, the predominance of RTC projects in low distress neighborhoods reinforces critiques that communities of color do not receive appropriate attention within planning and policymaking for legacy cities (see chapter 7). While preservation through the RTC is certainly taking place in legacy cities, there should be a concerted effort to examine carefully whose heritage is being preserved and consider whether preservation activity more broadly reflects the diverse histories of legacy cities, including the patterns of extreme race and class segregation. As this analysis indicates, more incentives may be necessary to support increased preservation-based activity in high distress neighborhoods, as higher levels of RTC activity in Richmond and St. Louis' high distress neighborhoods may be linked to their generous state-level RTC programs. While additional analysis is necessary to develop this link further, restructuring the federal program to target high need areas, similar to the process used to define eligible areas within the New Markets Tax Credit Program, could encourage preservation-based reinvestment in high distress neighborhoods.

The preservation community should also focus on proactively surveying and preparing National Register nominations for historic properties/districts in high distress places where there are more risks and likely less neighborhood-based capacity to survey/nominate. This would help lower the barriers to entry, since listing on the National Register of Historic Places is a precondition for RTC eligibility, into these neighborhoods for rehabilitation-oriented developers, and encourage the preservation of the distinctive legacies of culture, history, and heritage across all neighborhoods. Better connections between local officials and RTC developers, as described earlier, would also create opportunities to link developers with knowledge and experience of using historic tax credit to historic resources in high distress areas.

While the RTC is vital to the post–industrial transformation of legacy cities, as the current structure of the program readily supports large-scale projects adaptively reusing former commercial or manufacturing and converting these spaces to housing or mixed-used sites, the usefulness of this tool for other types of historic preservation projects is more limited. The need for architects, accountants, lawyers, and preservation consultants in order to qualify for the RTC often results in costs exceeding the tax benefits, which presents a barrier to using this incentive for small projects. Moreover, since non-income-producing buildings are not eligible for the federal RTC, the vast amounts of vacant, outmoded, single-family homes found across legacy cities are also not eligible for this incentive. Expanding the federal RTC to include non-income-producing, owner-occupied buildings within targeted, distressed neighborhoods, would more directly funnel federal funds toward the pressing needs and opportunities in legacy cities' historic built environments.

NOTES

1. The current 20 percent income tax credit structure took shape through the Tax Reform Act of 1986, which scaled back the RTC program from a 25 percent credit that was instituted with the Economic Recovery Tax Act of 1981 and created a 10 percent credit for non-historic buildings constructed prior to 1936 (Ryberg-Webster 2015a). The 10 percent credit was eliminated in 2017.

2. Eligibility requirements of the RTC include that the building must retain income-producing status for at least five years and the rehabilitation must be substantial (i.e., greater than $5,000 or exceed the building's adjusted basis). Income-producing uses include commercial, industrial, or rental apartments. Owner-occupied residential structures and public uses are not eligible for the federal RTC program.

3. Much of the gentrification literature focuses on urban contexts that differ greatly from the legacy city experience including high-growth places with tight housing markets such as New York (Freeman and Braconi 2004), Boston (Vigdor, Massey, and Rivlin 2002), or London (Atkinson 2000).

4. Hardest Hit Funds are a component of the Troubled Asset Relief Program that provides funding to states acutely affected by the Great Recession and foreclosure crisis. Demolitions supported by these funds are not required to complete the Section 106 review process. Established by the National Historic Preservation Act of 1966, Section 106 review "involves reviewing and commenting on federal and federally supported projects that affect historic properties . . . such review recognizes that federal policy and expenditures can cause great harm to historic properties" (Tyler, Ligibel, and Tyler, 2009, 51).

5. Hierarchical cluster analysis and discriminant analysis of pooled data (1970–2010) identified eight neighborhood types in these five cities across five census decades (1970–2010). This chapter focuses specifically on the neighborhood type of census

tracts with RTC activity in the year 2000, which is a proxy for their status prior to investment.

6. The data from NPS includes twelve cities. No full dataset of RTC activity is publicly available—thus other legacy cities are not included in the analysis. The NPS does maintain a searchable database that offers project addresses and approval dates, see http://tpsdev.cr.nps.gov/status/results.cfm.

7. Maryland, Ohio, and Pennsylvania also have state-level RTC programs, which are slightly less generous than those in Missouri and Virginia are. Maryland offers a 20 percent credit. In Ohio there is 25 percent credit with a competitive application process and a statewide cap of $60 million. In 2014 Pennsylvania created a state RTC program, which offers a 25 percent credit but is limited to $3 million of statewide annual program expenditures.

REFERENCES

Accordino, John, and Fabrizio Fasulo. 2013. "Fusing Technical and Political Rationality in Community Development: A Prescriptive Model of Efficiency-Based Strategic Geographic Targeting." *Housing Policy Debate* 23, no. 4: 615–42.

Advisory Council on Historic Preservation (ACHP). 2014. "Task Force on Rightsizing and Historic Preservation." Washington, DC, Advisory Council on Historic Preservation. http://www.achp.gov/achpTaskForceRightsizing.html.

American Assembly. 2011. *Reinventing America's Legacy Cities: Strategies for Cities Losing Population*. New York: American Assembly.

Atkinson, Rowland. 2000. "Measuring Gentrification and Displacement in Greater London." *Urban Studies* 37, no. 1: 149–65.

Bertron, Cara, and Donovan Rypkema. 2012. "Historic Preservation and Rightsizing." Advisory Council on Historic Preservation Report.

Brookings Institution. 2006. "Revitalizing Weak Market Cities in the U.S." http://www.brookings.edu/~/media/research/files/speeches/2006/5/08citiespercent20katz/20060508_weakmarketcities.pdf.

Campo, Daniel. 2016. "Historic Preservation in an Economic Void: Reviving Buffalo's Concrete Atlantis." *Journal of Planning History* 15, no. 4: 314–45.

Cohen, James R. 1998. "Combining Historic Preservation and Income Class Integration: A Case Study of the Butchers Hill Neighborhood of Baltimore." *Housing Policy Debate* 9, no. 3: 663–97.

Dubrow, Gail Lee. 1998. "Feminist and Multicultural Perspectives on Preservation Planning." In *Making the Invisible Visible: A Multicultural Planning History*, edited by Leonie Sandercock, 57–77. Berkeley: University of California Press, 1998.

Dynamo Metrics, LLC. 2015. "Estimating Home Equity Impacts from Rapid, Targeted Residential Demolition in Detroit, MI: Application of a Spatially Dynamic Data System for Decision Support." http://www.demolitionimpact.org/#thereport.

Freeman, Lance, and Frank Braconi. 2004. "Gentrification and Displacement New York City in the 1990s." *Journal of the American Planning Association* 70, no. 1: 39–52.

Galster, G. C. 2002. "Gentrification as Diversification: Why Detroit Needs It and How It Can Get It." *Journal of Law in Society* 4, no. 29: 29–43.

Hayden, Dolores. 1997. *The Power of Place: Urban Landscapes as Public History*. Cambridge, MA: MIT Press.

Hill, Edward W., Harold L. Wolman, Katherine Kowalczyk, and Travis St Clair. 2012. "Forces Affecting City Population Growth or Decline: The Effects of Interregional and Inter-Municipal Competition." In *Rebuilding America's Legacy Cities: New*

Directions for the Industrial Heartland, edited by Alan Mallach, 31–79. New York: American Assembly.

Hollander, Justin B. 2010. "Moving Toward a Shrinking Cities Metric: Analyzing Land Use Changes Associated with Depopulation in Flint, Michigan." *Cityscape* 12, no. 1: 133–51.

Hollander, Justin B., Karina Pallagst, Terry Schwarz, and Frank Popper. 2009. "Planning Shrinking Cities." *Progress in Planning* 72, no. 4: 223–32.

Howe, Kathryn Welch. 2003. "Private Sector Involvement in Historic Preservation." In *A Richer Heritage: Historic Preservation in the Twenty-First Century*, edited by Robert E. Stipe, 279–311. Chapel Hill: University of North Carolina Press.

Hyra, Derek. 2015. "The Back-to-the-City Movement: Neighborhood Redevelopment and Processes of Political and Cultural Displacement." *Urban Studies* 52, no. 10: 1753–73.

Kennedy, Maureen, and Paul Leonard. 2001. *Dealing with Neighborhood Change: A Primer on Gentrification and Policy Choices*. Washington, DC: Brookings Institution.

Kaufman, Ned. 2009. *Place, Race, and Story: Essays on the Past and Future of Historic Preservation*. London: Routledge.

Kinahan, Kelly L. 2016. "Neighborhood Revitalization and Historic Preservation in US Legacy Cities." PhD diss., Cleveland State University.

Legacy City Design (LCD). 2015. "Where Are Legacy Cities?" http://www.legacycitydesign.org/cities.

Legacy City Partnership (LCP). 2015. "What Are Legacy Cities? The Facts." http://www.legacycities.org/.

Listokin, David, Barbara Listokin, and Michael Lahr. 1998. "The Contributions of Historic Preservation to Housing and Economic Development." *Housing Policy Debate* 9, no. 3: 431–78.

Mallach, Alan. 2011. "Demolition and Preservation in Shrinking US Industrial Cities." *Building Research and Information* 39, no. 4: 380–94.

Mallach, Alan. 2012a. "Depopulation, Market Collapse, and Property Abandonment: Surplus Land and Buildings in Legacy Cities." In *Rebuilding America's Legacy Cities: New Directions for the Industrial Heartland*, edited by Alan Mallach, 85–110. New York: American Assembly.

Mallach, Alan. 2012b. "Reinventing America's Legacy Cities: Strategies for Cities Losing Population." In *Rebuilding America's Legacy Cities: New Directions for the Industrial Heartland*, edited by Alan Mallach, 323–43. New York: American Assembly.

Minner, Jennifer. "Revealing Synergies, Tensions, and Silences between Preservation and Planning." *Journal of the American Planning Association* 82, no. 2: 72–87.

National Park Service (NPS). 2017. *Federal Tax Incentives for Rehabilitating Historic Buildings: Annual Report for Fiscal Year 2016*. Washington, DC: US Department of the Interior, National Park Service, Technical Preservation Services.

Preservation Rightsizing Network (PRN). 2015. "Action Agenda for Historic Preservation in Legacy Cities." http://rightsizeplace.org/actionagenda/.

Ryberg-Webster, Stephanie. 2013. "Preserving Downtown America: Federal Rehabilitation Tax Credits and the Transformation of US Cities." *Journal of the American Planning Association* 79, no. 4: 266–79.

Ryberg-Webster, Stephanie. 2015a. "The Landscape of Urban Preservation: A Spatial Analysis of Federal Rehabilitation Tax Credits in Richmond, Virginia." *Journal of Urban Affairs* 37, no. 4: 410–35.

Ryberg-Webster, Stephanie. 2015b. "Urban Policy in Disguise: A History of the Federal Historic Rehabilitation Tax Credit." *Journal of Planning History* 14, no. 3: 204–23.

Ryberg-Webster, Stephanie. 2017. "Beyond Rust and Rockefeller: Preserving Cleveland's African American Heritage." *Preservation Education and Research* 9: 7–23.

Ryberg-Webster, Stephanie, and Kelly L. Kinahan. "Historic Preservation in Declining City Neighbourhoods: Analysing Rehabilitation Tax Credit Investments in Six US Cities." *Urban Studies* 54, no. 7: 1673–91.

Schilling, Joseph, and Jonathan Logan. 2008. "Greening the Rust Belt: A Green Infrastructure Model for Rightsizing America's Shrinking Cities." *Journal of the American Planning Association* 74, no. 4: 451–66.

Shilling, James, Kerry Vandell, Ruslan Koesman, and Zhenguo Lin. 2006. "How Tax Credits Have Affected the Rehabilitation of the Boston Office Market." *Journal of Real Estate Research* 28, no. 4: 321–48.

Smith, Neil. 1998. "Comment on David Listokin, Barbara Listokin, and Michael Lahr's 'The Contributions of Historic Preservation to Housing and Economic Development': Historic Preservation in a Neoliberal Age." *Housing Policy Debate* 9, no. 3: 479–85.

Tighe, J. Rosie, and Joanna P. Ganning. 2016. "Do Shrinking Cities Allow Redevelopment without Displacement? An Analysis of Affordability Based on Housing and Transportation Costs for Redeveloping, Declining, and Stable Neighborhoods." *Housing Policy Debate* 26, no. 4/5: 1–16.

Tighe, J. Rosie, and Joanna P. Ganning. 2015. "The Divergent City: Unequal and Uneven Development in St. Louis." *Urban Geography* 36, no. 5: 654–73.

Thomson, Dale E. 2008. "Strategic, Geographic Targeting of Housing and Community Development Resources: A Conceptual Framework and Critical Review." *Urban Affairs Review* 43, no. 5: 629–62.

Thomson, Dale E. 2011. "Strategic Geographic Targeting in Community Development: Examining the Congruence of Political, Institutional, and Technical Factors." *Urban Affairs Review* 47, no. 4: 564–94.

Thomson, Dale E. 2012. "Targeting Neighborhoods, Stimulating Markets: The Role of Political, Institutional, and Technical Factors in Three Cities." In *The City after Abandonment*, edited by Margaret Dewar and June Manning Thomas, 104–32. Philadelphia: University of Pennsylvania Press.

Tyler, Norman, Ted J. Ligibel, and Ilene R. Tyler. 2009. *Historic Preservation: An Introduction to its History, Principles, and Practice*. New York: W. W. Norton.

Vigdor, Jacob L., Douglas S. Massey, and Alice M. Rivlin. 2002. "Does Gentrification Harm the Poor?" *Brookings-Wharton Papers on Urban Affairs*: 133–82.

Werwath, Peter. 1998. "Comment on David Listokin, Barbara Listokin, and Michael Lahr's 'The Contributions of Historic Preservation to Housing and Economic Development.'" *Housing Policy Debate* 9, no. 3: 487–95.

5

Rental Housing Quality in Legacy Cities

WHAT DO WE KNOW AND WHAT CAN BE DONE?

MEGAN E. HATCH

The rental housing stock in legacy cities is often old and not well maintained. This lack of upkeep is the result of a variety of economic and housing market characteristics, and aggravated by split incentives. The split incentive occurs when landlords do not have an inducement to maintain their properties because they want to maximize their profits from renting the unit and renters do not want to invest in a home in which they cannot build equity. Thus, rental housing often suffers from a lack of repairs and upgrades that are common in owner-occupied homes. This absence of updates may be minor, such as not investing in new energy-efficient technologies, or major health and safety concerns such as not fixing broken bathroom plumbing. Vacant buildings, low rents, and limited municipal budgets all exacerbate the disincentive to invest in rental housing in legacy cities.

This chapter explores the conditions and causes of poorly maintained rental housing in legacy cities. It suggests possible policy solutions to help inform renters about the quality of a potential home as well as encourage landlords to maintain their properties. While all cities have some rental housing that is poorly maintained, the policy solutions to these problems in legacy cities must reflect their unique socioeconomic contexts. By identifying the state and sources of deteriorating housing stock, this chapter is a step toward understanding the consequences and solutions to poorly maintained rental housing in legacy cities. While much is still unknown about what policies will improve housing quality and what unintended consequences these policies may have, such as increasing rents or decreasing rental housing availability, the literature and programs already in place in some cities offer possible solutions for legacy cities seeking to address problems surrounding the quality of their rental housing stock.

THE PROBLEM: RENTAL HOUSING QUALITY IN LEGACY CITIES

As described by Guzman in chapter 3 and Krumholz in chapter 7, legacy cities are often characterized by an aging housing stock, financial instability, and persistent poverty. These factors, as well as others discussed later, increase the likelihood of low quality rental housing. This is particularly problematic for unsubsidized rental housing because that market is less regulated than the subsidized housing market, where units often undergo regular health and safety inspections by the government agencies providing the subsidies. In the unsubsidized sector, inspections are less likely to occur unless a specific violation is reported. Poor housing quality is associated with negative health outcomes (Krieger and Higgins 2002) as well as children's educational attainment and readiness for school (Coulton et al. 2016; Mueller and Tighe 2007). Coulton et al. (2016), in their study of Cleveland, find the negative effects on kindergarten readiness are particularly acute when considering cumulative exposure to poor housing quality. Furthermore, even nearby distressed properties may have a negative effect on children.

While not the primary focus of this chapter, high rent burdens and a lack of affordable housing are also reason for concern. In fact, Meltzer and Schwartz (2016) find high rent burdens are bad for health, often at a rate equal to or greater than negative housing quality conditions like cockroaches or the number of unit deficiencies. High rent burdens are defined as spending 30 percent or more of one's income on housing, with families spending more than 50 percent of their income on housing considered severely rent burdened (Newman 2008; Schwartz 2014). Since the 1990s renters have been getting poorer over time relative to homeowners, with real renters' income lower than in 1990 in almost all metropolitan statistical areas (Collinson 2011). High rent burdens are especially troublesome since the Great Recession because policy focus is on homeownership rather than unsubsidized rental housing (Colburn and Allen 2016).

Due to a lack of affordable housing, low-income populations are the most likely to live in low quality housing. While many scholars contend housing affordability is a bigger problem than housing quality in present-day US cities (Holupka and Newman 2011; Schwartz 2014), Desmond and Bell (2015) remind us the recent increase in rental housing prices has not gone hand in hand with increases in housing quality. Desmond (2016), in his Pulitzer Prize–winning book *Evicted*, gives many examples of low-income families in Milwaukee that were forced to take very low quality units (including nonfunctioning toilets and no stove) because it was either all they could afford or the only landlord who would rent to them with their rental history. Furthermore, renters who have been evicted or forced out of their homes are subsequently more likely to live in low quality housing (Desmond, Gershenson, and Kiviat 2015). Holupka and Newman (2011) find the number of children living in physically inadequate housing decreased by more than 50 percent between 1975 and 2005, although low-income children are still more than twice more likely to live in inadequate housing than the average for all children. Therefore, populations that are already vulnerable are most impacted by low quality rental housing, thus disproportionately suffering the negative consequences of poor housing quality.

DEFINING AND MEASURING RENTAL HOUSING QUALITY

Measuring substandard housing is a difficult task and, so far, a single valid and reliable measure has eluded researchers (Newman and Garboden 2013). A common measure of substandard housing is the American Housing Survey (AHS) inadequacy index, which categorizes housing as severely inadequate, moderately inadequate, and adequate (Schwartz 2014; US Census Bureau 2016). According to the 2015 AHS (US Census Bureau 2016), nationally, 1.3 percent of all housing units are severely inadequate and 4.4 percent are moderately inadequate, with rental units more than twice as likely to be severely or moderately inadequate. Despite the popularity of this measure of housing quality, Newman and Garboden (2013) warn researchers to use this index cautiously.

Another measure of housing quality comes from the American Community Survey (ACS) and is released by the US Department of Housing and Urban Development (HUD) as the Comprehensive Housing Affordability Strategy (CHAS) data. The CHAS data define housing quality two ways: substandard (with incomplete kitchen or plumbing facilities) and by the number of housing problems (none or one or more). The four housing problems are: incomplete kitchen facilities, incomplete plumbing facilities, crowding, and cost burden. The CHAS estimates of poor housing quality are higher than the AHS measures. For example, using data from the 2009–2013 ACS (US Department of Housing and Urban Development 2017), 36.2 percent of all households, 50.2 percent of renter households, and 28.6 percent of owner-occupied homes have at least one housing problem. Using the same data and the stricter definition of substandard as incomplete kitchen or plumbing facilities, the CHAS classifies 1.2 percent of all households, 2.1 percent of renter households, and 0.8 percent of owner households as substandard. The difference between the CHAS and AHS measurements are due to divergent definitions as well as the CHAS' inclusion of cost burden as a measure of a housing problem in one of their computations. For the purposes of this analysis, I use the CHAS data because it is available for all legacy cities and measures both housing quality and cost burden, providing both a conservative (the unit must be missing kitchen or plumbing facilities) and liberal (the unit must be missing kitchen or plumbing facilities, be overcrowded, or cause a rent burden) measure of poor housing quality. Together these two measures represent a range of ways to describe housing quality.

THE STATE OF RENTAL HOUSING QUALITY IN LEGACY CITIES

In order to understand the causes and potential solutions to low quality rental housing in legacy cities, it is helpful to have a snapshot of what the actual state of housing quality is in these cities. For this analysis, I consider the universe of legacy cities to be the eighty cities defined as "shrinking cities" by Ganning and Tighe (2018). Table 5.1 contains descriptive information from the 2009–2013 ACS five-year survey of these cities and the CHAS data based on that survey. On average, 50 percent of households in these cities rent their homes, with a range of 25 percent (Dearborn Heights, Michigan) to 77 percent (Newark, New Jersey), and a rental vacancy rate that averages 8.3 percent. Median income, education, and racial diversity vary greatly in the sample. The majority of the housing stock in these cities was built before 1960. Foreclosures are difficult to measure, but a proxy for the extent of foreclosures in a city is the number of properties identified as "other vacant" (Clark 2012). While this is only suggestive, on average, legacy cities have a per capita foreclosure rate of 0.04.

Table 5.1 presents two measures of housing quality: whether the ACS identifies the property as substandard or as having one or more identified problems (US Department of Housing and Urban Development 2017). The percentage of the rental stock defined as substandard in legacy cities ranges from zero (Lincoln Park, Michigan) to 4.2 percent (Springfield, Ohio), with a mean of 1.8 percent, which is below the national mean of 2.1 percent. This is in comparison to owner-occupied housing, where on average only 0.7 percent of housing is substandard. Substandard housing is a more conservative measure of housing quality than one or more problems, as the latter adds crowding and cost burden to the former's criteria of incomplete plumbing or kitchen facilities. Taking this more expansive view of housing quality, on average 53.8 percent of rental housing in legacy cities have at least one problem, a figure that ranges from 40.7 percent (Rome, New York) to 67.7 percent (Paterson, New Jersey). This is slightly higher than the national mean of 50.2 percent.

While the percentage of units with the strictest definition of substan-

TABLE 5.1: Population and housing characteristics of legacy cities

Characteristic	Mean	Standard deviation	Minimum	Maximum
Population				
Renters	50	10.3	24.5	77.3
Nonwhite	46	25.2	4.4	98.6
Bachelor's degree or higher	20	9.7	7.5	60.9
Median income	35,264	8,036	19,161	73,644
Population	175,996	355,199	26,830	2,706,101
Housing market				
Rental vacancy rate	8.3	3.4	1.7	20.1
Pre-1960 housing stock	65.9	11.9	28.5	87.8
Foreclosures per capita (proxy)	0.04	0.02	0.01	0.12
Housing quality				
Substandard owned	0.7	0.4	0	1.7
Substandard rented	1.8	0.8	0	4.2
One or more problems rented	53.8	5.0	40.7	67.7

dard housing are relatively low and the historical trend is towards improved housing quality (Schwartz 2014), these numbers still represent hundreds of thousands of households in legacy cities alone. When the measure of housing quality is expanded to include crowding and cost burden, over half of renters in legacy cities suffer from a housing quality problem. Thus, this represents a meaningful number of people in these cities, indicating a compelling need for a policy response to the problem of poor housing quality.

A DOUBLE THREAT: UNAFFORDABLE AND LOW QUALITY RENTAL HOUSING

A particularly vulnerable group are renters who live in substandard housing (using the definition of lacking complete kitchen or plumbing) and are cost burdened. While this represents less than 1 percent of renters on average in legacy cities, up to over 2.5 percent of renters live in substandard housing and spend 30 percent or more of their income on rent (Cleveland Heights, Ohio, and Springfield, Ohio). Figure 5.1 demonstrates the extent of this problem, and how it varies by income, measured as HUD Adjusted Median Family Income (HAMFI). The bars represent the mean percentage of renters in each city that are cost burdened. The income groups are not mutually exclusive, such that a person making 90 percent of HAMFI would be counted in each bar. On average, 0.96 percent of renters spend at least 30 percent of their income on rent and still live in substandard housing.

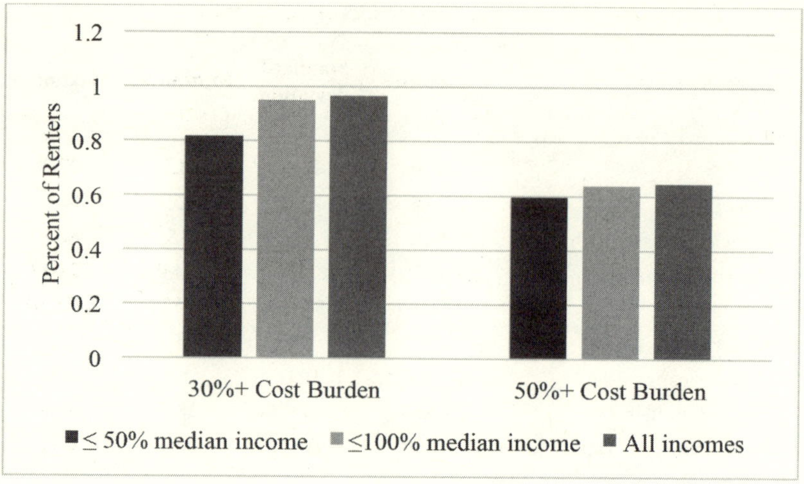

FIGURE 5.1: Mean percent of renters living in substandard housing, by income and rental cost burden

The majority of these cost-burdened renters make less than or equal to 50 percent of HAMFI. Severely cost-burdened renters (who spend 50 percent or more of their income on rent) are also most likely to have low incomes. While on average 0.65 percent of all renters are severely cost burdened and live in substandard housing, 0.60 percent make 50 percent or less of HAMFI. While being cost burdened and living in substandard housing is rare across legacy cities, those renters facing both cost and quality challenges are more likely to be low income.

CAUSES OF LOW QUALITY RENTAL HOUSING

The reasons why low quality rental housing exists in legacy cities are complex. Here I focus on several of the economic and housing market contextual factors that are especially prevalent in legacy cities. These problems are exacerbated by the split incentive phenomena present in any rental housing relationship. This lack of incentive for both landlords and renters to improve low quality units both explains why rental housing that does not meet basic health requirements exists and suggests a potential avenue for effective policy intervention to address this problem.

Old rental housing stock is susceptible to a host of problems. It is associated with higher maintenance costs, although the rate at which maintenance costs increase slows over time (Springer and Waller 1996). That is, in the short run, an older house may be more expensive to maintain than a new house, but in the long run, older houses may be cheaper to maintain because of factors such as more durable construction materials, and maintaining an older house is often cheaper than demolishing it and building a new house (Rypkema 2005). Older houses are more likely to have lead paint, and as older houses are demolished or updated, studies find that levels of lead poisoning among children decreases (Jacobs et al. 2009; Jacobs and Nevin 2006). With on average over 65 percent of rental housing in legacy cities built before 1960, the potential problems associated with older housing are of particular concern.

The housing bubble bursting and the Great Recession hit the housing stock in many US cities hard. Foreclosures not only negatively impacted homeowners but also their tenants and neighborhoods (Been and Glashausser 2009; Schuetz, Been, and Ellen 2008). The increase in the number of vacant properties and sheriff sales are noticeable and unequally distributed, as described by Mikelbank in chapter 10. As the foreclosure crisis unfolded, there was greater demand for rental housing (Joint Center for Housing Studies of Harvard University 2017) and a decrease in housing quality (Tilburg 2017), matched with an increase in the number of rent-burdened households (Colburn and Allen 2016). For example, Lens (2017) finds that between 2007 and 2010, the ratio of extremely low income households to affordable housing units increased in 70 percent of the United States' largest counties. Thus, the Great Recession and foreclosure crisis contributed to heightened demand for rental housing coupled with a decline in housing quality and affordability for many families in legacy cities.

Legacy cities often have strained municipal budgets. Due to years of shrinking populations and a loss of their tax bases, legacy cities must provide the same (or more) services with less revenue (see chapter 3). That means they must make difficult choices and prioritize policies. While cities may want to inspect all their rental housing, abate lead, and rehabilitate/tear down vacant properties, they might not be able to do those things. If ensuring high quality rental housing is a low priority, housing quality will continue to deteriorate over time.

One explanation for why private citizens do not address the quality issues on their own is the concept of a split incentive. Essentially, split incentive theory, which is also known as the landlord/tenant dilemma, occurs when two parties have different incentives and therefore cannot agree on a solution to a problem (Ástmarsson, Jensen, and Maslesa 2013). Mee et al. (2014) define it as a situation "where a landlord has to pay for an upgrade to a property but a tenant more directly benefits from that upgrade" (370). In the current context, split incentive theory holds no party in the rental relationship has the proper incentive to make repairs. For most landlords, the primary incentive is profit, and maintenance is part of that profit calculation (Springer and Waller 1996). Landlords will only invest in unit improvements if the modifications will not decrease their profits—meaning any improvement costs must be recouped in other ways, such as through a reduction in unit vacancy or an increase in rent. Rent increases in legacy cities may be impossible given the relatively low market rents compared to other cities (Tighe 2015). Renters, on the other hand, want to diminish their housing costs. Because renters do not gain equity in their homes, any investment they make in their unit will not be recovered later through resale value. Consequently, both parties have strong disincentives to make improvements to the property. The split incentive problem may be particularly acute for low-income renters (Bird and Hernández 2012), who have less information, incentives, and capital than higher income renters do. This does not mean, however, that neither party will do any property maintenance, as renters may make minor improvements as a coping mechanism (Hernández 2016) and landlords may make improvements if it will increase their profits (Springer and Waller 1996).

Split incentives are usually discussed in the context of energy efficiency and costs (Ástmarsson, Jensen, and Maslesa 2013; Bird and Hernández 2012; Gillingham, Harding, and Rapson 2012; Wrigley and Crawford 2017). However, increasing energy efficiency is similar to improving housing quality—it is something that will likely improve the lives of the people living in the homes, but is costly to do. In their study of Australian rental housing, Wrigley and Crawford (2017) find split incentives to be a key market failure explaining why neither party makes energy efficiency upgrades to rental properties. Gillingham, Harding, and Rapson (2012) observe if someone is paying the heating bill they will adjust the temperature during the day, suggesting the preference for energy efficiency (or any type of housing quality measure) varies depending on who is paying the costs and receiving the benefits. The lessons learned from the robust split incentive literature in the residential energy sector can offer opportunities for explanations of and solutions to the split incentive problem facing rental housing quality.

Rental housing quality is likely to remain a problem without policy intervention because of legacy cities' macro and micro challenges, including aged rental stock, high foreclosure rates, and strained municipal budgets, as well as the split incentive, whereby neither landlords nor renters are sufficiently compensated for property improvements. Within this context lies opportunity. The remainder of this chapter introduces existing and potential policy interventions to improve rental housing quality in legacy cities.

POTENTIAL POLICY SOLUTIONS

At the most basic level, the solution to low quality rental housing is to improve the quality of existing housing or to move populations into new, high quality housing. This can be done at the individual level through landlord and renter actions, although as argued earlier, this is unlikely because of the split incentive that discourages either party from investing in improvements. Individuals can move, although this does not appear to improve the housing quality of units where low-income children live (Holupka and Newman 2011). Therefore, legacy cities that want to address these problems need to design policies to facilitate improvements. Community engagement, particularly among affected renters, may also improve policy and housing quality outcomes (Hernández 2016).

Wrigley and Crawford (2017) attempt a similar charge as the one taken up here, by identifying possible policy solutions for overcoming split incentives and improving energy efficiency in rental housing in Australia. In their survey of landlords and renters, changes to the tax code and mandatory standards were the most supported potential policy solutions. Bird and Hernández (2012) assert an effective policy solution to the split incentive problem must have landlord and renter incentives, be voluntary, create savings, have durability such as thorough inspections, have costs covered by savings rather than grants, and be transparent. Ástmarsson, Jensen, and Maslesa (2013) concur, declaring any policy solution to a split incentive problem must be multidimensional and context specific. Local norms and standards are also important (Mee et al. 2014). It seems likely, then, that an effective approach to improving the quality of rental housing in legacy cities will need to be multifaceted and customized for each unique socioeconomic context.

One thing cities can do to improve rental housing quality is strengthen their renter protection laws. States already vary greatly in how much protection they offer renters, including the remedies available to renters if a property has health and safety violations (Hatch 2017). Less is known about city-level protections, but it is very likely these also vary substantially. Building and safety codes also provide important protections for households (Holupka and Newman 2011). However, as with all housing policies, there is a concern that additional regulation may lead to a reduction in the supply of affordable housing as landlords decide to leave the market rather than comply with the regulations (Been and Glashausser 2009; Burfurd, Gangadharan, and Nemes 2012). Future research should identify legacy city renter protection laws aimed at improving housing quality with the aim of recognizing best practices for adoption in other cities.

One form of renter protection is periodic unit inspections. One of the reasons rental housing quality is less of a problem in the subsidized rental sector (this is not to say all subsidized units meet health and safety standards—see, for example, Hernandez 2016) than in the unsubsidized rental sector is because of periodic health and safety inspections. For example, anyone wishing to move into a unit using a Housing Choice Voucher (colloquially known as a Section 8 voucher), must first have the unit inspected and designated by HUD to meet certain quality standards. While landlords often report the inspection process to be time-consuming and costly (Greenlee 2014), mandatory inspections for all rental properties may reduce landlord reticence to rent to voucher holders because the process would be the same for all rental units, regardless of the renter's source of income (Tighe, Hatch, and Mead 2017). Inspections, particularly targeted to high-risk areas, were effective in reducing rates of lead poisoning in children in Rochester, New York (Korfmacher and Hanley 2013). However, the challenge with inspections is implementation and enforcement (Krieger and Higgins 2002). Frequent inspections may be necessary as there is some evidence the number of housing problems increases over a household's tenure in the unit (Shuey, Leventhal, and Coley 2016).

In order for systematic inspections to be feasible, it is likely cities will have to introduce rental registries to aid with record keeping. In Maryland such a registry is associated with decreased levels of lead poisoning (Tilburg 2017). The challenge with registries is the need to constantly update them, which may pose an unsurmountable administrative burden on already resource-restricted legacy cities.

Whether or not regular unit inspections are feasible, another way to improve housing quality is to increase the information about housing quality and affordability, including utility bills, available to renters (Reina and Kontokosta 2017). One possible approach would be to mandate that landlords report the quality of their unit, including any deficiencies, before prospective renters sign a lease. This allows renters to make decisions about whether they want to live in a home with full knowledge of the quality (or lack thereof) of the unit. Philadelphia, for example, requires landlords of certain types of units to provide certifications that their properties are lead-free or lead-safe (Korfmacher and Hanley 2013). In their laboratory studies of energy upgrades, Burfurd, Gangadharan, and Nemes (2012) find that mandatory information sharing increases market efficiency, and the effect size for mandatory and voluntary information sharing is almost the same if information sharing is costless. Therefore, any policy aimed at making housing quality information available to potential renters will be most successful if the cost of sharing that information (such as on leases or vacancy advertisements) is low or zero.

Instead of mandating providing information about housing quality or requiring landlords to fix their properties, cities could incentivize landlords through the tax code. One policy already in place at the federal level is tax credits for window and door replacement through the residential property energy tax credit. Jacobs and Nevin (2006) argue that window replacement is the largest contributing factor to the reduction in childhood lead poisoning between 1990 and 2000. Additional city-level subsidies for window replacement may help overcome the split incentive problem by reducing the cost to landlords of the improvement. Similar incentives to encourage homeowners to invest in modern insulation to reduce air leakage through the basement and attic may also produce positive outcomes. In legacy cities, which are often in colder climates, this would mean lower utility bills for renters, thus also addressing part of the housing affordability problem. Tax credits or deductions may be an effective way to encourage landlords to improve the quality of their homes by lowering the costs of those improvements. The tax incentives could be expanded from energy to include health and safety upgrades to rental properties, such as completing plumbing or kitchen facilities. However, this policy solution may be more effective at the state or federal level than at the city level because not all cities have municipal taxes where they can provide the credits or deductions. If tax incentives are not possible, similar solutions that cities may be able to enact are interest-free or low-interest loans for property repairs. One such program is the Detroit 0% Home Repair Loans Program (Poethig et al. 2017). These types of financing programs lower the cost to landlords of renovating their properties, thus helping to diminish the split incentive problem.

Two main policy challenges remain. First, there is likely a tradeoff between housing quality and price. Families may choose to live in lower quality housing to decrease their rent burden (Desmond 2016). In studies of housing market regulations, Been and Glashausser (2009) find regulation is associated with higher rental prices. Increasing quality (and therefore prices), may intensify rental burdens, particularly for low-income unsubsidized renters who already face many challenges to finding a place to live. Mandatory standards may also decrease the availability of rental housing (Burfurd, Gangadharan, and Nemes 2012). As Shuey, Leventhal, and Coley (2016) explain: "policies and programs designed to improve housing conditions for low-income families do not have a complete picture of how various aspects of housing may interrelate, and thus efforts to help low-income families in one domain of housing may have unintended consequences in other domains" (104). Therefore, policymakers in legacy cities should carefully consider these trade-offs and unintended consequences of any policy, including the ones discussed earlier, before initiating any policies or programs aimed at addressing rental housing quality.

This relates to the second challenge: housing scholars, advocates, and policymakers do not know a lot about what works to improve housing quality. Most of the recent literature focuses on housing instability among low-income renters (Holl, van den Dries, and Wolf 2016; Desmond and Gershenson 2017) rather than the quality of that housing. In a meta-analysis of eviction-prevention practices, Holl et al. (2016) identify a paucity of high quality evaluations. Therefore, what is needed is large-scale empirical evaluations of existing policies legacy cities are already implementing to develop best practices for other cities to emulate. For example, it is not clear if universal rental housing registries and inspections are feasible. Cleveland Heights, Ohio, requires that all rental units be inspected every three years (City of Cleveland Heights 2017). Other cities mandate at least some inspections of their rental stock, although the inspections may only be of certain types of housing (e.g., multifamily), a sample of units, and not annually (Newman 2008) or compliance-based, meaning they only occur when someone files a complaint (Tilburg 2017). Evaluations of this type of program remain elusive (Poethig et al. 2017), so it is unclear whether and to what extent the policies are enforced, and if they are enforced, what effect they have on unit price, quality, and available quantity.

CONCLUSION

As in all cities, renters in legacy cities face a plethora of challenges to finding high quality, affordable rental housing. What makes these challenges unique in legacy cities is the context of strained municipal budgets, aging housing stock, and low rents. The combination of problems and contexts are unique in legacy cities, so public policy must focus on how to address these problems within this context. As Korfmacher and Hanley (2013) explain: "local policy makers may need assistance to identify key features of their local physical, economic, and legal environment, to adapt tools from other areas, and to provide for a robust system of ongoing evaluation" (810). This chapter provided some examples of policies legacy cities are already using to address housing quality, but there is much we still do not know about what works to improve rental housing quality, particularly without increasing rents and making units even less affordable for already rent-burdened populations. Local policy experimentation and adoption with careful evaluation may be the most effective way to address housing quality concerns in legacy cities.

REFERENCES

Ástmarsson, Björn, Per Anker Jensen, and Esmir Maslesa. 2013. "Sustainable Renovation of Residential Buildings and the Landlord/Tenant Dilemma." *Energy Policy* 63 (December): 355–62.

Been, Vicki, and Allegra Glashausser. 2009. "Tenants: Innocent Victims of the Nation's Foreclosure Crisis." *Albany Government Law Review* 2: 1–28.

Bird, Stephen, and Diana Hernández. 2012. "Policy Options for the Split Incentive: Increasing Energy Efficiency for Low-Income Renters." *Energy Policy* 48 (September): 506–14.

Burfurd, Ingrid, Lata Gangadharan, and Veronika Nemes. 2012. "Stars and Standards: Energy Efficiency in Rental Markets." *Journal of Environmental Economics and Management* 64, no. 2: 153–68.

City of Cleveland Heights. 2017. "Rental Property Inspections." http://www.clevelandheights.com/index.aspx?page=1137.

Clark, Sandra Luckett. 2012. *Understanding Differences in ACS and 2010 Census Information on Occupancy Status—Data Collection Methods*. Washington, DC: US Census Bureau.

Colburn, Gregg, and Ryan Allen. 2016. "Rent Burden and the Great Recession in the USA." *Urban Studies* 55, no. 2: 226–43.

Collinson, Rob. 2011. "Rental Housing Affordability Dynamics, 1990–2009." *Cityscape* 13, no. 2: 71–103.

Coulton, Claudia J., Francisca Richter, Seok-Joo Kim, Robert Fischer, and Youngmin Cho. 2016. "Temporal Effects of Distressed Housing on Early Childhood Risk Factors and Kindergarten Readiness." *Children and Youth Services Review* 68 (September): 59–72.

Desmond, Matthew. 2016. *Evicted: Poverty and Profit in the American City*. New York: Crown/Archetype.

Desmond, Matthew, and Monica Bell. 2015. "Housing, Poverty, and the Law." *Annual Review of Law and Social Science* 11, no. 1: 15–35.

Desmond, Matthew, and Carl Gershenson. 2017. "Who Gets Evicted? Assessing Individual, Neighborhood, and Network Factors." *Social Science Research* 62 (February): 362–77.

Desmond, Matthew, Carl Gershenson, and Barbara Kiviat. 2015. "Forced Relocation and Residential Instability among Urban Renters." *Social Service Review* 89, no. 2: 227–62.

Ganning, J., and J. R. Tighe. Forthcoming. "Moving toward a Shared Understanding of the US Shrinking City." *Journal of Planning Education and Research*.

Gillingham, Kenneth, Matthew Harding, and David Rapson. 2012. "Split Incentives in Residential Energy Consumption." *Energy Journal* 33, no. 2: 37–62.

Greenlee, Andrew J. 2014. "More Than Meets the Market? Landlord Agency in the Illinois Housing Choice Voucher Program." *Housing Policy Debate* 24, no. 3: 500–524.

Hatch, Megan E. 2017. "Statutory Protection for Renters: Classification of State Landlord–Tenant Policy Approaches." *Housing Policy Debate* 27, no. 1: 98–119.

Hernández, Diana. 2016. "Affording Housing at the Expense of Health: Exploring the Housing and Neighborhood Strategies of Poor Families." *Journal of Family Issues* 37, no. 7: 921–46.

Holl, Marieke, Linda van den Dries, and Judith R. L. M. Wolf. 2016. "Interventions to Prevent Tenant Evictions: A Systematic Review." *Health & Social Care in the Community* 24, no. 5: 532–46.

Holupka, C. Scott, and Sandra J. Newman. 2011. "The Housing and Neighborhood Conditions of America's Children: Patterns and Trends over Four Decades." *Housing Policy Debate* 21, no. 2: 215–45.

Jacobs, David E., and Rick Nevin. 2006. "Validation of a 20-Year Forecast of US Childhood Lead Poisoning: Updated Prospects for 2010." *Environmental Research* 102, no. 3: 352–64.

Jacobs, David E., Jonathan Wilson, Sherry L. Dixon, Janet Smith, and Anne Evens. 2009. "The Relationship of Housing and Population Health: A 30-Year Retrospective Analysis." *Environmental Health Perspectives* 117, no. 4: 597–604.

Joint Center for Housing Studies of Harvard University. 2017. "The State of the Nation's Housing." Harvard University, Cambridge, MA. http://www.jchs.harvard.edu/sites/jchs.harvard.edu/files/harvard_jchs_state_of_the_nations_housing_2017_0.pdf.

Korfmacher, Katrina S., and Michael L. Hanley. 2013. "Are Local Laws the Key to Ending Childhood Lead Poisoning?" *Journal of Health Politics, Policy and Law* 38, no. 4: 757–813.

Krieger, James, and Donna L. Higgins. 2002. "Housing and Health: Time Again for Public Health Action." *American Journal of Public Health* 92, no. 5: 758–68.

Lens, Michael C. 2017. "Extremely Low-Income Households, Housing Affordability and the Great Recession." *Urban Studies* 55, no. 8: 1615–35.

Mee, Kathleen J., Lesley Instone, Miriam Williams, Jane Palmer, and Nicola Vaughan. 2014. "Renting Over Troubled Waters: An Urban Political Ecology of Rental Housing." *Geographical Research* 52, no. 4: 365–76.

Meltzer, Rachel, and Alex Schwartz. 2016. "Housing Affordability and Health: Evidence From New York City." *Housing Policy Debate* 26, no. 1: 80–104.

Mueller, Elizabeth J., and J. Rosie Tighe. 2007. "Making the Case for Affordable Housing: Connecting Housing with Health and Education Outcomes." *Journal of Planning Literature* 21, no. 4: 371–85.

Newman, Sandra J. 2008. "Does Housing Matter for Poor Families? A Critical Summary of Research and Issues Still to Be Resolved." *Journal of Policy Analysis and Management* 27, no. 4: 895–925.

Newman, Sandra J., and Philip M.E. Garboden. 2013. "Psychometrics of Housing Quality Measurement in the American Housing Survey." *Cityscape* 15, no. 1: 293–306.

Poethig, Erika C., Joseph Schilling, Laurie Goodman, Bing Bai, James Gastner, Rolf Pendall, and Sameera Fazili. 2017. "The Detroit Housing Market." Urban Institute, March 3, 2017. http://www.urban.org/research/publication/detroit-housing-market.

Reina, Vincent J., and Constantine Kontokosta. 2017. "Low Hanging Fruit? Regulations and Energy Efficiency in Subsidized Multifamily Housing." *Energy Policy* 106 (July): 505–13.

Rypkema, Donovan D. 2015. *The Economics of Historic Preservation: A Community Leader's Guide*. 2nd ed. Washington, DC: National Trust for Historic Preservation.

Schuetz, Jenny, Vicki Been, and Ingrid Gould Ellen. 2008. "Neighborhood Effects of Concentrated Mortgage Foreclosures." *Journal of Housing Economics* 17, no. 4: 306–19.

Schwartz, Alex F. 2014. *Housing Policy in the United States*. London: Routledge.

Shuey, Elizabeth A., Tama Leventhal, and Rebekah Levine Coley. 2016. "Housing Characteristics over Time: Identifying Patterns for Low-Income Families." *Journal of Poverty* 20, no. 1: 102–25.

Springer, Thomas M., and Neil G. Waller. 1996. "Maintenance of Residential Rental Property: An Empirical Analysis." *Journal of Real Estate Research* 12, no. 1: 89–99.

Tighe, J. Rosie. 2015. "Affordable Housing in Legacy Cities." Paper presented at the University of San Francisco School of Law Conference, San Francisco, CA, January 2015.

Tighe, J. Rosie, Megan E. Hatch, and Joseph Mead. 2017. "Source of Income Discrimination and Fair Housing Policy." *Journal of Planning Literature* 32, no. 1: 3–15.

Tilburg, William C. 2017. "Policy Approaches to Improving Housing and Health." *Journal of Law, Medicine & Ethics* 45, no. 1: 90–93.

US Census Bureau. 2016. "American Housing Survey for the United States: 2015." https://www2.census.gov/programs-surveys/ahs/2015/2015%20AHS%20Definitions.pdf.

US Department of Housing and Urban Development. 2017. "Consolidated Planning/CHAS Data | HUD USER." https://www.huduser.gov/portal/datasets/cp.html.

Wrigley, Koel, and Robert H. Crawford. 2017. "Identifying Policy Solutions for Improving the Energy Efficiency of Rental Properties." *Energy Policy* 108 (September): 369–78.

6

From Brown to Green

SUSTAINABLE BUILDINGS IN LEGACY CITIES

ROBERT SIMONS AND EUNKYU LEE

What we now call legacy cities in the United States were once the envy of the industrializing world: jobs were plentiful and population growth followed. However, in the mid-twentieth century, many industrial powerhouse cities experienced shuttered factories as the global post–World War II economy and globalization took hold (see Ryberg-Webster and Tighe's introduction to this volume). Some of these legacy cities have recovered—others have not.

At the same time, servicing urban buildings has played an increasingly important role in human society, increasing their impact on the environment. US buildings account for 41 percent of the total US energy consumption, which is more than the energy consumption from the transportation and industrial sectors, while contributing 40 percent of the nation's total carbon dioxide emissions (US Department of Energy 2012).

In this context, a main focus of our research interest is to examine the installation of sustainable (green) property development, typified by Leadership in Energy and Environmental Design (LEED) certification in legacy cities in comparison to non-legacy cities. According to the Environmental Protection Agency (EPA), green buildings represent resource-efficient models for construction and operation that are designed to use fewer resources and generate less pollution.

Over the past decade, the green building movement has gained substantial strength and momentum in global society, and the United States is one of the world's leaders. A growing body of literature reveals the positive and rejuvenating effects of sustainable buildings in terms of economic, environmental, and occupant benefits (Biblow 2009; Miller et al. 2009; Eichholtz et al. 2010). These economic benefits can be categorized into two parts: those benefits related to the sustainable property itself and those pertinent to the role of those buildings in regional economies. The second aspect is of interest here, to see if legacy cities are bouncing back with green growth.

In this context, this study examines the incidence and development of green buildings in the United States. We specifically compare the presence of both new green construction and retrofit projects between legacy cities and non-legacy cities across the country. The green projects analyzed in this study include LEED-certified commercial, residential, industrial, for-profit, and nonprofit (e.g., public schools) buildings and neighborhood development (LEED-ND) projects. LEED-ND is particularly designed for neighborhood-scale urban development projects taking a green design approach that reduces the environmental harms of the built environment and also restores the balance of natural systems.

The general idea of a legacy city is that past industrial activity has left a "legacy" of urban problems, including lost manufacturing jobs, brownfields with contaminated land, and general decline, often coupled with fiscal stress and population loss. Although the definition of a legacy city is not universally agreed upon, this chapter follows the empirically justified list of legacy cities identified by Tighe and Ganning (2018).[1]

The green building movement as one aspect of sustainable development is described in the next section, followed by data analyses on the association between the green building movement and legacy cities. This chapter particularly analyzes green building market penetration rates and two types of green building incidence: new construction and retrofits. Our analysis tests if more green building retrofits are found in legacy cities. Finally, we draw policy implications for future sustainable real estate development in legacy cities.

GREEN BUILDING MOVEMENT

The basic concept of sustainable development emerged from the notion that the environmental crisis is inseparably linked with the economic crisis and can be resolved only through a revolutionary change in our understanding of the relationship between economic activities, the ecosystem, and our perception of nature (Korten 1991). From this point of view, sustainable development strategies emphasize that sustainable economic growth is key to achieving both agendas: economic growth and environmental protection. In the same context, Mega (1996) simply defines sustainable cities as places trying to develop in order to meet the increasing environmental, economic, and social challenges.

In this context, the general idea of sustainable (green) building can be traced to the 1970s, when the energy crisis emerged as one of the most urgent social issues in the global society. *The Limits to Growth* (1972) initially sounded an alarm on the global energy crisis through an elaborate computer simulation (Meadows, Meadows, Randers, and Behrens 1972). Since the 1970s, public knowledge and concerns of general environmental issues have grown (Bord, Fisher, and O'Connor 1998). Dunlap and Van Liere (1978) and Milbrath and Fisher (1984) explain that there was a worldwide revolution in public awareness of a new environmental paradigm that pursues the need for humans to live in harmony with nature and the balance between economic growth and environmental protection (Scott and Willits 1994).

GREEN BUILDING CERTIFICATION

Given this background, green building practices have been widely adopted by both the public and private sectors over the past decade, worldwide. In the United States the federal government and many states (notably California) and local governments (including large East Coast cities and those in California) lead the movement by offering financial incentives for green buildings, by establishing mandatory green building standards, and/or by locating government offices in green-certified buildings.

The certification of green buildings has been driven by a wide variety of organizations around the world (Kebert 2004). The world leader is the US Green Building Council (USGBC), who developed and continued to certify LEED standards, a well-known building rating system that verifies environmental performance of new and existing commercial, institutional, and residential buildings, and community development projects. On the operating (rather than design) side, the Energy Star certification program was established by the EPA in 1992 under the Clean Air Act. Energy Star provides a certification for consumer products, homes, buildings, and plants that are designed to be energy efficient.

At the federal level, President Obama introduced in 2011 the Better Buildings Initiative, intended to make commercial and industrial buildings 20 percent more energy efficient over the next ten years, as well as to accelerate private-sector investment in energy efficiency. This initiative has encouraged state and local governments to adopt their own sustainable building policies, and has resulted in the rapid diffusion of green-certified buildings.

Currently, more than 20 percent of US cities with populations greater than fifty thousand have their own green building programs, such as financial incentives and grants, and approximately fifty-five million people live in cities with green building programs (American Institute of Architects 2009). In a broader geographical context, twenty-four out of the twenty-five most populated US metropolitan areas include cities with their own green building policies such as tax incentives and grants. The true number of green building-supportive communities continues to increase nationwide.

In the private sector, a growing number of companies are motivated to relocate into green-certified buildings for reasons that include marketing and public relations opportunities, additional property premiums, lower carbon footprints, and increased employee productivity, in terms of the concept of corporate social responsibility (Kaplow 2009; Eichholtz, Kok, and Quigley 2009). Furthermore, real estate developers and property owners are motivated to invest in green building construction as it provides financial benefits from tax credits and/or deduction programs as well as subsidies (Fuerst and McAllister 2011).

Cleveland, Ohio, is one of the cities committed to encouraging green buildings and has appointed a sustainability coordinator to facilitate these efforts. The city promotes green structures that provide safe, affordable, and healthy environments for residents and workers. A key part of the green building movement in Cleveland is energy efficiency, which lowers operating costs and reduces greenhouse gas emissions. In 2003 private-sector developers built their first green building at 3500 Lorain Avenue, and now downtown Cleveland contains a substantial cluster of LEED-certified and registered buildings, with about twenty green buildings scattered from the Flats East Bank to East 9th Street, an area of about 3.2 square miles. Furthermore, fifteen LEED-certified buildings are located along Euclid Avenue, which is "the largest concentration of green building" in Cleveland. According to the national LEED database, one hundred projects had been certified by LEED in Cleveland as of December 2016.[2] These LEED-certified projects include fifty-two commercial, eleven residential, and seven government buildings. The city government has adopted green-supportive policies, such as a Sustainable Municipal Building requirement, and also set carbon footprint-reduction goals as part of its Climate Action Plan.[3]

GREEN BUILDING PREMIUMS

When it comes to the economic benefit of building sustainable properties, a large number of studies find that buildings certified by green building assessment systems, such as LEED and Energy Star, have property value premiums of up to 26 percent, compared with noncertified buildings (Fuerst and McAllister 2011). Specifically, Fuerst and McAllister find a rental premium of 5 percent for LEED-certified buildings and 4 percent for Energy Star buildings, compared to noncertified conventional buildings. Furthermore, the same study finds a price premium of 25 percent for LEED buildings and 26 percent for Energy Star buildings with higher levels of certification providing a higher premium.

Kok, Miller, and Morris (2012) find that LEED-certified buildings have a 7.1 percent rental premium over noncertified buildings. Additionally, their study shows that when buildings have both LEED and Energy Star certifications together, their rental premium is even higher. Additionally, Wiley et al. (2010) find a rental premium of 17 percent for LEED buildings and 8 percent for Energy Star-labeled buildings.

Furthermore, a growing body of literature reveals the positive effect of green certification on rents and occupancy rates (e.g., Wiley et al. 2010). Additionally, several case studies show that the financial benefits offset the initial construction cost, which is generally higher than conventional building construction due to relatively higher costs of green materials and technology (Rehm and Ade 2013). Thus, green construction should exert upward pressure on commercial property values, sustaining economic recovery.

GREEN BUILDINGS AND LOCAL ECONOMIES

As the green building movement has attracted worldwide attention during the past decade, studies have provided evidence of the relationship between the diffusion of green-certified buildings and regional economies (Fitzgerald, 2010). Some initial work indicates that the proliferation of green-certified buildings promotes local economic growth by facilitating green product- and service-related industries (Allen and Potiowsky 2008).

A report from McKinsey and Company (2009) reveals that improvements in energy efficiency for the residential and commercial real estate sector is expected to create six hundred thousand to nine hundred thousand stable and ongoing green jobs in the United States by 2020. Specifically, the report explains that sustainable building-related job growth can be driven in two ways: from the labor-intensive construction sectors, and from the implementation and enforcement of sustainable building standards and codes, such as LEED and Energy Star. For example, General Electric hired an additional 150 employees for energy-efficient light bulb production in Ohio and Illinois in 2013 (McKinsey and Company 2009).

The energy-efficiency industry has rapidly become one of the major economic drivers in the United States, and this is supported by federal, state, and local policies. According to a report from the Lawrence Berkeley National Laboratory, employment in the energy-efficiency sector will increase to three times its current size by 2030, when it will reach 1.2 million employees (Goldman 2010). It should be noted that building and construction-related workers currently account for about 70 percent of the total employment in the energy-efficiency sectors. In 2013 sustainable buildings supported about eight million workers in various occupational areas, including construction, management, architecture, engineering, and finance. Booz Allen Hamilton (2009) estimated that sustainable construction added $554 billion to the national GDP in that same year.

In this context, we pose the notion that legacy cities could benefit from green buildings when it comes to their economic recovery, at least in the construction sector. This study is the first piece of our research series addressing this question.

GREEN BUILDINGS IN LEGACY CITIES

This study utilizes the national LEED-certified project inventory data as a measure of green buildings. As of December 2016, 49,360 projects (including building construction, retrofits, and community development projects) had been certified by LEED in the United States. Among them, 40,877 projects are included in the analysis of the current study. Due to confidentiality concerns, the data for 8,484 projects are missing key information, such as the address and size (square feet) of the project and the date of certification, and thus were eliminated from consideration.[4] Of the 40,877 projects, 3,757 projects (9.2 percent) are retrofits (i.e., green renovations).[5] The most common types of LEED-certified projects in the United States are residential (43 percent) and commercial (32 percent). Other types include educational properties, government-owned buildings, health-care facilities, hotels, and community development projects, including parks.[6] The average size of LEED-certified projects is 74,911 square feet, with the smallest project just 13.27 square feet, and the largest project at 26 million square feet.

Table 6.1 contains an examination of the rates of green building adoption, for both the top ten legacy cities and top ten non-legacy cities in the United States, sorted by LEED-certified square feet per capita. Table 6.1 combines legacy cities together, regardless of their past population growth rates. The average adoption rate for LEED projects overall appears higher among non-legacy cities (fifty-eight vs. sixty-three square feet per capita), but for the median value, legacy cities have a higher green building adoption rate (forty-five vs forty square feet per capita). Thus, at first glance, there is no clear trend among these top ten cities.

GREEN RETROFITS VS. NEW GREEN CONSTRUCTION

Broadly, green retrofits are defined as any kind of upgrade at an existing building that is wholly or partially occupied to improve energy and environmental performance, reduce water use, and improve the comfort and quality of the space in terms of natural light, air quality, and noise—all

TABLE 6.1: Top ten legacy and non-legacy cities by LEED project

		Legacy Cities	
Rank	City, State	Number of Projects	Per capita LEED-certified sq. ft.*
1	Washington, DC	1,129	200.4
2	Chicago, IL	577	81.8
3	Cincinnati, OH	449	63.6
4	Pittsburgh, PA	155	59.5
5	Syracuse, NY	107	46.4
6	Cleveland, OH**	100	42.8
7	Baltimore, MD	133	23.3
8	Dayton, OH	40	23.1
9	Philadelphia, PA	480	18.6
10	New Orleans, LA	419	15.8
	Average	359	57.5
	Median	287	45

* Rank is sorted by per capita LEED-certified space.
** For example, the total building area of the one hundred LEED-certified projects in Cleveland was 16.6
LEED space was 43 square feet.

done in a way that it is financially beneficial to the owner.[7] Applying the general concept of green retrofits to a building's assessment system, LEED has developed a subcategory of its certification, LEED for Building Operations and Maintenance (O+M), under the idea that the greenest building is the one already built. This concept aligns with the research question of the current study testing if green retrofits are geographically concentrated in legacy cities, compared to non-legacy cities. Therefore, this study starts from an assumption that green retrofits in legacy cities are more desirable than building new green properties, both economically and environmentally.

LEED O+M is applied to any type of the existing built environment, from retail stores and schools to hotels, data centers, and warehouses. In this study LEED projects are designated as "green retrofits" when a project belongs to any type of the LEED O+M certification (see appendix 1 for a breakdown of LEED O+M categories).

Green retrofits represent only 9.2 percent of total LEED projects. Thus, only a small portion of building rehabilitation projects are certified by LEED. However, it does not imply that green retrofits are less important in the green building movement, particularly in legacy cities, where many

Non-Legacy Cities		
City, State	Number of Projects	Per capita LEED-certified sq. ft.*
Atlanta, GA	408	153.8
Seattle, WA	369	126.7
San Francisco, CA	473	114.5
Irving, TX	264	51.7
Las Vegas, NV	270	46.1
Fort Worth, TX	335	34.6
Portland, OR	483	27.5
Austin, TX	547	26.7
Denver, CO	356	26.1
Houston, TX	544	26
Average	405	63.4
	389	40

lion square feet as of December 2016. The city's population was 385,800 in 2016; therefore, per capita

prominent and historic buildings were already built, and the number of new construction projects is relatively limited. This enables us to address the main research question: do green retrofits appear more frequently in legacy cities than in non-legacy cities?

Comparing the number of green LEED retrofit projects in legacy and non-legacy cities, 17.4 percent of LEED projects in legacy cities are retrofits, while 8 percent of LEED projects in non-legacy cities are retrofits. This simple comparison supports our main research question because the numbers (17.4 percent vs. 8 percent) shows that green retrofits are much more active in legacy cities compared to non-legacy areas. However, these simple figures do not hold constant other important factors.

In an effort to further explore the incidence of green buildings in legacy cities, we ran two multiple regression models. The first model is designed to examine which type of legacy city is implementing green building practices (including both new construction and green retrofits) faster than non-legacy cities by using a green building market penetration rate as a dependent variable and different types of legacy cities as independent variables. We also control for other factors that affect the green building market penetration rate, including type of project, project size, project owner, proj-

TABLE 6.2: Summary of regression outputs from green building penetration model

Variable	Coefficient*
Huge legacy cities	-1.92 (7.551)
Recovered legacy cities	46.53* (4.230)
Recovering legacy cities	13.77* (2.746)

The coefficient values in this table indicate the extent to which each legacy city group has LEED-certified square feet per capita, in comparison to non-legacy city group, for all types of LEED projects.

Huge legacy cities are not statistically different from non-legacy cities, while recovered legacy cities have forty-seven square feet more per capita than non-legacy cities, all else held constant. Recovering legacy cities had eighteen square feet more LEED projects per capita than non-legacy cities.

ect LEED score, city population, and state dummy variables to control for green policies. In the second model, we split green building projects into two groups (new construction vs. green retrofits), and examine what types of legacy cities have more green retrofits than new construction, compared to non-legacy cities.

GREEN BUILDING PENETRATION RATES

For more detailed analysis, we break out the legacy cities based on population changes into three categories: huge, recovered, and recovering legacy cities.[8] According to the statistical results, both recovered and recovering (or languishing) legacy cities have more LEED-certified green building space per capita than non-legacy cities. So, holding other factors constant, recovered legacy cities have 46.5 square feet more LEED space per capita than do non-legacy cities, while recovering legacy cities have 13.8 square feet more LEED space per capita than non-legacy cities (see table 6.2).

These results might be contrary to the general perception that non-legacy cities would have more green buildings since they are developing faster than legacy cities, and thus have stronger construction and real estate markets overall. However, our analysis uses per capita space of green buildings to compare the penetration rates between city groups. It should be noted that the average population size of legacy cities is relatively smaller than that of counterpart cities. Thus, as expected, the number of LEED projects is positively associated with legacy city status.

GREEN RETROFIT PROJECTS

Although the first regression analysis informs us that more green buildings per capita are found in legacy cities than non-legacy cities, it is hard

TABLE 6.3: Summary of regression outputs from green retrofit model

Variable	IRR (Odds Ratio)
Huge legacy cities	0.64* (0.062)
Recovered legacy cities	1.13* (0.057)
Recovering legacy cities	0.70* (0.065)

IRR is the Incidence-Rate Ratio. A value of 1.0 represents neutral odds: >1 means more likely, thus recovered legacy cities are more likely to have green retrofit projects than are non-legacy cities, while huge and recovering legacy cities are less likely.

Note 1: Control variables are omitted in panels 2 and 3 due to shortage of space. The complete outputs are available upon request.
Note 2: Standard errors in parentheses in panels 2 and 3.
* Statistically significant at a 95 percent confidence level.

to tell what types of green buildings they are. For example, we question if more green retrofits are found in legacy cities and if nonprofit organizations are more likely to rehab existing buildings with green technologies than for-profit organizations. Thus, the aforementioned model is based on a simple assumption that legacy cities already have well-constructed built environments as part of their legacy, regardless of its energy efficiency or sustainability. As mentioned earlier, we ask the research question because we believe that green retrofits are preferable to building new green space, particularly in legacy cities, because these cities are older, more built-up, and not currently experiencing population growth as quickly as non-legacy cities. To answer the question, we employ Poisson regression analysis at the individual project level looking just at green LEED retrofit projects.[9]

As in the first regression analysis, three legacy city categories are added in the model (huge, recovered, and recovering legacy cities). The model controls for project characteristics including the size of project (measured by square foot), the type of project (e.g., commercial, residential, public, etc.), the ownership status (e.g., public vs. private), and the LEED certification score.

According to the results of the Poisson regression model, which shows probabilities of adoption, a LEED project in a recovered legacy city is 1.13 times more likely to be green retrofit than a similar project in a non-legacy city. The odds ratio is 0.64, hence less than one, for huge legacy cities, and is statistically significant. A similar significant result of .70 is found for recovering legacy cities, Thus, green retrofits are less likely to be found in both huge legacy cities and recovering legacy cities than in non-legacy cities (see table 6.3).

The Poisson regression model also controls for other factors that might affect the incidence of green retrofits. Those factors include LEED points achieved, the type of LEED project, the ownership of the project, and the size of population at the city level. Commercial properties are 2.4 times more likely to be green retrofits compared to the reference category including all other project types except commercial, residential, and government projects, while residential properties more likely to be new construction. When it comes to the type of ownership, for-profit organizations, including publicly traded companies, are more interested in new green building construction compared to counterpart property owners such as nonprofit and educational organizations and governments from the local to the federal level.

CONCLUSIONS

As the concept of sustainability in the built environment has gained substantial attention over the past decade, this chapter examined the incidence of green buildings and community development projects in legacy cities compared with non-legacy cities. First, we used regression analysis to examine which type of legacy city is implementing green building practices faster than non-legacy cities, by using a green building market penetration rate as a dependent variable, for three types of legacy cities based on their population, controlling for other factors that affect the penetration rate. We find that recovered and recovering legacy cities implement aggregated LEED projects (combining new construction and retrofits) at a higher rate than non-legacy cities in terms of per capita LEED-certified space. More specifically, recovered legacy cities uniformly perform above their legacy city peers in green building adoption across the board.

After comparing the presence of green buildings between legacy cities and non-legacy cities across the United States, we split green building projects into two categories: new construction and green retrofits. The analysis revealed that 13 percent more green building retrofits are likely to be found in recovered legacy cities than non-legacy cities, while green retrofits are less likely to be found in huge legacy cities and recovering legacy cities.

Considering the idea that "the greenest building is the one already built," green retrofits could be a more desirable approach to real estate development in legacy cities than building new green structures. This idea is also in line with the literature on the economic advantage of historic preservation. Specifically, Rypkema (2014) emphasizes the role of historic buildings in comprehensive sustainable development because of the cost-effective use of resources as well as environmental issues associated with demolishing existing buildings.

The statistical results from this study show that the desirable real estate development (i.e., green retrofits) has already been achieved in recovered legacy cities. In this context, we argue that legacy cities, particularly in the category of recovering legacy cities (where population growth has not yet returned to its prior earlier level in 1960), should consider supporting financially viable green retrofit projects wherever possible.

Recovering legacy cities should take note that their adoption rates of new projects could bc improved. They should emulate the activities of recovered legacy cities for both new and retrofit green projects. Given the potential upside for both property values and green employment growth, urban policy makers could encourage redevelopment of green buildings perhaps with financial incentives.

NOTES

1. Detailed discussions of the definition are left out of this chapter since it is covered in Ryberg-Webster and Tighe's introduction to this volume.

2. In Cleveland, Ohio, about eighty additional projects have been registered in LEED with the intent of earning LEED certification for their projects once it is complete.

3. For more on Euclid Avenue as Cleveland's top green building corridor, see www.gcbl.org.

4. Of the 40,877 LEED-certified projects, 37,172 (91 percent) projects are located in metropolitan statistical areas (MSAs). Our data set included 365 MSAs.

5. The average LEED score is 55.8, which is in the LEED silver category.

6. When a project covers more than two types of properties, such as residential and retail stores, the project is assigned to a major type of the project. Unfortunately, the data do not provide breakdown information.

7. See Building Retrofits, Urban Land, November/December 2009, www.esbnyc.com.

8. Huge legacy cities have populations of more than one million people as of 2010; recovered legacy cities have recovered their population loss and reached more than 95 percent level of their 1960 population size as of 2016; the remaining cities are categorized as recovering.

9. In the Poisson regression model, a binary dependent variable is coded as 1 if a project is a LEED-certified retrofit project, otherwise coded as 0. Although logistic regression is the most popular method for a model with a binary response variable, we use the Poisson regression model instead of logistic analysis because the proportion of green retrofit projects is relatively rare, representing only 9 percent in the data set. Extensive discussions in the literature conclude that the Poisson regression model is preferable to logistic analysis when the rate of event is less than 10 percent (Greenland 1987).

REFERENCES

Allen, Jennifer H., and Thomas Potiowsky. 2008. "Portland's Green Building Cluster: Economic Trends and Impacts." *Economic Development Quarterly* 22, no. 4: 303–15.

American Institute of Architects. 2009. *Local Leaders in Sustainability—Green Building*

Policy in a Changing Economic Environment. Washington, DC: American Institute of Architects.

Booz, Allen Hamilton. 2009. *U.S. Green Building Council Green Jobs Study.* Washington, DC: US Green Building Council. http://www.usgbc.org/ShowFile.aspx?DocumentID=6435.

Biblow, Charlotte A. 2009. "Going Green in Construction Offers Environmental Benefits and Significant Financial Savings." *Real Estate Finance* 26, no. 3: 13–15.

Bord, Richard J., Ann Fisher, and Robert E. O'Connor. 1998. "Public Perceptions of Global Warming: United States and International Perspectives." *Climate Research* 11, no. 1: 75–84.

Dunlap, Riley E., and Kent D. Van Liere. 1978. "The 'New Environmental Paradigm.'" *Journal of Environmental Education* 9, no. 4: 10–19.

Eichholtz, Piet, Nils Kok, and John M. Quigley. 2010. "Doing Well by Doing Good? Green Office Buildings." *American Economic Review* 100, no. 5: 2492–2509.

Fitzgerald, Joan. 2010. *Emerald Cities: Urban Sustainability and Economic Development.* New York: Oxford University Press.

Fuerst, Franz, and Patrick McAllister. 2011. "Green Noise or Green Value? Measuring the Effects of Environmental Certification on Office Values." *Real Estate Economics* 39, no. 1: 45–69.

Ganning, J., and J. R. Tighe. Forthcoming. "Moving toward a Shared Understanding of the US Shrinking City." *Journal of Planning Education and Research.*

Goldman, Charles. 2010. *Energy Efficiency Service Sector: Workforce Size and Expectations for Growth.* Berkeley Hills, CA: Lawrence Berkeley National Laboratory.

Greenland Sander. 1987. "Interpretation and Choice of Effect Measures in Epidemiologic Analyses." *American Journal of Epidemiology* 125, no. 5: 761–68.

Kaplow, Stuart. D. 2009. "Does a Green Building Need a Green Lease?" *Baltimore Law Review* 38, no. 3: 375–409.

Kibert, Charles J. 2004. "Green Buildings: An overview of Progress." *Journal of Land Use and Environmental Law* 19, no. 2: 491–502.

Kok, Nils, Norman G. Miller, and Peter Morris. 2012. "The Economics of Green Retrofits." *Journal of Sustainable Real Estate* 4, no. 1: 4–47.

Korten, David. 1991. "Sustainable Development." *World Policy Journal* 9, no. 1: 157–90.

Lee, Eunkyu. 2017. "The Impact of Sustainable Building Projects on Regional Green Economies." Unpublished working paper.

McKinsey and Company. 2009. *Unlocking Energy Efficiency in the US Economy.* New York: McKinsey and Company.

Mallach, Alan, and Lavea Brachman. 2013. *Regenerating America's Legacy Cities.* Cambridge, MA: Lincoln Institute of Land Policy.

Meadows, Donella H., Dennis L. Meadows, Jorgen Randers, and William W. Behrens. 1972. *The Limits to Growth.* New York: Universe Books.

Mega, Voula. 1996. "Our Cities, Our Future: Towards Sustainable Development in European Cities." *Environment and Urbanization* 8, no. 1: 133–54.

Miller, Norm, Dave Pogue, Quiana Gough, and Susan Davis. 2009. "Green Buildings and Productivity." *Journal of Sustainable Real Estate* 1, no. 1: 65–89.

Milbrath, Lester W., and Barbara V. Fisher. 1984. *Environmentalists: Vanguard for a New Society.* Albany: State University of New York Press.

Rehm, Michael, and Rochelle Ade. 2013. "Construction Costs Comparison between 'Green'and Conventional Office Buildings." *Building Research and Information* 41, no. 2: 198–208.

Rypkema, Donovan D. 2014. *The Economics of Historic Preservation: A Community Leaders' Guide.* 3rd ed. Washington, DC: National Trust for Historic Preservation.

Simons, Robert A. 1998. *Turning Brownfields into Greenbacks.* Washington, DC: Urban Land Institute Press.

Scott, David, and Fern K. Willits. 1994. "Environmental Attitudes and Behavior: A Pennsylvania Survey." *Environment and Behavior* 26, no. 2: 239–60.

US Department of Energy. 2012. *Buildings Energy Data Book.* Washington, DC: US Department of Energy. http://buildingsdatabook.eren.doe.gov/docs/DataBooks/2011_BEDB.pdf.

Wiley, Jonathan A., Justin D. Benefield, and Ken H. Johnson. 2010. "Green Design and the Martket for Commercial Office Space." *Journal of Real Estate Finance and Economics* 41, no. 2: 228–43.

APPENDIX 1.

GREEN RETROFITS: LEED BUILDING OPERATIONS AND MAINTENANCE (O+M) CATEGORIES

- *Existing Buildings*: Specifically, projects that do not primarily serve K–12 educational, retail, data centers, warehouses and distribution centers, or hospitality uses.
- *Retail*: Guides existing retail spaces, both showrooms and storage areas.
- *Schools*: For existing buildings made up of core and ancillary learning spaces on K–12 school grounds. Can also be used for higher education and nonacademic buildings on school campuses.
- *Hospitality*: Existing hotels, motels, inns, or other businesses within the service industry that provide transitional or short-term lodging with or without food.
- *Data Centers*: Existing buildings specifically designed and equipped to meet the needs of high density computing equipment such as server racks, used for data storage and processing.
- *Warehouses and Distribution Centers*: Existing buildings used to store goods, manufactured products, merchandise, raw materials, or personal belongings (such as self-storage).

Source: http://www.usgbc.org/.

THE LEGACY OF DECLINE

PART TWO

IN CLEVELAND

7

Cleveland's Neighborhoods in Black and White

2000–2014

NORMAN KRUMHOLZ

This chapter's deliberately stark title highlights a similarly stark fact: Cleveland's neighborhoods have been, and continue to be, intensively polarized along racial lines. Racial segregation in housing is a tragic legacy in this legacy city. Black residents are not only segregated within the city of Cleveland, but within the Cleveland-Elyria-Mentor metropolitan area as well. For decades planners and academics have mapped and documented the extent of racial segregation and the various inequalities among Cleveland's black and white citizens, but significant positive changes have been glacial. Yet racial discrimination and racial segregation are key factors in racial inequality, income and educational disparities, spatial distortions in land use, and the ability of the city to redevelop itself. It is no longer a question of straightforward acts of discrimination; rather, subtler institutional racism, cloaked in softer language and innocuous-seeming legislation, results in black and white Americans having different starting points in their quest for individual success.

Although central to Cleveland's future, issues of race and concentrated poverty have been largely overlooked as the city responds to the global economic restructuring that began in the 1970s. Instead, the city has increasingly been preoccupied with enhancing its competitiveness. The shockingly rapid decline of population, manufacturing industries, and the massive shedding of jobs made a commitment to economic growth seem imperative. As a result, from 2000 to 2014 Cleveland used a mix of efforts to not only cope but to transform the downtown space while deep-seated economic and social problems persisted in poor black and white neighborhoods. As with many other legacy cities, Cleveland can point to progress on certain issues and remaining challenges as it attempts to identify a new role for its future in the face of seemingly intractable obstacles.

Most legacy cities reflect periods of intensive urban growth up until about 1950 and decades of severe decline thereafter. But while this dreary pattern repeats itself often, it also nurtures unusual examples of executive and administrative leadership as political and civic leaders tried to deal with shrinking resources and reverse industrial decline. The administration of Cleveland mayor Carl B. Stokes (1967–1971), the first African American mayor of a major American city, provides a stellar example of executive leadership on the crucial issues of housing segregation and the environment that have been mostly overlooked by history. During his short tenure, Mayor Stokes provided support for the nascent federal housing voucher program and also attempted to decentralize racially impacted neighborhoods in Cleveland and Cuyahoga County by supporting a number of housing-integration initiatives:

- In 1970 Mayor Stokes supported the successful construction of new public housing in white neighborhoods on Cleveland's west side—a nontraditional approach, especially in this era;
- He supported a fair-share plan for low rent housing in Cuyahoga County where fifty-eight suburban communities had used exclusionary laws and declined to accept any public housing at all, leaving Cleveland with about twelve thousand units (Cleveland City Planning Commission 1971);
- He supported the Warren's Ridge New Town—a mixed-use plan that included proposals for the development of new, low rent public housing in a suburban location (Cleveland City Planning Commission 1971);
- At the national level, Mayor Stokes provided support for the proposed Housing Allowance Program, which passed into law as the Section 8 rent subsidy program. He made his support explicit in Congressional testimony and in a published article (Stokes 1971a);
- In 1971 Mayor Stokes challenged the members of the American Society of Planning Officials to broaden their focus and include social equity issues like housing, education, and poverty in their plans (Stokes 1971b).

Mayor Stokes also led an ecological thinking that emphasized the connectedness of social and environmental problems and the need for regional solutions (Stradling and Stradling 2015). In a city known for its "caretaker" low tax and low service mayors, Stokes fought for and passed a $100 million bond issue to clean up Lake Erie and the Cuyahoga River. Stokes also joined a regional coalition that stopped the Clark Freeway saving, in the process, numerous Cleveland neighborhoods and the Shaker Lakes ecological system.

On these issues Mayor Stokes won some, and he lost some, but he led boldly in a way that should be emulated by other local and state officials.

PROGRESS, 2000–2014

The early years of the twenty-first century saw progress in Cleveland in many areas. The city's first and (so far only) female mayor, Jane Campbell, was elected. She supported building a new downtown convention center, reforming the troubled Cleveland Municipal School District (CMSD), and improving transit along Euclid Avenue, the city's most important commercial street, from downtown to University Circle. This support was echoed by her successor, Frank Jackson, the city's third black mayor, elected in 2006 and still in office as of 2019.

Throughout the decade city leaders achieved many key objectives for Cleveland, especially in the downtown neighborhood. The RTA completed its $200 million bus-rapid transit line, funded mostly by the federal government, and investment, for the first time in decades, began flowing back into the Euclid corridor. Making a bid for more tourist-related business, the city and county completed a new $450 million convention center and the Global Center for Health Innovation, along with a new $275 million hotel adjacent to the convention center. All were funded by a county-wide sales tax as was a new county administration building. The city's historic Public Square was the target of a mostly taxpayer-funded $50 million makeover in anticipation of the Republican National Convention in 2016. Following approval of a statewide ballot initiative, Cleveland's first casino opened in a remodeled department store on Public Square and promised to generate new tax revenues for the city, county, and state. All these public improvements were on top of the new Rock and Roll Hall of Fame and the new football, baseball, and basketball venues the city and county built in the 1990s for Cleveland's three professional sports teams at a cost of almost $1 billion. Cleveland State University, which had been a commuter school, expanded with new buildings and added hundreds of student housing units to its campus, changing the character of the university. The city also completed a large privately funded mixed-use development on the east bank of the Cuyahoga River.

Partially as a result of these investments, downtown Cleveland's population grew for the first time in decades. From 1990 to 2010 the downtown population grew by 96 percent (from 4,562 residents to 9,098 residents), and stood at 9,464 in 2014. Much of the population growth was facilitated by the conversion of office space into residential units, which were in high demand; in 2016 the occupancy rate for downtown units was over 90 percent. Additionally encouraging, this new population included a significant component of well-educated young adults living and working downtown and in nearby neighborhoods (Piiparien and Russell 2014).

Significant school reform efforts also took place as the Cleveland Metropolitan School District (CMSD) prepared, and the state legislature adopted in 2012, the Cleveland Plan for Transforming Schools. Later in 2012 the city's voters approved a new $15 million levy for Cleveland schools, the first operating levy approved since 1996. It was argued that a substantial property tax increase was essential in order to implement the Plan for Transforming Schools and improve the low performance of its students.

Progress downtown was matched by progress in the University Circle neighborhood, which also saw major investments and growth during this period. Located about four miles east of downtown and surrounded by some of the most poverty-stricken and racially segregated neighborhoods in the region, University Circle is home to many of Cleveland's great institutions: the Cleveland Orchestra, the Museums of Art and Natural History, and forty other arts, cultural, educational, and health nonprofit institutions. It is the home of the Cleveland Clinic and University Hospitals—the number one and number two employers in the region—as well as Case Western Reserve University, a major educational and research institution. Combined, the latter three institutions employ over sixty thousand people and annually spend over $3 billion in goods and services. In 2016 all three institutions were undergoing massive expansion programs (Wright et. al. 2016).

University Circle also saw the new Museum of Contemporary Art, built as part of a new high density residential and commercial district called Uptown. In 2016 a new highway, the Opportunity Corridor, was under construction to improve access from the west side and airport to University Circle. Demand in the neighborhood for upscale housing was such that in 2016, ground was broken for a new $116 million twenty-story building with 280 luxury apartments. In order to stimulate demand for more moderate housing, an employer-assisted program began offering financial assistance to University Circle employees who worked in the neighborhood and wished to buy or rent property there. Also, to try to build employment opportunities for local residents, the Cleveland Foundation launched its Evergreen Cooperative Program, a worker-owned model in three businesses: Evergreen Commercial Laundry; Evergreen Energy Solutions, which manufactures solar collectors; and Green City Growers, a large hydroponic greenhouse. In 2016 over one hundred persons were employed in these three cooperatives.

Progress and growth downtown and in the University Circle neighborhood was clear, but these are only two neighborhoods, not the entire city of Cleveland. However, positive signs were emerging in other neighborhoods as Cleveland struggled to transformation itself from an old industrial economy into a service economy with important educational and health-care components. Cleveland was well positioned for this transformation with 36.5 percent of all jobs in 2011 in these two sectors, compared with 15 percent nationally. Institutions like Cleveland State University, Case Western Reserve University, the Cleveland Clinic, and University Hospital were functioning as export industries, drawing money into the community and multiplying its effect through secondary spending. By reasonable estimates, about two-thirds of the growth in the local economy was driven by the education and medical sectors.

Although Cleveland's overall net population has been falling steadily since 1960 and continues to fall, new in-migration is now growing slowly. It is dominated by millennials—mostly single, well-educated, white young people who are increasingly drawn to urban living. As magnets to these young people, legacy cities like Cleveland are not doing as well as other cities such as Seattle or Washington, DC, where 17.5 percent of the population is made up of millennials, but Cleveland is beginning to catch up. The young in-migrants are looking for specific environments: high density, mixed-use clusters with high levels of activity, good public transit options, and strong architectural and historic character. In many cities, including Cleveland, these needs are satisfied by downtowns and nearby historic neighborhoods commonly referred to as "the core."

However, core areas make up only a small part of the typical US city. Outside of Cleveland's downtown, which was historically almost entirely made up of nonresidential land uses and University Circle, which is mostly institutional, Cleveland is largely a patchwork of single-family and two-family homes. Eighty-three percent of all the residential structures in the city are single-family homes and 15 percent are two-family homes. Only a small number of structures have three or more residential units, and four out of five units were built before 1960.

Currently there are three contrasting dynamics of neighborhood change underway in Cleveland: gentrification, stable/revitalizing, and decline. There are clearly a few neighborhoods in the city that are drawing new, well-educated residents in the twenty-five to thirty-four age range and where new housing is being built as well as being extensively renovated. These neighborhoods are gentrifying by any reasonable definition. On the west side, these mostly white neighborhoods include some parts of Edgewater (70 percent white), Detroit Shoreway (55 percent white), Ohio City

(51 percent white), and Tremont (60 percent white) (Cleveland City Planning Commission 2014). The gentrifying process may be an indication that the efforts of local community development corporations to brand themselves as attractive places for young professionals is succeeding. East of the Cuyahoga River, gentrifying neighborhoods include downtown and University Circle. In all these neighborhoods incomes are rising, and rents and home prices are also rising. This is welcome news because Cleveland has far too few neighborhoods that can be described in those terms for the city's economic well-being. Gentrification, the displacement of lower income families by higher income newcomers, is not seen as a problem at this time. The number of people who are potentially at risk of displacement is small and the regional housing market is extremely soft, with high vacancy rates and relatively cheap rents in many stable city and suburban neighborhoods.

While a few Cleveland neighborhoods are gentrifying, more neighborhoods are stable and slowly revitalizing. These tend to be located in in the city's outer reaches following the historic pattern of city development further out from the core. These neighborhoods featuring older housing in relatively good condition and some new housing developments include Buckeye-Shaker, Little Italy, Euclid-Green, North Collinwood, and Lee-Miles. Also on the east side new tax-credit housing in the Central neighborhood has improved the aesthetics if not residents' incomes of the city's largest concentration of public housing, and new housing construction in Hough has not changed the overall poverty of the neighborhood. On the west side Edgewater, Kamm's Corners, West Boulevard, Bellaire-Puritas, Old Brooklyn, Jefferson, and Riverside are stable neighborhoods. Some very recent new housing developments have been built in Detroit Shoreway, Ohio City, Tremont, and Broadway–Slavic Village. Many of the improvements in these neighborhoods can be credited to the work of the city's many community development corporations; nonprofit housing developers such as the Cleveland Housing Network; and several intermediaries that have become national models for effectiveness. In sum, housing demand is booming downtown and in the University Circle neighborhood, and a few of Cleveland's neighborhoods are either gentrifying, as in Detroit Shoreway, Ohio City, and Tremont, or are showing signs of stabilization and growth.

These signs of optimism and progress must be tempered, however, by the continuing reality of the city's many remaining challenges.

CHALLENGES, 2000–2014

First among these challenges is Cleveland's declining population. Since 1960 the city's population has been in decline. In 1950 Cleveland's population peaked at 914,000—in 2010 the US Census reported a population of 396,000. From 2010 to 2014 population losses continued down to a count of 378,000, a loss of 17 percent, making the city's population almost equal to its 1900 level. During the 2000–2010 decade, suburban Cuyahoga County also declined, losing 2.3 percent of its population. Population projections for the future of the entire five-county Cleveland-Elyria-Mentor metropolitan region envision a loss of 4.5 percent over the next thirty years, while other regions in the United States were projected to grow up to 35 percent. Losses of such magnitude make inevitable a redundancy of residential, commercial, and industrial structures and put heavy strains on the city's ability to provide basic services and keep up with essential rehabilitation or demolition. It also raises questions about the possible uses of a growing inventory of vacant land.

A second major problem is one of poverty and the hollowing out of the middle class. This is a national phenomenon that has had a devastating effect on urban neighborhoods. Today's Cleveland has far fewer middle-class families than it had thirty or forty years ago. In 1960 nearly half of the city's families earned between 80 percent and 150 percent of the citywide median—today it is only a quarter. With respect to poverty, the poverty rate in Cleveland remains high at 36 percent, and the city's median income is only 54 percent of the state's average. Employment fell by 2 percent between 2010 and 2013 (Economic Innovation Group 2016).

The trends on income disparity are also ominous. The American Community Survey for 2005–2009, completed by the US Census Bureau, found that white families in Cuyahoga County had a median income of $55,808, while black families had a median income of just $35,534.

Poor people—especially poor minorities, who must deal with prejudice as well as lack of income—tend to lack mobility and are locked into their isolation. For instance, "two-thirds of black children who were raised in the poorest quarter of US neighborhoods a generation ago, now raise their own children in similarly poor neighborhoods. About half of all black families have lived in the poorest American neighborhoods over the last two generations, compared to just 7 percent of white families" (Florida, 2013). In Cleveland twelve neighborhoods were over 90 percent black in 2000, and eleven were over 90 percent black in 2014. Two of these neighborhoods, Hough and Glenville, were the sites of racial riots in the 1960s.

Where a person lives—their access to schools, jobs, food, health services, public transit, and other resources—determines their chances in life. Unfortunately, black residents in Cleveland have seen a significant increase in high poverty neighborhoods—that is, neighborhoods where over 40 percent of the residents are poor. In 2000, 38 percent of Cleveland's poor, black residents lived in high poverty neighborhoods; in 2013, 45.5 percent lived in such neighborhoods. In terms of concentrated poverty for black residents, Cleveland ranks sixth highest in the United States (Jargowski 2016).

Coupled with this depressing picture is a drop in homeownership. Homeowners are now being replaced by absentee owners, vacancy, and increasing renter populations, as Mikelbank describes in chapter 10. From 2000 to 2010 Cleveland lost over 22,000 homeowners, a 25 percent drop. This has powerful implications not only for the physical quality of structures in the neighborhoods but also for their social dynamics.

Concentrated poverty also has the effect of challenging educational progress. Although the Cleveland Board of Education is addressing school reform through its Cleveland Plan for Transforming Schools, and although the voters passed a $15 million property tax levy to implement the plan, Cleveland students continue to lag near the bottom on state achievement tests. Court-ordered busing was abandoned in the 1990s and schools have re-segregated on a neighborhood basis. Yet research shows that moving children from a high poverty neighborhood to one with lower poverty results in better school performance, more college attendance, and higher lifetime earnings (Chelly et al. 2015).

A significant third problem has to do with economic shifts. Many legacy cities have started to see job growth, but it does not translate into opportunity. The urban population is being decoupled from the economy. Cleveland is not short on jobs, but most city residents do not hold them. Currently there are two jobs in the city for every resident jobholder; 76 percent of the jobs in Cleveland are held by commuters (Mallach 2015). In many neighborhoods, there are many fewer people who actually hold jobs living there than there were fifteen or twenty years ago. This is one of the reasons why the Evergreen project of worker-owned cooperatives is both innovative and important.

The next problem concerns the physical condition of the housing stock in many neighborhoods. As noted earlier, Cleveland is an old city. Most homes are modest, wood-framed structures, built for a working-class population. As Hatch further described in chapter 5, many homes are substandard and fall below the city's housing and building codes; many have suffered from years of deferred maintenance, and are hard to maintain and expensive to rehabilitate.

Cleveland was hit hard by Great Recession. Property owners in Hispanic and black neighborhoods were targeted by subprime lenders and lured into buying bad mortgages. When the market collapsed, the average black family lost 31 percent of its wealth (Desmond 2016). The collapse engulfed many of the city's neighborhoods and left many thousands of vacant and abandoned homes in its wake. For example, the Slavic Village neighborhood (then one of Cleveland's most successful redeveloping neighborhoods) became a national example of the devastating impact of subprime lending experienced by urban neighborhoods (Kotlowitz 2009). In many neighborhoods, market prices are below replacement cost. In 2016 a city-wide survey found that some 6,100 homes were distressed or vacant and awaiting rehabilitation or demolition. A residential unit costs approximately $10,000 to demolish, so the total would be about $60 million. In addition, 1,400 buildings have been condemned by the city; their demolition costs would be much higher depending on size and any necessary environmental remediation (Cleveland Property Inventory 2015). Fortunately, Cuyahoga County established a land bank in 2009, which is able to acquire tax-delinquent and foreclosed properties and demolish or rehabilitate them. By May 2016, using the federal government's Neighborhood Stabilization Program and other resources, the Land Bank had acquired about 6,400 abandoned homes, rehabilitated 1,400, and demolished 4,330 (Whitney 2016; Keating 2011). The extensive demolition likely to take place in the next few years raises the question of the future use of all the vacant land, an issue the city has been unable to effectively address.

Adding to the problem of abandoned housing is regional competition. Cleveland is surrounded by incorporated suburbs, many of which offer at least marginally safer environments and better schools. In many of these suburbs the median home price is under $100,000. If a prospective buyer has an income of $30,000–$40,000, good credit and a down payment, or can get an FHA loan, they can move to the suburbs. As Figure 7.1 indicates, rising percentages of black residents in close-in eastern suburbs like, Euclid, Warrensville Heights, Cleveland Heights, Shaker Heights, Maple Heights, and Bedford Heights make clear that many relatively higher income black households are choosing that option.

Finally, in the litany of Cleveland's problems, one of the most significant is the racial segregation of its people and neighborhoods. Based on one calculation of dissimilarity of index scores, Cleveland's metropolitan area ranks fifth nationally in racial segregation amongst metropolitan areas with populations over five hundred thousand people, with a score of 74.1 (Denvir 2011). Another study ranked Cleveland's metro area as the most segregated area in the United States (Kent 2015).

Income segregation is also a problem in Cleveland. In 2015 the Cleveland metropolitan area was ranked as number one in income segregation among large metropolitan areas (Florida 2015). Median household income among black families in Cleveland is $35,416, compared to white families, which is $57,000. Disparities in wealth are even greater with wealth among

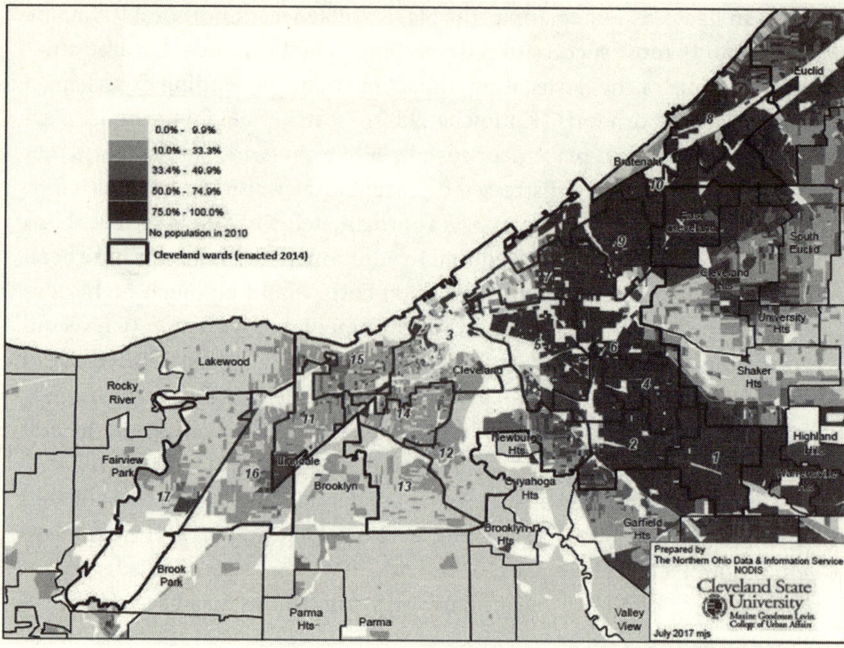

FIGURE 7.1: Percent African American population, 2010 US Census, by census block

white households at $116,000, compared with black wealth, at just $1,700. Low incomes may be the result of a sluggish labor market. In 2013, 20.2 percent of black Cleveland residents were unemployed—nearly four times the white unemployment rate of 5.4 percent. As a key element in the vicious cycle of racial prejudice and inequality, segregation has had particularly devastating consequences for the black poor. It influences polarization in two ways. First, the homes of poor black residents and the sites of the unskilled or semi-skilled jobs that might be available to them are in different places in the Cleveland metropolitan area. Between 2000 and 2014, 90 percent of the new semiskilled jobs in the region were situated in suburban factories, fast-food outlets, and shopping malls. Because of racial segregation, most of the black poor are concentrated in inner-city neighborhoods. Because information about most jobs is passed by word of mouth, the inner-city poor are less likely to know about job openings and, therefore, less likely to apply. If they do apply and are hired, the pay for semiskilled jobs is often not sufficient to compensate for the cost of the commute.

The joblessness and economic deprivation of the black population contributes to their disadvantages in housing and health care. Also, as middle- and upper-income black and white families tend to move away from areas of rampant poverty, segregation contributes to the out-migration of Cleveland's tax base and nullifies the city's efforts to encourage reinvestment and redevelopment in those areas.

There are also lasting indirect effects of segregation on school performance. Both the social composition of the classroom and the amount of money spent on public education depend on the municipality in which the school is located. Racial segregation affects the educational quality that black children receive both due to the socioeconomic makeup of the classroom and Cleveland's weakened economic capacity. The often-evicted black poor move from place to place and school to school while their children are unable to form long-lasting relationships with teachers, friends, or role models.

AN ALTERNATIVE POLICY FOR CLEVELAND AND THE UNITED STATES

It is clear that Cleveland is pursuing an urban policy based on downtown growth and development in the hopes of shedding its reputation as a declining industrial city and becoming a regional tourist destination. From 2000 to 2014 the city doubled down on investments downtown. There is merit to this strategy: older cities need to be renewed to remain attractive to investment and the new jobs and taxes investment creates. In addition, a tourist-based strategy provides many service jobs in restaurants and hotels that can be filled by poorly educated workers (Fainstein and Gladstone 1999).

However, a downtown-focused policy is too narrow. It concentrates on growth downtown and ignores the true underlying causes of urban distress: racial segregation and concentrated poverty. Since racial discrimination, segregated housing, and concentrated poverty are core elements in Cleveland's many problems, direct antidiscrimination and antipoverty measures should be the cornerstone of local, state, and national policies. Policies to increase minority incomes, as well as educational and employment opportunities, cannot be fully effective so long as black residential choices remain restricted. Additionally, policies to encourage broad private investment into redeveloping Cleveland will fail as long as many of the city's neighborhoods are blighted by the shadow of segregated neighborhoods.

The amelioration of poverty and the elimination of racial barriers to open housing must attack racial discrimination in private housing markets, where 98 percent of all dwellings are located. This will involve direct institutional involvement of the federal government—particularly the US Department of Housing and Urban Development (HUD). As a first step, HUD should substantially expand the subsidized rental voucher program to enable poor black residents and others to access units in the private market.

The ultimate goal should be a universal voucher program for all qualified low income families. Every family below a certain income level would be eligible for a housing voucher, which could be used for housing anywhere in the metropolitan area. Currently the pattern of voucher use in Cleveland makes clear that voucher-holders are being steered into racially segregated neighborhoods (Healy and Lepley 2016). To discourage racial discrimination, all landlords would have to accept vouchers. Carefully developed regulations would guarantee that housing units were safe and sanitary, and that rents would not be excessive. Families would pay 30 percent of their income for rent, with the voucher paying the balance.

Such a program would allow black demand to spread more evenly around the metropolitan housing market. As it now stands, black residents who want to live outside black neighborhoods must be prepared to spend an inordinate amount of time house-hunting and be prepared to accept frequent humiliations. If they actually find a house in a white-majority neighborhood, they must be prepared for possible hostile or violent reactions. As a result, black populations have been reluctant to enter white neighborhoods. A well-regulated universal housing voucher program would do much to overcome these fears.

Next, to further weaken racial barriers to open housing, HUD should increase its financial assistance to local fair housing organizations to increase their ability to investigate and prosecute individual complaints of housing discrimination. If these organizations identified realtors engaging in a pattern of persistent discrimination, evidence of such patterns should be turned over to the attorney general for vigorous—and highly visible—prosecution. HUD should also scrutinize lending data for unusually high rates of rejection among minority applicants, and when evidence of discrimination is discovered, the case should be referred to the attorney general, or an equal-opportunity lending plan should be implemented.

A universal voucher program would do much to reduce housing poverty where families with limited income are forced to spend unreasonable amounts of their income on housing, leaving very little left over for other necessities. If regulated to assure that all landlords would have to accept vouchers with a limited return on their investment, it should greatly ease the effects of racial discrimination and the concentrations of poverty. If segregated neighborhoods were eliminated and black residents were distributed among residential areas in the same proportion as the metropolitan population, there would be no serious quality disparity among neighborhood schools. At the same time there would be no concern about black populations being trapped in declining city neighborhoods distant from expanding job opportunities in the region. Housing developers, too, would consider the possibilities for new developments closer to the core and no longer feel threatened by the many problems of neighborhoods overwhelmed by segregation and poverty.

THE LEGACY OF EQUITY PLANNING

Any alternative policy for Cleveland or similar legacy cities should also include a system of values and strategies called *equity planning*, which evolved in Cleveland during the 1970s. During this period, advocacy or equity planning became less of a hortatory theory than a tangible effort undertaken within the political system and directed toward and achieving real ends of redistribution and social justice. The central goal adopted by Cleveland's equity planners was that, in the context of limited resources, first and priority attention should be "to provide a wider range of choices for those Cleveland residents who have few, if any, choices" (Krumholz 1982, 163). Operating within this framework, Cleveland's equity planners tried to move resources, political power, and participation toward the city's lower income, disadvantaged people.

Cleveland's planners justified their goal with three arguments. First, they argued that a long-standing, historic, and moral commitment existed to seek greater equity in the social, economic, and political relations among people. Second, building on the ideas of the philosopher John Rawls (1971) they used reason as a means of justifying a more equitable society—the kind of society that free, equal, and rational people would establish to protect their own self-interest. Finally, they justified their goal with reality: making explicit the imbalances and gaps in income, education, health, housing, and other social and economic variables that existed in Cleveland between black and white citizens and the city and suburbs.

To move their agenda forward, Cleveland planners adopted a number of strategies, including coalition-building, extensive writing, and framing. They created or joined a number of coalitions, including a network of neighborhood-based advocacy groups to plan and develop poor neighborhoods, an anti-highway coalition to stop a proposed ruinous freeway, a business-based coalition to lobby progressive tax-foreclosure changes through the state legislature, and an environmental coalition to facilitate the transfer of Cleveland's rundown lakefront parks to the Ohio Department of Natural Resources, among others.

In contrast to other practicing city planners, who write little for general publication, Cleveland's planners wrote a great deal. Articles and op-eds were written for local publications to clarify the planners' plans, policies, and programs. Other pieces were used to discredit or hurt rivals in the public sphere or to serve as trial balloons to test the popularity of an idea. A significant op-ed can get a story onto the front page and strengthen a mayor's (or a planner's) agenda. More scholarly articles were written and published in professional planning journals both to spread Cleveland's story and to encourage other planning professionals to try their own models of redistributive justice.

Cleveland's planners took care to properly frame the issues before them. For example, when opposing a taxpayer-funded sports stadium, it was never "build the stadium or lose the team"—it was "here is the impact of the stadium expenditure on the essential needs of the neighborhoods." When proposing the expansion of the city-owned electric power company, it was never "power to the people" or similar slogans (which might have been seen as too radical), but "this is a good business proposition that will produce lower rates, jobs, and taxes."

During the 1970s and under three mayors who could not have been more different—a black liberal Democrat, a white conservative Republican, and a self-described urban populist—the efforts of Cleveland's equity planners helped produce an expansion of new public housing into nontraditional wards in the city; progressive changes to Ohio's property laws, allowing the city to land bank abandoned properties; the establishment of a network of competent community development corporations working to revitalize poor neighborhoods; improvements in public-service delivery; the establishment of a regional transit authority and the enhancement of transit services to the transit-dependent population; the rescue of Cleveland's lakefront parks; and many other improvements. In what might be called entrepreneurial networking, Cleveland's planners forged links, built alliances, and cooperated with and strengthened local advocacy groups without worrying about their right to do so.

Cleveland's equity planners also developed a four-point work program to help the city (and similar legacy cities) to provide a reasonable level of services even as resources shrink:

1. Imposition of restraints: Don't buy every proposal for large-scale redevelopment, and make sure the ones you buy offer a sure prospect of benefits for the maximum possible number of struggling residents and neighborhoods;
2. Creative investments: Make the investments needed to maintain current physical assets in good repair and help existing systems work efficiently, and leverage public funds to achieve these goals;
3. Constructive shrinkage of responsibilities: Identify city responsibilities, such as public transit and lakefront parks, that state and metropolitan regions can assume and will find it in their self-interest to do so;

4. Build strong community organizations: They should be fostered as useful allies to emphasize the needs of their neighborhoods. They should also bring a skeptical eye to politically appealing but expensive proposals for new investment based on unreasonable growth assumptions.

Other US cities, some with minority mayors (as of this writing), such as Cleveland and Chicago, and cities with white mayors, such as Boston, Denver, Hartford, Jersey City, Berkeley, and Santa Monica have adopted an equity-oriented approach designed to aid lower income residents (Krumholz and Clavel 1992). Minority or liberal mayors are more likely to provide equity planners with essential support, but progressive planning ideas have also been implemented under more conservative political leadership.

This is not to suggest that equity planning can restore the legacy city to its former status of greatness or reverse industrial decline, yet it can be an important step in the right direction to move toward a better future for Cleveland and other legacy cities.

REFERENCES

Chelly, Raj, Nathaniel Hendren, Lawrence E. Katz. 2015. "The Effects of Exposure to Better Neighborhoods on Children: New Evidence in the Moving to Opportunity Experiment." Harvard University and National Bureau of Economic Research, August.

Cleveland City Planning Commission. 1970. "A Fair-Share Plan for Low-Rent Housing in Cuyahoga County."

Cleveland City Planning Commission. 1971. "Warren's Ridge New Town: A Pre-Application Proposal."

Cleveland City Planning Commission. 2014. "SPA 2014 Fact Sheets." http://planning.city.cleveland.oh.us/2010census/factsheets.php.

Denvir, Daniel. 2011. "The Ten Most Segregated Urban Areas in America." Solon Media Group, Inc., March 29.

Desmond, Mathew. 2016. *Evicted*. New York: Crown.

Economic Innovation Group. 2016. "The 2016 Distressed Community Index." https://eig.org/wp-content/uploads/2016/02/2016-Distressed-Communities-Index-Report.pdf.

Fainstein, Susan S. and David Gladstone. 1999. "Evaluating Urban Tourism." In *The Tourist City*, edited by Dennis R. Judd and Susan S. Fainstein, 21–34. New Haven, CT: Yale University Press.

Florida, Richard, and Charlotta Melander. 2015. "Segregated City: The Geography of Economic Segregation in America's Metros." Martin Prosperity Institute, University of Toronto, February.

Florida, Richard. 2013. "The Persistent Geography of Disadvantage," CityLab, July 25, 2013. https://www.citylab.com/equity/2013/07/persistent-geography-disadvantage/6231/.

Healy, Lenore, and Michael Lepley. 2016. "Housing Voucher Mobility in Cuyahoga County." Housing Center. http://www.thehousingcenter.org/wp-content/uploads/2016/02/Cuyahoga-County-Voucher-Mobility-Report.pdf.

Jargowski, Paul A. 2016. *Architecture of Segregation: Civil Unrest, the Concentration of Poverty and Public Policy*. New York: Century Foundation.

Keating W. Dennis. 2011. "Cuyahoga County Land Revitalization Corporation: The Beginning, the Present, and Beyond." Cuyahoga County Land Bank. http://www.cuyahogalandbank.org/articles/CCLRC_2009_2011_Report.pdf.

Kent, Alex, and T. C. Frohlich. 2015. "America's Most Segregated Cities." 24/7 Wall Street.

Kotlowitz, Alex. "All Boarded Up." 2009. *New York Times Magazine*, March 4, 2009.

Krumholz, Norman. 1982. "A Retrospective View of Equity Planning: Cleveland 1969–1979." *Journal of the American Planning Association* 48, no. 2: 163–74.

Krumholz, Norman, and Pierre Clavel. 1994. *Reinventing Cities: Equity Planners Tell Their Stories*. Philadelphia: Temple University Press.

Mallach, Alan. 2015. "The Challenge of Cleveland's Neighborhoods." Address at Levin College of Urban Affairs, Cleveland State University, Cleveland, OH, March 26, 2015.

New York Times. 2016. "Poorest Areas Have Missed out on Boons of Recovery, Study Finds," February 2, 2016.

Piiparien, Richey, and Jim Russell. 2014. "Globalizing Cleveland: A Path Forward." *Urban Publications*, paper 1164, Levin College of Urban Affairs, Cleveland State University, Cleveland, OH.

Rawls, John. 1971. *Theory of Justice*. New York: Belknap Press.

Sharkey, Patrick. 2013. *Stuck in Place: Urban Neighborhoods and the End of Progress toward Racial Equality*. Chicago: University of Chicago Press.

Stokes, Carl B. 1971a. "Public Housing and the Urban Crisis." *George Washington Law Review* 39, no. 4: 662–73.

Stokes, Carl B. 1971b. "On Reordering the Priorities of the Planning Profession." In *Planning 1971: Selected Papers from the ASPO National Planning Conference*, 1–6. Chicago: American Society of Planning Officials.

Stradling, David, and Richard Stradling. 2015. *Where the River Burned: Carl Stokes and the Struggle to Save Cleveland*. Ithaca, NY: Cornell University Press.

Whitney, William. 2016. Personal conversation with the CEO of Cuyahoga County Land Revitalization Corporation, May 2016.

Wright, Walter, Kathryn W. Hexter, and Nick Downer. 2016. "Cleveland's Greater University Circle Initiative." Cleveland Foundation. https://www.clevelandfoundation.org/wp-content/uploads/2014/01/Cleveland-Foundation-Greater-University-Circle-Initiative-Case-Study-2014.pdf.

8

Race and Policing in Ohio

THE LOSS OF HOPE CROSS THE RIVER JORDAN

RONNIE A. DUNN, TERRANCE ALLEN, AND AHMED WHITT

The state of Ohio once held special significance for blacks enslaved in the antebellum South relative to their quest for freedom. As encrypted in Negro spirituals used as code by runaway slaves seeking freedom on the Underground Railroad and their abolitionist conductors, "stealing away cross the Jordan River" to the "Promised Land" of Canada meant crossing the Ohio River into the sanctuary of the free state of Ohio. One of the last stops along this clandestine network of passageways and safe houses for fugitive slaves before reaching Canada and unrepressed self-determination was the city of Cleveland, referred to as *Hope*. Today Ohio's status as a safe haven for blacks is in question, as a number of police-involved shootings of unarmed African Americans in cities across the country, including Cleveland, are indicative of the problematic relationship between blacks and the police, which catalyzed the Black Lives Matter movement. As noted by the preeminent policing scholar Samuel Walker (2001), "the problem of police abuse is primarily a problem of race relations and is one of the most volatile aspects of the national race crisis" (4). Ohio leads the nation in the number of police agencies that have come under the federal oversight of the US Department of Justice's Civil Rights Division with five, more than double that of California and Montana, the states with the next highest number of law enforcement agencies coming under Department of Justice guidance with two each. In 2013 Cleveland became the latest city in the state—along with Steubenville, Cincinnati, Columbus, and Warren—to earn this ignominious distinction.

This chapter examines policing in Cleveland to analyze the relationship, dynamics, and interactions between the police and African Americans and, by extension, minority groups in general, in twenty-first-century America. The history of community-police relations, the state of police-community relations in Cleveland, and the status of agreed-upon police reforms there and in the state in general are examined. This examination includes a review of news reports and official documents pertaining to patterns of policing practices—for example, the use of force, including deadly use of force, arrests, traffic stops, etc., and their racial implications. It also includes information on the work of two bodies established by Ohio's governor to address the crisis between law enforcement and African Americans and other underrepresented groups within the state.

THE RELATIONSHIP BETWEEN BLACKS AND THE POLICE

To fully comprehend the dynamic forces and complexities entailed in the problematic interactions between police and the African American community, each deadly encounter cannot be examined as an isolated incident, or as a late twentieth-, early twenty-first-century phenomenon, but rather must be placed and examined within the holistic, sociohistorical context within which this relationship exists. The relationship between blacks and the police as an institution was forged during slavery and evolved from the interactions between the enslaved population and the slave patrols, referred to as *patterollers* (Wintersmith 1974; Dulaney 1996; Dunn and Reed 2010). Patterollers were responsible for enforcing the Slave Codes, which governed the prevailing mores and social interactions between blacks and whites. They were typically poor, young, white males responsible for regulating the movement of the enslaved and free blacks by checking the passes of slaves outside their home plantation and the papers of free blacks identifying them as such (Dunn 2016), capturing runaway slaves, checking slave quarters for stolen property, and administering discipline, typically through whipping (Gabbidon and Greene 2013). Although American policing is traced to England, with the adoption of the night-watch system in the colonies, slave patrols, which had been established in every Southern colony by the mid-1700s, are the precursor to modern police in the American South, where the majority of blacks lived until after 1950 (Dulaney 1996). It is within this legacy of racial antipathy that we must examine the relationship between the African American community and police officers.

THE STATUS OF BLACKS IN THE FREE STATE OF OHIO

Despite Ohio's admission to the Union as a free state, whose northern banks of the Ohio River symbolized freedom for runaway slaves, the state was not particularly progressive on the issue of slavery and the treatment of blacks—free or enslaved (Dunn and Reed 2010). According to George Knepper (2003), "Ohio's blacks, many of them legally free, and many others fugitives from slavery, were kept in their place," but in some sections lived under fewer restraints than blacks commonly endured in free states (196). The Ohio legislature enacted legislation in 1804 to deter black migration to the state by requiring blacks entering the state "to post bond for $500 (presumably to deter their becoming a public charge)" and "file evidence of his free status with local authorities" (197).

Just prior to the Civil War, Ohio had a "colored" population of 36,700—the majority of whom lived in the southwestern counties of Hamilton (Cincinnati), Ross, Gallia, and Franklin (Columbus). Few blacks lived in the state's northern counties, with the majority (1,277) living in Cuyahoga County (Cleveland) in 1850. The northwestern region had fewer blacks, therefore they were not perceived as an economic threat in the region. Scholars suggest that free blacks in Cleveland, Akron, and surrounding towns in the Western Reserve experienced a more liberal environment and opportunities than blacks in other parts of the state due to its early settlers' New England conscience (Knepper 2003). As immigrants swelled the populations of cities such as New York, Philadelphia, Chicago, Milwaukee, and Detroit throughout the 1800s, Ohio emerged as the state with the largest concentration of urban centers—Cleveland, Cincinnati, Columbus, Toledo, Dayton, Youngstown, Akron, Canton—and a constellation of small industrialized towns, such as Warren and Steubenville (Dunn et al. 2016).

CLEVELAND: AKA HOPE

Blacks' presence in Cleveland preceded that of all European ethnic groups, except the German and Irish, as the first blacks settled in the city in 1809 (Dunn et al. 2016). Prior to the Civil War approximately 2 percent of the city's population of 43,000 were black. Cleveland, on the southern shores of Lake Erie, served as a port by which slaves seeking freedom on the Underground Railroad stowed away on ships bound for Canada. Analogous to how their African ancestors were held in dungeons of slave castles along the Slave Coast of West Africa until there was enough human cargo to fill the hulls of slave ships that lay in wait in the bay, runaway slaves, with the aid of white and free black conductors, hid in the basement, the bell tower, or sanctuary of St. John's Episcopal Church, code-named "Station Hope," on West 26th and Church Street. They waited there until receiving a signal from the docks to secret their way the short distance to the lake to steal away aboard a ship to Canada.

After the Civil War, while small numbers of blacks migrated west, the majority remained in the South, 75 percent of whom lived and worked on rural farms (Dunn et al. 2016). Between World War I and the Great Depression (1914–1929) more than 1.5 million blacks migrated to northern industrial centers to fill vacancies in the industrial wartime economy created by restrictions on European immigration (Dunn et al. 2016). By 1920 Cleveland was a major industrial-manufacturing center and the fifth largest US city. No northern city, with the exception of Detroit, experienced greater growth in its black population during the 1920s than Cleveland. With the onset of the Great Depression, black migration slowed, but did not stop; as America entered World War II the second wave of the Great Migration was ignited. This mass exodus of blacks to urban areas in the Northeast, Midwest, and West represents the greatest internal human migration in world history as more than six million African Americans migrated to northeastern, midwestern, and western cities and towns between 1915 and 1970 (Dunn et al. 2016; Wilkerson 2010).

Like the immigrants that preceded them, blacks were confined to the sections of town with the worst housing, inadequate schools, poor health care, and high poverty, unemployment, and crime rates that were further compounded by pervasive police brutality and racial bias (Bowen, Dunn, and Kasdan 2010). As the noted sociologist William Julius Wilson (1987) observed, many of the second-wave black migrants arrived in northern cities seeking jobs in the manufacturing-based economy as the US economy was restructuring to a service- and technology-based economy.

As these dire socioeconomic conditions coalesced, black anger and frustration festered, ultimately exploding in a series of more than one hundred race riots throughout the nation from the mid- to late 1960s. President Johnson convened the Kerner Commission in 1967 to study the root causes of the riots, which concluded, "The riots were the result of blacks' profound dissatisfaction with an American society in which racism was deeply embedded." As Wintersmith (1974) noted, "virtually every urban rebellion that took place during the sixties was immediately preceded by police-black-citizen confrontations" (44). Since the turbulent 1960s, Ohio has had race riots in each of its major cities—Cleveland (1966 and 1967), Cincinnati (1967, 1968, and 2001), Columbus (1969), and Toledo (2005), all of which are legacy cities, except Columbus.

RACE AND US DEPARTMENT OF JUSTICE INTERVENTION

Erik Luna (2003) notes, "Police officers still embody the initial contact between African Americans and the criminal justice system," and these, "negative confrontations become 'race-making situations,' constructing what it means to be black through interaction with police—namely, second-class citizens under constant surveillance and subject to abusive enforcement"

(185). According to Van Maanen (1978), the police "represent the visible aspect of the body politic and is that aspect most likely to directly intervene in the daily lives of the citizenry" (115). While police-citizen interactions take place in various contexts, the most frequent contact the average citizen has with police comes occurs through a traffic stop (Eith and Durose 2011; Dunn 2015). Although routine, traffic stops are fraught with uncertainty and represent one of the most potentially volatile encounters between police and citizens. This is evident in a number of incidents of police officers using deadly force against black motorists caught on video over the past several years—for example, Philando Castile in Falcon Heights, Minnesota; Walter Scott in North Charleston, South Carolina; Samuel Dubose near the University of Cincinnati; and, the first such incident captured on video, the 1991 beating of Rodney King in Los Angeles.

Following the acquittal of four white Los Angeles Police Department officers involved in the videotaped beating of King and the ensuing 1992 Los Angeles riots, Congress granted the Department of Justice (DOJ) authority to investigate and intervene when local law enforcement agencies are found to engage in unconstitutional policing (Kelly et al. 2016). The Violent Crime Control and Law Enforcement Act of 1994 makes it illegal for any governmental authority, or person acting on its behalf, to deprive a person of the rights, privileges, or immunities secured or protected by the Constitution or laws of the United States.

The decision to investigate a law enforcement agency, made by the assistant attorney general of the US Department of Justice Civil Rights Division, depends on whether the allegations are verified, whether they violate the Constitution or federal law, and whether they constitute a pattern or practice of behavior. Where such misconduct is confirmed, the DOJ can obtain a federal court order that mandates local or state law enforcement agencies remedy the institutional deficiencies that give rise to the systemic unconstitutional policing practices. Since its inception in 1994, the DOJ has opened sixty-nine formal investigations of local or state law enforcement agencies and entered into forty reform agreements. As of January 2017, the DOJ had eighteen active reform agreements, five investigations underway, and cases in litigation in Colorado City, Arizona, and Hildale, Utah (US Department of Justice Civil Rights Division 2017).

As noted earlier, Ohio has the unenviable distinction of leading the nation in the number of police agencies that have come under federal investigation by the Department of Justice, with five investigations: Steubenville (1997–2005), Columbus (2002–2004), Cincinnati (2002–2008), Warren (2012–present), and Cleveland (1999–2005; 2015–present). And while the size, socioeconomic conditions, and racial demographics in each jurisdiction have differed, race has been a salient factor in the events that ultimately led to federal intervention in their respective police departments. Most of these cities, big and small, share many of the characteristics of legacy cities, which Cleveland epitomizes. It has the largest black/minority population (54 percent) and is the only large majority black/minority city in Ohio. We will thus examine community-police relations and the federal intervention in Cleveland.

RACE AND POLICING IN CLEVELAND

Cleveland and its police department have an interesting and complicated history that intersects policing and race. In the 1950s and 1960s two landmark US Supreme Court rulings pertaining to the Fourth Amendment and police search and seizure procedures emanated from encounters between Cleveland police officers and African Americans. *Mapp v. Ohio* (1957) stemmed from an incident where three Cleveland police officers, using a fake search warrant, forced their way into the home of Dollree Mapp, an African American woman suspected of harboring a suspect and possessing gambling slips. The officers did not find the suspect or gambling slips, but they did find pornographic materials, for which Mapp was arrested and convicted. The case reached the US Supreme Court, which ruled, "the right to be free from unreasonable search and seizure applied in the state courts as well as the federal and evidence obtained in violation of the Fourth Amendment was inadmissible" (Stokes and Chanoff 2016, 51).

The second case, *Terry v. Ohio* (1968), stems from a 1963 encounter in downtown Cleveland in which a white police officer, Martin McFadden, searched and arrested John Terry and Richard Chilton, both black, for carrying concealed weapons after observing them for ten minutes walking back and forth looking into store windows at 14th Street and Euclid Avenue. McFadden suspected the pair, along with an unarmed white male acquaintance, of "casing a job" (Dunn and Reed 2011, 14). Terry, represented by the late congressman Louis Stokes, appealed the case all the way to the Supreme Court, alleging that his Fourth Amendment right against unreasonable search and seizure was violated. The Supreme Court upheld the lower courts' ruling but used its decision to establish the legal limits by which police may use stop-and-frisk procedures to prevent unreasonable search and seizure and constrain police discretion in determining when there is probable cause to believe that a crime has occurred for which an arrest can be made (Dunn and Reed 2011). The ruling defined the procedure police refer to as a *Terry frisk*. Collectively, the cases are germane to the pervasive problem of racial profiling, and the inadmissibility of evidence obtained in a search that violates the Fourth Amendment.

By this time, Cleveland's racial dynamics had changed as this once racially progressive and liberal city had become increasingly segregated and reflected the racially stratified patterns found in other metropolitan areas in the country. Blacks continued to migrate to industrial centers as the process of deindustrialization was well under way, resulting in precipitous job losses and white out-migration from the urban core to the burgeoning suburban periphery. The forced residential segregation of blacks in Cleveland culminated in race riots in the city's Hough and Glenville neighborhoods in 1966 and 1968, respectively.

Paradoxically, this segregation and the concomitant dire living conditions had the unintended effect of consolidating and galvanizing black political voting power in the city. Coupled with the racial anxiety created by the Hough riots, Carl Stokes was elected mayor of Cleveland in 1967, becoming the first African American mayor of a major US city. Whereas blacks only represented 37 percent of Cleveland's population at the time, Stokes garnered the support of the white business community, which viewed him as an insurance policy against future racial unrest, and contributed to this historic victory (Stokes 1989).

Cleveland again experienced racial unrest on July 23, 1968, nine months after Stokes's election, with the Glenville riot, which started when a black nationalist leader, Ahmed Evans, opened fire on a police stakeout, thinking his organization's headquarters was being attacked. When the rioting ended five days later, three white police officers, three black nationalists, and one black civilian were dead. Amidst reports of police violence against black residents, Stokes removed all white officers from the Glenville area and sent in the National Guard and black police officers, along with "peace patrols," comprised of black public officials, clergy, and community leaders, to help quell the violence. This infuriated the white rank and file and further exacerbated the adversarial relationship between the administration and the police, which persisted throughout Stokes's two terms in office (1967–1971). The Cleveland Police Patrolmen's Association (CPPA), the union for the rank and file, established in 1969, cites the Glenville riot in its mission statement as "The most tragic day in the history of the Cleveland Police Department," and the catalyst of its origins (CPPA 2017).

Against the backdrop of a number of questionable police-involved shootings and death in custody cases involving blacks, an emergency ordinance was passed in Cleveland in 1985 establishing a civilian police review board for the expressed purpose of maintaining the peace, as racial tensions were once again heightened in the city. In 2000 Mayor Michael White called on the FBI to investigate the department for "organized racist activity." While sufficient evidence was not found to substantiate "organized racist activity" within the department, the voluminous investigation file contained a four-page memo from the deputy chief of operations, which explicitly stated, "we the Cleveland Division of Police racially profile African Americans, particularly young black males," and detailed the manner in which it occurred. Media reports made no mention of the memo and readily dismissed the investigation (Dunn 2010).

Racial tensions rose in the African American community during the administration of Jane Campbell (2002–2006), the city's only female mayor, as five unarmed black males were shot by police officers, four of which resulted in fatalities, and three of which occurred within a one-month period in 2005 (Dunn 2010). Upon taking office in 2006, Campbell's successor, current mayor Frank Jackson, immediately issued a revised use of force policy directive, which stated, "excessive and unnecessary use of deadly force would not be tolerated," (Dunn 2010, 127). The policy initially seemed to reduce the use of deadly force, but its effect soon waned, resulting in two of the most egregious use of deadly force cases in US police history.

The first is the November 2012 shooting of Timothy Russell and Malissa Williams, two unarmed African Americans killed in a hail of 137 bullets following a twenty-five-minute, high-speed chase involving 63 police cruisers, and more than 115 officers from five jurisdictions. Thirteen Cleveland police officers, twelve white and one Hispanic, fired 137 rounds into Russell's car, striking him and his passenger, Williams, twenty-three and twenty-four times, respectively, in the head, neck, and upper torso. One Cleveland police officer, Michael Brelo, who jumped on the hood of the disabled car and fired forty-nine rounds into the vehicle, was indicted for manslaughter. He was acquitted in May 2015. The city fired Brelo, but the CPPA appealed his firing and sought his reinstatement to the department (Blackwell 2016).

Although the DOJ announced the opening of an investigation of the Cleveland Police Department (CPD) in March 2013, there was a considerable skepticism in the community relative to the effect of an investigation. The DOJ and the city had signed a memorandum of agreement calling for revision and enforcement of the CPD's use-of-force policy and development of a police accountability system (i.e., Early Warning System) to monitor, track, and correct officer performance in 2004. The memorandum was terminated in March 2005.

On November 23, 2014, weeks before the DOJ concluded its investigation of the Cleveland Police Department, a rookie Cleveland police officer shot and killed twelve-year-old Tamir Rice, a black youth playing with a replica BB gun in a city park. Responding to a call of an armed suspect, Timothy Loehmann and his partner, Frank Garmback, pulled their cruiser within feet of Rice. Loehmann fired two shots within two seconds as he exited from the passenger side, striking Rice in the abdomen. Tamir Rice died at the hospital the next day.

It was discovered that Loehmann had resigned from the Independence Police Department, a Cleveland suburb, after it was determined he was unfit to serve as a police officer. His personnel file from the Independence Police Department contained a memo from the deputy chief that detailed multiple emotional breakdowns that Loehmann had during weapons training and concluded that no amount of training would rectify these deficiencies. The Cleveland Police Department failed to check the Independence personnel file as part of the hiring process. Tamir Rice's death sparked demonstrations and protests in Cleveland and in other cities throughout the country, and while the Cleveland protests remained peaceful, tensions were heightened as the city awaited the verdict in the Brelo murder trial. The Tamir Rice case struck an emotional chord deep within the African American community, as well as across the nation and world, as he was seen as a modern-day Emmitt Till and his death further galvanized the Black Lives Matter Movement.

With the release of its findings letter, the DOJ reported, "we have reasonable cause to believe that CDP [CPD] engages in a pattern or practice of the use of excessive force in violation of the Fourth Amendment of the United States Constitution," and "determined that structural and systemic deficiencies and practices—including insufficient accountability, inadequate training, ineffective policies, and inadequate engagement with the community—contribute to the use of unreasonable force" (US Department of Justice Civil Rights Division 2014). And although "there was not a finding of racial profiling," the agreement does call for bias-free policing, which is critically important in Cleveland—a city that is 54 percent black and 64 percent people of color, and in which public officials have been remiss in addressing the issue of racial profiling (Diaz et al. 2015).

The reforms in the subsequent consent decree agreed upon by the DOJ and the city cover fourteen broad areas, including revised use of force policies; crisis-intervention training; community engagement and building trust; community and problem-oriented policing; bias-free policing; search and seizure training; a revamped accountability system with enforcement, robust data collection and analysis; and transparency and oversight, including the hiring of a police inspector general. The agreement also requires that officers have the necessary equipment and resources to perform their jobs effectively and safely. Of particular note in the agreement is the establishment of a thirteen-person Community Police Commission, composed of ten community members representing diverse groups within the city and three police representatives, and the department-wide adoption of a community- and problem-oriented policing philosophy and strategy rather than a designated Community Policing Unit or officers.

THE STATUS OF THE CLEVELAND CONSENT DECREE REFORM EFFORTS AFTER ONE YEAR

According to the federal monitoring team overseeing the implementation of the consent decree's second semiannual report, "The City of Cleveland has reached several critical milestones in the Consent Decree process—including new use of force policies, forthcoming crisis intervention policies, and new manuals for complaint investigation and review" (Monitor's Report 2017, 1). The most notable challenges identified are the backlog of uncompleted investigations of 439 citizen complaints filed with the Office of Professional Standards and the Police Review Board. According to the report, 81 percent of complaints filed in 2016, 68 percent of complaints filed in 2015, and even complaints filed in 2014 are unresolved. The report incredulously states, "At this point, the Monitor Team struggles for language sufficiently strong to communicate how unacceptable and appalling the state of OPS as an entity is," and adds, "all efforts to date by OPS to outline mechanisms for addressing the backlog have been patently insufficient in all respects and in form and content, not serious proposals," (Cleveland Police Monitoring Team 2017, 3–4).

A review of traffic enforcement and arrest records since 2013 reveal a 55 percent decrease in ticket-writing and a 42 percent drop in arrests by CDP officers, indicative of "depolicing" by patrol officers, (Meyer 2017). CPPA president Steve Loomis acknowledged as much, stating, "We're not doing it because we don't want to be accused of being unconstitutional. We don't want to be accused of being biased of who we're stopping and why." He added that officers are still responding to radio calls, but are less likely to engage in "proactive policing," or respond to anything that does not come from a 911 call (Meyer 2017). The CPPA endorsed Donald Trump for president—the first time in the union's forty-eight-year history that it endorsed a political candidate—and Loomis made a number of campaign appearances with Trump. Given Trump's racially inflammatory rhetoric, calls for "law and order" and the use of "stop-and-frisk," the union leadership's actions have exacerbated the already inimical community-police relations in this racially segregated, majority black city (McGreal 2017).

EFFORTS TO IMPROVE COMMUNITY-POLICE RELATIONS ACROSS THE BUCKEYE STATE

In the wake of the deadly police shootings of John Crawford III and Tamir Rice, Ronnie A. Dunn urged two state legislators from Cleveland to implore Governor John Kasich, who was also running for the 2016 Republican presidential nomination, to commission a statewide task force on policing. Within a week's time, Governor Kasich signed an executive order and was making the rounds on the Sunday morning political talk shows announcing the establishment of a twenty-four-person Ohio Task Force on Community-Police Relations. The task force, compromised of elected officials, law enforcement, community leaders, clergy, and academics held four public forums throughout the state and produced a six-hundred-page report, which included testimony from residents as well as research and recommendations on policing best practices provided by expert witnesses. The report's recommendations fell within six broad areas: use of force/deadly force, recruitment and hiring, accountability and oversight, community education, community involvement, and the grand jury process.

Governor Kasich then signed another executive order establishing the Ohio Collaborative Community-Police Advisory Board. This standing board is charged with developing statewide standards to guide the approximately 877 law enforcement agencies across the state, and to provide greater police transparency and accountability and build mutual understanding, trust, and respect with the communities they serve. To date seven statewide standards have been established, which include policies on the use of force, including deadly force; recruitment and hiring; community engagement; radio-dispatch training; body cameras; and bias-free policing, which requires data collection on all traffic stops (Ohio Collaborative Community-Police Advisory Board 2017). A certification process was established, allowing police agencies across the state to provide documentation demonstrating their agency's adoption and implementation of the standards to the Ohio Office of Criminal Justice Services, and undergo an onsite assessment. The first compliance report, released in March 2017, assessed the number of agencies in the certification process relative to the first two standards established, which addressed the use of force/deadly force and recruitment and hiring. Across the state, 58 percent of law enforcement agencies are in the process of being certified—27,740 of the state's 34,807 law enforcement officers work in these agencies, and 80 percent of the state's eleven-million-plus people are covered by agencies in the certification process (Ohio Collaborative Community-Police Advisory Board 2017).

Although it is not mandatory that law enforcement agencies adopt these standards, they establish for the first time in Ohio history uniform minimum standards for police agencies across the state and provide a criterion that citizens can reasonably expect their local police and public officials to adhere to. These standards were developed in partnership with the Ohio Association of Chiefs of Police and the Buckeye State Sheriffs Association, which should minimize law enforcement's resistance to the reform efforts and state legislators' reluctance to enact laws to address systemic problems such racial profiling—that is, bias-free policing.

DISCUSSION

Race is still a salient characteristic that colors and defines the prevalence and outcomes of interactions between persons of color and law enforcement, as evidenced by the persistent number of police-involved shooting deaths of unarmed African Americans, across the country over the past several years. It is apparent that the troubled relationship between blacks and police officers remains one of the most impermeable social and political domestic problems confronting American society more than 150 years after slavery was abolished. While this relationship has been contentious throughout most of US history, it has seemingly reached a critical tipping point within the last quarter century with the increase of federal investigations of troubled police agencies and the signing of consent decrees to reform departments, from the Los Angeles Police Department in 1992 to the Baltimore Police Department in 2016.

Although there are a limited number of studies that demonstrate the effectiveness of consent decrees in cities in which they have been implemented, studies of Los Angeles and Cincinnati have shown the effectiveness of consent decrees in bringing about constitutional policing practices, enhanced operational infrastructures, and improved police-community relations (Ross 2009). Both cities' police departments, which once epitomized the stigmatized image of racially biased and abusive police agencies that plagues many urban police departments, today are hailed as national models of effective police reform and enjoy much-improved community-police relations (Stone et al. 2009; Semuels 2015). Despite the momentum for police reform that has evolved nationally in the aftermath of the rash of deaths of unarmed citizens at the hands of police officers across the country, this compulsion might recede with the election of President Trump and the confirmation of a new attorney general. After less than two months in office, Sessions, whom many view as an ardent opponent of civil rights and has stated his belief that consent decrees impede police work, ordered a review of all police reform agreements signed under the Obama administration. This includes eighteen signed consent decrees, including those in Warren and Cleveland. The federal judge overseeing Cleveland's consent decree stated that the agreement's enforcement is a matter of the court. Additionally, Cleveland's mayor has reiterated his administration's intention to adhere to the terms of the agreement. Yet, without the backing of the Department of Justice, the enforcement of such agreements becomes much more tenuous, particularly in the face of emboldened police obstruction. Already, the CPPA's president has reportedly viewed this as an opportunity to "pull back," (Heisig 2017).

These dynamics create a volatile situation, particularly at this time in our nation's history, given the deep racial divisions that still persist in the United States, which the 2016 presidential election unequivocally exposed. With the unremitting loss of black lives at the hands of police officers, as evidenced by the recent shooting death of Jordan Edwards, a fifteen-year old African American honor student, by a suburban Dallas police officer, and the retaliatory killing of five police officers in Dallas in July 2016 followed by the killing of three police officers in Baton Rouge ten days later, and that of a New York City police officer in July 2017.

CONCLUSION

Since the abolition of slavery, African Americans and other marginalized and oppressed groups have primarily looked to the federal government to safeguard and enforce their constitutional rights and protections. Relative to the current crisis in policing which, given the recent events cited show no signs of abating, these protections have typically been sought and come through the enforcement of Department of Justice consent decrees. It appears however, that may no longer be the case, given the recalcitrance of the Trump administration and the DOJ under Attorney General Sessions to use federal investigations and consent decrees to reform troubled and abusive police agencies.

Accordingly, the impetus to transform policing in the United States must shift to the state and local levels. Ohio offers a template for such reform efforts with the introduction of statewide policing standards established by the Ohio Collaborative Community-Police Advisory Board. This model provides residents with measures and expectations that they can hold their local officials and police departments accountable to through the political process. Additionally, it affords law enforcement another means of reassuring the communities they serve of their commitment and dedication to the principles of just, equitable, and constitutional policing regardless of one's background or zip code.

Cincinnati and Cleveland were both once key points on the Underground Railroad. They were places of sanctuary for blacks escaping slavery. Cleveland was also where blacks could board ships bound for uncontested freedom in Canada. Today, these two cities represent the polar extremes in policing in America relative to community-police relations in urban communities of color. The Queen City (Cincinnati) provides a sense of optimism for the future of policing, whereas conditions in the city once referred to as *Hope* by runaway slaves does not inspire that emotion, particularly for people of African, and other non-European descent. Yet, the policing standards being adopted by jurisdictions across Ohio offer a way forward for the Buckeye State and the nation.

REFERENCES

Blackwell, Brandon. 2016. "Cleveland Police Officer Michael Brelo Fired over 2012 Chase, Shooting." Cleveland.com. http://www.cleveland.com/metro/index.ssf/2016/01/cleveland_police_officer_micha.htm.

Bowen, William M., Ronnie A. Dunn, and David O. Kasdan. 2010. "What is Urban Studies? Context, Internal Structure, and Content." *Journal of Urban Affairs* 32, no. 3: 199–227.

Cleveland Police Monitoring Team. 2017. "Second Semiannual Report." http://www.clevelandpolicemonitor.net/resources-reports/.

Cleveland Police Patrolmen's Association (CPPA). 2017. "History of the CPPA." http://www.cppa.org/about-us.html.

Diaz, Shakyra, Carole Rendon, Terry Gilbert, Jonathan Witmer-Rich, Ronnie A. Dunn, and Craig M. Boise. 2015. "Ferguson, Staten Island, and Cleveland: A Legal Discussion about the Use of Lethal Force by Law Enforcement Officers." Cleveland State University, Cleveland-Marshall College of Law, Cleveland, OH. http://engagedscholarship.csuohio.edu/law_other_events/31.

Dulaney, W. Marvin. 1996. *Black Police in America.* Bloomington: Indiana University Press.

Dunn, Ronnie A. 2010. "Race and the Relevance of Citizen Complaints against the Police." *Administrative Theory & Praxis* 32, no. 4: 577–97.

Dunn, Ronnie A., and Wornie L. Reed. 2010. *Racial Profiling: Causes & Consequences.* Dubuque, IA: Kendall-Hunt Publishing.

Dunn, Ronnie A., Donna M. Whyte, James Hardiman, Mittie Davis Jones, and Adrienne Hatten. 2016. *Boycotts, Busing, and Beyond: The History and Implications of School Desegregation in the Urban North.* Dubuque, IA: Kendall-Hunt Publishing.

Eith, Christine, and Matthew Durose. 2011. "Contacts Between Police and the Public, 2008." Washington, DC, US Department of Justice, Office of Justice Programs. https://www.bjs.gov/content/pub/pdf/cpp08.pdf.

Gabiddon, Shaun L., and Helen Taylor-Greene. 2013. *Race and Crime.* Thousand Oaks, CA: SAGE.

Heisig, Eric. 2017. "Why They Believe Cleveland Police Reform Is Critical." *Plain Dealer* (Cleveland, OH), April 28, 2017.

Kelly, Kimbriell, Sarah Childress, and Steven Rich. 2015. "Forced Reforms, Mixed Results." *Washington Post,* November 13, 2015.

Knepper, George W. 2003. *Ohio and Its People.* Kent, OH: Kent State University Press.

Luna, Erik. 2003. "Race, Crime, and Institutional Design: The Political Geography of Race Data in the Criminal Justice System." *Law and Contemporary Problems* 66, no. 3: 183–220.

Manning, Peter K., and John Van Maanen, eds. *Policing: A View from the Street*. 1978. Santa Monica, CA: Goodyear.

McGreal, Chris. 2017. "Cleveland's Dividing Lines over Race Issues Come to Light under Trump." *Guardian* (UK), March 3, 2017.

Meyer, Tom. 2017. "Investigator: Cleveland Police Ticketing and Arresting a Lot Fewer." WKYC.com, February 6, 2017. http://www.wkyc.com/news/investigations/investigator-cleveland-police.

Morrison, Aaron. 2017. "Jeff Sessions May Have Doubts about Police Reform Agreements: But They Actually Work." Mic, April 13, 2017.

Ohio Collaborative Community-Police Advisory Board. 2017. "Standards." http://www.ocjs.ohio.gov/ohiocollaborative/standards.html.

Ross, Darrel L., and Patricia A. Parke. 2009. "Policing by Consent Decree: An Analysis of 42 USC § 14141 and the New Model for Police Accountability." *Police Practice and Research: An International Journal* 10, no. 3: 199–208.

Semuels, Alana. 2015. "How to Fix a Broken Police Department." *Atlantic*, May 28, 2015. https://www.theatlantic.com/politics/archive/2015/05/cincinnati-police-reform/393797/.

Stokes, Carl B. 1989. *Promises of Power*. Cleveland: Friends of Carl B. Stokes.

Stokes, Louis, and David Chanoff. 2016. *The Gentleman from Ohio*. Columbus: Trillium.

Stone, Christopher, Todd Foglesong, and Christine M. Cole. 2009. "Policing Los Angeles under a Consent Decree: The Dynamics of Change at the LAPD." Harvard Program in Criminal Justice Policy and Management, Cambridge, MA.

US Department of Justice Civil Rights Division. 2017. "The Civil Rights Division's Pattern and Practice Police Reform Work: 1994–Present." https://ucr.fbi.gov/nibrs/2015.

Van Maanen, John. 1978. "Kinsmen in Repose." In *Policing: A View from the Street*, edited by Peter K. Manning and John Van Maanen. Santa Monica, CA: Goodyear.

Walker, Samuel. 2001. *Police Accountability: The Role of Citizen Oversight*. Belmont, CA: Wadsworth.

Wilson, William Julius. 1987. *The Truly Disadvantaged: The Inner City, the Underclass, and Public Policy*. Chicago: University of Chicago Press.

Wintersmith, Robert F. 1974. *The Police and the Black Community*. Lexington, MA: Lexington Books.

9

Urban Neighborhood Main Streets in Legacy Cities

CHALLENGES AND OPPORTUNITIES

KIRBY DATE

While the foundation of urban neighborhood revitalization is a sustainable base of quality housing, retail development is nevertheless a pressing issue facing urban neighborhoods in legacy cities. Population, household income, and property decline, combined with competing commercial centers in surrounding suburbs and now increasing e-commerce, have decimated retail opportunity in urban neighborhoods. The result in legacy city neighborhoods is a pattern of low-density, deteriorating retail establishments spread out over long commercial strips, punctuated by dollar stores, drugstores, convenience, and predatory businesses. And yet, retail development holds opportunities for local community resident investment and entrepreneurship, training of youth in entry-level jobs, and resident and business interaction.

This chapter explores retail activity, shopping habits, and supply and demand for retail space in six Cleveland neighborhoods. The findings characterize four important markets that urban neighborhood retail main streets serve and highlight the importance of critical mass and strategic investment. The chapter first characterizes the challenges and opportunities present in legacy city neighborhood main streets. It then addresses various aspects of the urban retail market. Key findings, recommendations, and implications for policy conclude the chapter.

LEGACY CITY NEIGHBORHOOD MAIN STREETS

Population decline, loss of economic base, growing household income inequality and poverty, and falling property values are signifying characteristics of legacy cities' urban neighborhoods (see Ryberg-Webster and Tighe's introduction to this volume). Together they result in soft housing markets with too much supply and falling demand, too little property-owner equity, too little investment in rebuilding and restoring housing stock, and a changing land-use pattern characterized by decreasing density and increasing vacancy and abandonment (see chapters 5 and 10). Occupied and maintained houses are interspersed with vacant lots and poorly maintained or abandoned homes; neighborhood density and walkability diminish; infrastructure (utilities, roads, sidewalks, lighting, transit) is less efficient. Lower household incomes and fewer people mean greatly reduced municipal revenues, making it difficult for the public sector to maintain neighborhood infrastructure (see chapter 3).

These same principles apply to the commercial environment on urban main streets. Since household income within an establishment's trade area drives retail success, population decline and low household income results in reduced capacity to support retail. For example, Cleveland's Slavic Village neighborhood was once home to seventy thousand people, with a robust local retail environment clustered on three main streets (Broadway Avenue, East 55th Street, and Fleet Avenue), and included many small, corner retail establishments embedded throughout the neighborhood. With a current population of just twelve thousand, the majority of Slavic Village's once-thriving retail establishments are gone, leaving behind gap-toothed corridors mixed with successful businesses, vacant and dilapidated storefronts, storefronts renovated for nonretail uses, and vacant lots. Corner retail on residential streets is largely renovated for residential use, with a few isolated businesses, some with longstanding clientele who continue to return after moving elsewhere, still in operation.

Declining property values on urban neighborhood main streets negatively affects business success. An oversupply of retail space results in very low rents, which may appear to be a boon to business owners, but gives property owners no incentive to upgrade and maintain spaces. Many property owners choose to leave properties vacant and report a tax loss (Accordino and Johnson 2000). Conversations with local community development corporation staff indicate that the recent housing foreclosure crisis has had a parallel effect on commercial property. Speculative absentee landowners sought rent without much investment, abandoning and/or vacating buildings when maintenance and debt service costs exceeded income generated. These vacant, abandoned, and poorly maintained buildings reduce the quality of neighborhood commercial environments, pulling stronger properties down with them. Vacant land and buildings resulting in a wide spacing of businesses, interspersed with deteriorated properties, reduces the quality of the walking and shopping environment. A spread-out line of businesses inhibits the critical mass required for vibrancy, walkability, and thriving retail. Infrastructure deterioration—in particular, roads, lighting, and sidewalks, contributes to the problem. The quality of the environment is especially important as shoppers must feel safe and comfortable walking, parking their cars, carrying goods, and moving from place to place (Cachinho 2014).

The legacy city retail spaces that remain, whether occupied or vacant, are highly variable in quality. There are two distinct types of legacy city retail areas. Urban main streets that were once major centers of commerce may contain stately multistory historic buildings, with masonry facades, detailed architectural features, tall ceilings, and well-built, upper-floor office space. These main streets likely housed banks, central post offices, furniture stores, restaurants, clothing stores, dry goods stores, haberdasheries, law and professional firms, and medical offices. While these former grand main streets may now suffer from deferred maintenance and vacancy, they remain important symbolic components of neighborhood identity. Yet, finding tenants is challenging when building footprints and the overall square footage are too large to support typical neighborhood entrepreneurial businesses.

A second, more common, type of legacy city retail district is found in pedestrian-scale neighborhood main streets that generally served their immediate neighborhoods. Former uses might have included butcher and bakery shops, hardware stores, produce vendors, smoke shops, tailors, dry goods, pharmacies, and delis. These main streets are well suited to restoration to meet the current trend for walkable neighborhoods with local entrepreneur-driven cafés, restaurants, gift and novelty shops, beauty shops, yoga and fitness shops, and the like. However, some of these retail clusters developed via an incremental transformation from residential uses, with family-owned businesses adding retail storefronts in front of the family home. These add-ons, dating from the late 1800s to the 1950s, were often hastily and inexpensively built, with limited foundations, inadequate structures, and do-it-yourself wiring and finishes. While they contribute to the historic character and identity of neighborhoods, the work involved in restoration is often cost prohibitive.

As with most urban main streets, legacy city neighborhoods now face competition with typical suburban big-box commercial development and increasing internet sales. In many communities across Ohio, big-box stores have effectively monopolized retail purchasing capacity, with huge footprints selling virtually every household good. Suburban retail complexes border Cleveland, pulling residents' dollars and sales tax revenue from the city. At the same time, internet sales are challenging big-box stores, suburban shopping malls, and even highly vibrant urban retail. Nationwide, e-commerce retail sales (excluding motor vehicles) rose from 5 percent in 2010 to 8.5 percent in 2015 (US Department of Commerce 2016), and are expected to continue to expand (Thompson 2017). The retail environment is undergoing a revolution, and legacy city urban neighborhoods are not exempt from the impacts. However, there is potential hope in three current trends: the steady increase in consumer appetite for dining outside the home; consumer interest in unique, local shopping experiences; and market demand for walkable neighborhoods (US Bureau of Labor Statistics 2016a; Mahalaha and Damicis 2017; Cisneros 2015). All three are well met by neighborhood main streets, in a way that cannot be met by suburban shopping malls, big-box stores and internet vendors.

As the proportion of low-income families increases in an urban neighborhood, the mix of local businesses shifts. This phenomenon applies to any low-income neighborhood, legacy city or not, but is especially prevalent in legacy city communities with severe population loss (Cachinho 2014). Dollar stores, convenience stores, discount groceries and drugstores, fast-food restaurants, and secondhand goods stores provide affordable food, clothing, health and beauty supplies, and other needs. Laundromats, daycares, auto parts and repair stores, and beauty and barbershops meet residents' needs for affordable services within a convenient location to their homes and jobs. Social services offices and religious organizations provide needed support and opportunities for community life and participation.

At the same time, some common businesses in low-income neighborhoods take advantage of residents' financial fragility and lack of financial knowledge. These predatory businesses profit by leveraging low-income households' basic needs and include tax-refund services, payday loan establishments, and/or pawn shops and consignment shops. For-profit education programs may encourage residents to take out loans to pay high tuition for services provided more affordably elsewhere (Ford and Beveridge 2004). Dollar stores and convenience stores provide affordable options, but do not provide quality or selection, and often have a higher price per unit than shopping opportunities available in suburban and higher income areas (Block and Kouba 2006). In addition, many national chain businesses that do operate in urban neighborhoods typically build new, inexpensive buildings, which deteriorate quickly over time. Following longtime national trends favoring obsolescence in construction, within ten years, and certainly within thirty, these buildings are deteriorated and abandoned for newer ones (Abramson 2016). Easy and fast obsolescence in urban neighborhoods further hinders neighborhood revitalization and stabilization.

The barriers faced by entrepreneurs are an additional challenge for neighborhood retail success. Entrepreneurship is difficult under any circumstances, with an average 43 percent business failure rate after five years in the retail industry nationally (US Bureau of Labor Statistics 2016b). Low property values, struggling personal finances, multilevel city review processes, and lender/investor bias against many older neighborhoods and retail clusters greatly reduces access to needed capital, further exacerbating entrepreneurial success in urban neighborhoods. Low property values and low rent potential also reduce the collateral available to secure small business loans. For a startup company, the business and personal finances of the owner are the same. An entrepreneur challenged by underemployment and underpaid status may never have the time, funds, or credit score needed to launch an independent business, no matter the potential of their vision or marketing savvy. More often, entrepreneurs struggle with gaining the financial, business management, and marketing knowledge, along with capital, necessary to succeed.

And yet, in most urban neighborhoods some businesses thrive. Some of these are long-standing neighborhood enterprises that generate sufficient profit to properly maintain a quality retail space, attract customers from near and far, weather market fluctuations, and provide stable employment and training to workers. Those who succeed can grow their wealth and equity, keep profits local, and employ and train residents. These businesses strengthen a neighborhood's overall retail environment by contributing to a critical mass of vitality that invites consumers to shop, linger, and return.

Neighborhood main streets are critical to long-term neighborhood vitality, providing a central space where businesses, institutions, and diverse residents intersect. Neighborhood main streets are a "third place" (outside of home and work) for social interaction and engagement within the community, while meeting local residents' need for goods and services (Oldenburg 2002). This is especially important in low-income neighborhoods, where a sizeable proportion of households have no access to a car. While the national and Ohio averages of households without a car are at 9 percent and 8.5 percent, respectively, 25.5 percent of Cleveland's households lack access to a private automobile (US Census Bureau 2014). This factor provides strong justification for the need for local businesses that serve residents.

Neighborhood revitalization is an assumed positive goal, but it raises concern about the potential displacement of longtime, low-income residents and businesses. Commercial gentrification is both a blessing and a curse for legacy cities, as it indicates growing economic vitality, with increased rents and property values. It also brings an increase in the cost of goods and services, a change in the types of goods and services sold, and a change in clientele. While overall business success may increase, longtime residents and businesses, especially those without equity in their property, may find themselves priced out of their community and unable to find affordable goods and basic services. Economic development efforts aimed at attracting business to main streets capitalize on unique specialty stores that draw outside visitors and new residents who seek a local experience and who can pay higher rents and maintain quality retail spaces. Without careful attention to the potential for gentrification and local resident/business displacement there is a sizeable risk that the neighborhood will lose its place as home to existing residents.

In legacy cities revitalization, repopulation, and renewed main street vitality are not possible in every neighborhood in the immediate future. Those with locational, cultural, environmental and/or anchor institution assets have the greatest potential. However, every urban neighborhood would benefit from a commercial center, even if small, that provides opportunity for wealth and equity building, employment, the exchange of goods and services, and social/community interaction. The challenge in legacy city neighborhoods is to strengthen economic and social vitality by meeting residents' needs, attracting new residents, and bringing in outside dollars in a way that is sustainable and serves all residents.

NEIGHBORHOOD MAIN STREETS IN CLEVELAND

There are many unexplored questions about the condition and possible future for legacy cities' neighborhood main streets. The remainder of this chapter draws on an analysis of six Cleveland neighborhoods, which have varying population, household, and employer-business characteristics, and are not fully revitalized. Analyzing the retail environment in these neighborhoods helps establish a base of data and understanding that can drive solutions and best practices for legacy city neighborhoods, providing an important advancement in planning and decision-making for retail development. Most of the existing data that developers, investors, and entrepreneurs use focuses on the shopping and sales patterns of suburban and mall shoppers, high vitality urban shopping districts in East or West Coast cities, and/or revitalizing and gentrifying neighborhoods that are often anomalies in legacy cities. This analysis used data generated via detailed inventory, visitor surveys, and interviews with merchants, neighborhood nonprofits, civic leaders, and developers, along with retail market analysis, to begin to characterize the unique conditions, markets, and business environment in urban neighborhood main street commercial areas.

The six neighborhoods include three each on the city's east (Buckeye-Shaker Square, Slavic Village, Union Miles) and west (Clark-Fulton, Detroit Shoreway, Westown) sides (table 9.1). Each set of three included one neighborhood poised to revitalize and two others further behind in the revitalization process.[1] All of the neighborhoods retain unique assets, such as clusters of vital businesses; longtime individual businesses with established clientele; dining establishments with unique character; proximity to freeways, transit hubs, and areas of commerce and employment; substantial employment opportunities; strong neighborhood schools; and/or historic and anchor institutions.

Buckeye-Shaker Square, located on the eastern edge of Cleveland, has three distinct shopping districts: Shaker Square, Larchmere, and Buckeye Road. Centrally located Shaker Square has the highest traffic volume and is home to the Shaker Square Cinema, Dave's Supermarket, and several longstanding full-service restaurants. It is organized around a commuter rail hub and is also the site of the region's oldest and largest Saturday farmer's market. Larchmere, home to a mix of small specialty shops, galleries, and antique stores, is one block north of Shaker Square. Buckeye Road is just south of Shaker Square and has a few longtime businesses, but more disinvestment and transience than the other two districts.

Slavic Village was home to seventy thousand residents in the mid-twentieth century. The neighborhood contains both types of urban main streets identified earlier in this chapter. The intersection of Broadway and East 55th Street was the largest commercial center in the county outside of downtown Cleveland, with multistory buildings providing space for banks, department stores, other retail, and professional offices. With a current population around twelve thousand, the Broadway and East 55th Street district declined, and revitalization of its larger retail spaces is challenging. Fleet Avenue, a secondary main street in the southern portion of Slavic Village, is smaller in scale and is seeing slow revitalization; the street has much potential due to excellent freeway access. Fleet Avenue has a few substantially built structures, but also many storefronts that were added to family homes. Slavic Village has several anchors, including Third Federal Savings' headquarters, a MetroHealth center, two prominent historic Catholic churches, and a full range of Catholic schools. Slavic Village was an early epicenter of the foreclosure crisis. However, recent housing and revitalization efforts are slowly increasing property values.

Union Miles was originally known as Newburgh Village, a historic nineteenth-century community that was once larger than Cleveland. The area had a traditional village green and was home to a lumber mill and associated industry. Once a thriving, middle-class African American neighborhood, the area has seen substantial disinvestment. Neighborhood anchors include the Earl B. Turner Recreation Center, the Mather Daycare Center

TABLE 9.1: Study neighborhood characteristics

	Buckeye-Shaker Square	Clark-Fulton	Detroit Shoreway	Slavic Village	Union-Miles	Westown
Primary market area characteristics						
Population	16,329	11,571	10,660	15,324	19,486	13,308
Number of households	7,904	4,375	4,773	6,127	7,892	5,248
Households with a member sixty or over	35%	27%	25%	30%	43%	26%
Households with a member under eighteen	21%	26%	23%	31%	25%	28%
Households without access to a car	23.50%	28.30%	30.40%	35.30%	22.30%	17.40%
Mean household income [1]	$65,134	$30,486	$36,672	$26,156	$31,495	$40,516
Household purchasing power (millions)	$514.80	$133.40	$175.00	$160.30	$248.60	$212.60
Total retail square footage [2]	271,431	469,450	382,700	633,061	358,185	635,302
Vacancy rate [3]	15.20%	6.30%	12.50%	20.50%	20.10%	14.70%
Grocery capture rate [4]	34%	32%	25%	49%	41%	78%
Main street average daily traffic	21,080	19,166	10,131	16,835	17,250	16,323
One-mile radius characteristics						
Employment	5,176	20,728	7,700	8,941	2,328	7,259
Median household income	$27,971	$23,379	$24,276	$18,685	$28,078	$30,006
Median home value	$89,489	$60,077	$71,177	$52,238	$54,536	$56,356

[1] Mean household income is generated using GIS clip within neighborhood PMA boundary; median household income for clipped area not available

[2] First floor retail/services space only

[3] Vacancy measured only on main street properties appearing to be suitable for retail with moderate renovation

[4] As collected via visitors surveys. Note the very small sample size in Westown (n = 40)

of the Center for Families and Children, and two public library branches. A new development at East 131st Street and Miles Avenue at the intersection of two former "Main Streets" includes an independent grocery store, a Fifth Third Bank branch, and health service center.

Clark-Fulton, located on Cleveland's near west side has a growing Hispanic and international population, with associated specialty food shops and restaurants. Anchors include several major employers, including MetroHealth, which draw a large population from outside the neighborhood during the day. At twenty thousand workers within a one-mile radius, Clark-Fulton has the largest daytime population of the six neighborhoods. St. Rocco's Church, a prominent anchor, hosts an annual three-day Labor Day weekend festival, which attracts several thousand visitors from throughout northeast Ohio.

Detroit Shoreway is the smallest of the six neighborhoods in population. Recent investment in historic building restoration and the Gordon Square Arts District anchors the neighborhood. Along with substantial housing investment, Detroit Shoreway is experiencing retail revitalization on Detroit Avenue, its main street. Gentrification concerns are most prominent here; the neighborhood has good walkability and bicycle/public transit access to downtown and the adjacent thriving neighborhoods of Ohio City and Tremont.

The center of commercial activity in Westown is Lorain Avenue and West 117th Street. A cluster of big-box stores to the north creates nearby retail competition. At the same time, West 117th has excellent freeway access for attracting outside business. This district has substantial historic assets, including the Variety Theatre. Current plans to restore the theater and surrounding area include a restaurant, movie theater, retail, and apartments. The neighborhood is home to growing Arab and Central American populations, with specialty groceries, restaurants, and professional offices serving them. Other neighborhood assets include Halloran Park and a public library branch.

NEIGHBORHOOD MAIN STREETS: CONDITIONS, MARKETS, AND BUSINESS POTENTIAL

This study characterizes the conditions unique to neighborhood businesses in six Cleveland neighborhoods that are not yet fully in the revitalization/gentrification cycle. In Cleveland legacy city characteristics of population decline, disinvestment, and economic restructuring intersect with evolving market demands and trends for consumer retail goods and services. The impact to the built environment, consumer markets, and business environment are unique to legacy cities.

NEIGHBORHOOD MAIN STREET CONDITIONS

In these neighborhood commercial corridors, exterior building condition is highly variable. A citywide survey by the Western Reserve Land Conservancy, completed in 2015, rated each building in Cleveland ranging from "A, Excellent" ("no visible signs of deterioration"), to "B, Good" ("needs basic improvements"), to "C, Fair" ("needs major work") to "D, Deteriorated" ("major cracking of brick, wood rotting"), "to "F, Unsafe/Hazard" ("house is open and a shell").[2] The building conditions in the six neighborhoods were typically rated about one-third *A*, one-third *B*, one-third *C*, and smaller proportions of *D* and *F*. All six neighborhoods contain underutilized historic buildings that are in poor repair and/or in a poor location for future retail occupancy. This issue is widespread and must be addressed by policymakers, planners, and neighborhood developers, given the significant contribution historic buildings make to neighborhood character, identity, and unique experience—critical factors for main street viability. In each neighborhood a substantial amount of building space originally used for retail is now used for another purpose, such as community spaces, nonretail businesses, churches, daycares, or residential. Building space dedicated or repurposed to other uses ranged from 3.6 percent of all retail space in Clark-Fulton to 12.6 percent of all retail space in Union Miles. The highest rate of conversion is in Buckeye-Shaker Square, where 20 percent of original retail space is now used for nonretail purposes.

Local-serving neighborhood retail spaces (the more common of two types outlined earlier) are typically substantially smaller than mainstream retail footprints.[3] Many storefronts range from 500 to 1,500 square feet, although some businesses combine two or three storefronts together to achieve larger spaces. This provides an opportunity for smaller businesses to get a foothold with less investment in space and inventory, a retail environment at a walkable scale, and the intimacy that goes with the personal service of independent businesses.[4]

Traffic volumes are a key statistic for investors evaluating the viability of a commercial retail street. Average daily traffic volumes on the main streets in each neighborhood were in line with generally understood main street retail attraction levels of eight thousand to twenty thousand vehicles per day. This means that traffic volumes are high enough to attract drive-through demand, in addition to neighborhood resident and destination visitor demand.

NEIGHBORHOOD RETAIL MARKETS

Recognizing the costs and benefits of revitalization and the competition from large retail centers, it is important for neighborhood retail economic development to strategically target potential customer markets. Urban neighborhoods must serve four basic markets: (1) "first market" neighborhood residents, (2) "new local" residents, (3) outside visitors, and (4) employees. While the mix and location of businesses serving each of these markets should vary, all provide an opportunity for retail success. Merchants and economic developers can target these markets to maximize marketing success and provide an appropriate mix of goods and services.

First market neighborhood residents include existing, often lower income, households that seek affordable basic daily goods. These are the customers patronizing dollar stores, convenience stores, discount clothing stores, and affordable restaurants. Neighborhood revitalization strategies that lead to gentrification risk pushing this market out of the neighborhood. This market is often ignored in retail analyses and economic development efforts, yet these residents hold significant buying power in spite of their lower household income due to the higher density of urban neighborhoods. The second group, termed *new locals*, seek unique experiences, products, and services. These residents have more disposable income and seek unique urban experiences within their neighborhoods, and are often identified as *gentrifiers*. The third market, *outside visitors*, also seek unique experiences, products, and services, but travel to a neighborhood from other city neighborhoods or from the suburbs. They are drawn to restaurants and shops, especially those that are locally owned, that provide a unique experience and/or specialized customer services, and unique neighborhood identity. The fourth market, *employees*, work in the neighborhood or nearby. These consumers often eat lunch or other meals in the neighborhood and conduct daily convenience errands. They may stay late for after-work meals or entertainment and become "outside visitors" at that point. This market plays an important role in urban neighborhoods, bringing in outside dollars on a daily basis. Local workers play an important role in the purchasing capacity of certain goods in urban neighborhoods, as evidenced by the large number of nearby employees in the Clark-Fulton neighborhood and its ability to support multiple fast-food restaurants. While the number of workers within each primary market area (PMA) varies, most neighborhoods had a sizeable number of workers within one mile.[5]

Neighborhood buying power in the six PMAs is based on the number of households and the mean household income for each area. Given competitor locations, lower mean household incomes, and smaller PMAs, urban neighborhood buying power is much lower than is typical for suburban shopping areas. For example, a study of exurban Middlefield, Ohio, showed primary market area household buying power of over $1 billion, compared to the $133–$513 million given for the neighborhoods in table 9.1 (Date 2014). This lower buying power may be a barrier to attracting national chains, which have strict requirements for the number of households and millions of dollars of household income in their trade areas. However, other forces can increase sales in legacy city neighborhoods to the point of viability, including:

- The presence of substantial nearby employment
- Traditional main street walkability and vibrancy
- Customer preferences for shopping in their neighborhoods

- High proportions of households without access to a car and with an associated need to shop close to home
- Consumer trends toward dining outside the home
- Interest of suburban shoppers in experiencing urban neighborhood retail
- Significant and unique neighborhood asset
- Continuing growth of housing over time
- Trends toward buying local

This study's shopper surveys of residents demonstrated overall capture rates lower than 50 percent. Mainstream market analysis might consider that these neighborhoods have little demand for business within the neighborhood.[6] However, the availability of local goods and services ultimately drives capture rates. For instance, if there is no neighborhood clothing store, the capture rate will be 0 percent. For this reason, I assess overall leakage rates simultaneously. Leakage rates for total household spending on particular goods were consistently high for general merchandise, hardware/home and garden, clothing and shoes, and full-service restaurants. Of interest, the Union-Miles neighborhood also exhibited high leakage rates for grocery stores. Low and negative leakage rates (oversupply) varied widely from neighborhood to neighborhood, ranging from grocery, auto parts, convenience stores, to gifts/novelties, depending on location.

MAIN STREET BUSINESS: SUCCESSES AND DIFFICULTIES

Despite decades of decline, legacy city neighborhoods do contain successful businesses. Across all six neighborhoods, the largest square footage of businesses was in six categories: (1) auto repair and parts, (2) beauty salons and barber shops, (3) convenience stores, (4) general merchandise dollar and drug stores, (5) grocery stores, and (6) dining. Businesses in some of these categories are also often the oldest and most established enterprises, with funds to maintain quality spaces and offer steady employment. These are mainstays of community expenditure in hard times as well as good times, providing for longtime business owners with stable incomes. Chain dollar and convenience stores, while bearing national brands, are often franchises owned by local or regional residents. A substantial proportion of the income and profit from these strong neighborhood businesses remains in the local economy. Yet, lenders, private-sector developers, and economic developers often overlook or undervalue these establishments.

The neighborhoods demonstrated very distinctive patterns of retail activity. For instance, in Buckeye-Shaker Square, 16 percent of the total retail activity is full-service restaurants, with additional concentrations of salons and barber shops. Detroit Shoreway also had concentrations of restaurants, mixed with high levels of convenience retail. Union-Miles and Westown had high rates of salons and barber shops. Overall, dining is a consistent strength. Restaurants, bars and taverns, main street mainstays, command a sizeable and growing proportion of household income. In 2016, for the first time, national household expenditure on "food consumed outside the home" (restaurants, bars) exceeded expenditure on "food consumed at home" (grocery, takeout) (USDA Economic Research Service 2016). This pattern is similar for low- and high-income households (US Bureau of Labor Statistics 2016a).

Neighborhood convenience stores typically center their sales on liquor, cigarettes, lottery tickets, and snack foods with low nutritional value. However, there are many of them in these neighborhoods, often occupying longtime older storefronts on side streets that likely housed corner stores for generations. Many of them are very compact with limited space for a variety of produce and other fresh goods. In Philadelphia and New Jersey the nonprofit Food Trust's Healthy Corner Store Initiative works with store owners to optimize use of space in order to facilitate fresh food sales. The program is multifaceted and includes training and education for store owners, workers, and customers ("The Food Trust: In Corner Stores" n.d.). Continued work on innovative programs to introduce fresh produce and other fresh and quality goods to local neighborhood convenience stores would be useful in improving the benefit that these stores can provide.

The neighborhoods studied had no pattern of total retail square footage in relation to population, household numbers, or buying power. Retail success is highly variable based on multiple factors including business acumen, access to capital, and entrepreneur vision and marketing savvy. And yet, critical mass and density are heralded as key factors to retail business district success (Mahalaha and Damicis 2017). Critical mass occurs when businesses are near each other. Creating critical mass requires businesses to align their operating hours, stay open longer in order to meet the widest range of customer needs, and locate in close proximity. This remains a challenge for main street businesses with varying interests and suggests the need for local economic developers or planners to serve in a coordinating role.

Despite ongoing vacancies and property deterioration, these neighborhoods demonstrate that independent businesses can do well, and sometimes thrive, in Cleveland. Successful neighborhood businesses offer stability, employment, consumer goods and services, and ongoing investment. The specifics of each business that succeeds varies widely based on location, retail category, and clientele, speaking to the personal service and unique experience advantages offered by independent businesses. Factors involved in business success also include merchant vision and ability to position the business in its intended market, overall marketing knowledge and competency, capitalization, business management knowledge, and collaboration with other merchants on a variety of issues.

IMPLICATIONS FOR POLICY

Neighborhood main street revitalization in legacy cities must focus on key strategies, including strengthening businesses and providing targeted, strategic investment. Strengthening businesses includes supporting them through capitalization assistance, developing financial/market/business management knowledge, and assisting them in developing realistic marketing visions. Providing strategic investment in target areas should start with small concentrations of existing viable retail and grow incrementally outward. Economic developers should consider locational, environmental, and cultural/historic assets, building conditions, and the presence, proximity, and participation of nearby businesses and anchor institutions. Strategic planning should address alternative uses to complement and fill in gaps between target areas. These might include new housing, landscape and streetscape elements, outdoor uses, small-scale food and goods production, nonretail businesses, and parks and open spaces. Neighborhood housing development and restoration remains a critical component and foundation of successful main streets, providing customers and neighborhood activity to support a vibrant retail business environment. City- and state-level policy must address issues of predatory businesses to protect consumers. Local planners and economic developers can help through programs to educate residents and improve their financial knowledge and decision-making capacity.

Economic developers, funders, and businesses need to address all four neighborhood markets. Retaining first market residents in their neighborhoods involves providing affordable housing but also goods and services to meet daily needs, especially since many of them (particularly seniors and those with disabilities) may not have access to a car. A strong anti-gentrification strategy must leverage convenience, grocery, and general merchandise stores to provide better quality and selection for nearby first market residents. Dollar stores can play a role in retaining affordable goods—in Cleveland, Ohio City Incorporated, the neighborhood's community development corporation, has purchased a building leased to a dollar store in order to ensure its continuation on a key street corner (Jarboe and Dealer 2018).

Historic assets and dining options are important for neighborhood character and key to unique experiences—critical factors in successful neighborhood retail activity in the digital age. More and more, retail patrons choose unique experiences that are "un-Amazonable," including dining, unique local services, and shops in places with unique character. At the very least, street-level and parcel-level strategies for revitalization should prioritize building evaluation and stabilizing historic buildings until future uses or redevelopment opportunities emerge. As dining is a new anchor for retail districts nationwide, a strong strategy must recognize the role that a variety of dining, drinking, and other "food outside the home" opportunities plays in strengthening neighborhood retail activity. In particular, dining provides a tremendous opportunity to bring outside dollars into legacy city neighborhoods.

Recognizing the viability and important role of the six strongest business categories has several implications. These are the foundation of retail goods and services utilized by the first market and are crucial to neighborhoods that have not yet revitalized, but are often disparaged by economic developers. Such businesses are often recession-proof as people consistently have basic needs and prioritize repair in hard times. They can be the strongest businesses in the neighborhood, providing stable employment and maintaining their storefronts. Beauty salons, barbers, and auto repair shops meet neighborhood needs for "third places," beyond bars and drinking places, where neighborhood residents can connect and engage with community affairs. Cultural and racial biases can result in devaluing the role that such businesses play in neighborhoods, and make it more difficult for these businesses to obtain working capital, technical assistance, and business district collaboration.

NOTES

The author would like to thank and acknowledge Matthew Martin Thomas, Rachel Oscar, and Larry LaPrade for their diligent assistance in collecting surveys and data, street-checking inventory, conducting merchant interviews, and helping with GIS analysis. In particular, many thanks are due to Dr. Robert Simons for his guidance in designing and implementing the study.

1. Neighborhood selection considered geographic, economic, and demographic criteria, as well as the recommendation of key informants and local experts.

2. The Western Reserve Land Conservancy survey only evaluated exterior, not interior, conditions.

3. Typical business sizes, for example, are around 10,000 square feet for a drugstore, 7,000 square feet for an auto supply store, and up to 120,000 or more for a large general merchandise store.

4. Main Street business advisors note that inventory-control software can now help small businesses maintain the right proportion of inventory within a small space to optimize the investment of space and capital to maximize sales.

5. More research is needed to define the role that workers play, the types of goods they support, and how far they are willing to travel to reach desired goods and services.

6. Capture rate information should be verified through extended merchant interviews, since there were discrepancies between visitor and merchant capture reports.

REFERENCES

Abramson, Daniel. M. 2016. *Obsolescence: An Architectural History*. Chicago: University of Chicago Press.

Accordino, John, and Johnson, Gary T. 2000. "Addressing the Vacant and Abandoned Property Problem." *Journal of Urban Affairs* 22, no. 3: 301–15.

Block, Daniel, and Joanne Kouba. 2006. "A Comparison of the Availability and Affordability of a Market Basket in Two Communities in the Chicago Area." *Public Health Nutrition* 9, no. 7: 837–45.

Cachinho, Herculano. 2014. "Consumerscapes and the Resilience Assessment of Urban Retail Systems." *Cities* 36: 131–44.

Cisneros, Henry. 2015. "13 Urban Trends to Watch." *Urban Land*, March 26, 2015. http://urbanland.uli.org/economy-markets-trends/13-urban-trends-watch/.

Date, Kirby. 2014. "Retail Market Study: Village of Middlefield, Ohio." *Urban Publications*, Cleveland State University. http://engagedscholarship.csuohio.edu/urban_facpub/1175/.

Food Trust. n.d. "What We Do: In Corner Stores." http://thefoodtrust.org/what-we-do/corner-store.

Ford, Julie M., and Andrew A. Beveridge. 2004. "'Bad' Neighborhoods, Fast Food, 'Sleazy' Businesses, and Drug Dealers: Relations between the Location of Licit and Illicit Businesses in the Urban Environment." *Journal of Drug Issues* 34, no. 1: 51–76.

Jarboe, Michelle. 2018. "Family Dollar Sale in Cleveland's Ohio City is Bid to Preserve Affordable Retail Amid Growth." *Plain Dealer* (Cleveland, OH), April 13, 2018. http://realestate.cleveland.com/realestate-news/2018/04/family_dollar_sale_in_clevelan.html.

Mahalaha, Hrishue, Jim Damicis, and Alexandra Tranmer. 2017. "The Case of Disappearing Main Street Retail." Camoin Associates, Innovation Economy Partners. https://www.camoinassociates.com/sites/default/files/THE%20CASE%20OF%20DISAPPEARING%20MAIN%20STREET%20RETAIL.pdf.

Oldenburg, Ray, ed. 2002. *Celebrating the Third Place: Inspiring Stories About the "Great Good Places" at the Heart of Our Communities*. New York: Da Capo Press.

Thompson, Derek. 2017. "What in the World Is Causing the Retail Meltdown of 2017?" *Atlantic*, April 10, 2018. https://www.theatlantic.com/business/archive/2017/04/retail-meltdown-of-2017/522384/.

US Bureau of Labor Statistics. 2016a. "Consumer Expenditure Survey." http://www.bls.gov/cex/.

US Bureau of Labor Statistics. 2016b. "Establishment Age and Survival Data." https://www.bls.gov/bdm/bdmage.htm#RETAIL.

US Census Bureau. 2014. "American Community Survey (ACS)." https://www.census.gov/programs-surveys/acs.

US Department of Commerce. 2016. "US Census Bureau Monthly and Annual Retail Trade." https://www.census.gov/retail/index.html.

USDA Economic Research Service. 2016. "Food Expenditures." https://www.ers.usda.gov/data-products/food-expenditures.aspx.

10

What's Changed and What Does It Matter?

LESSONS FROM A LEGACY CITY HOUSING MARKET

BRIAN A. MIKELBANK

Two fundamental changes are occurring within the housing markets of legacy city regions as they struggle to settle into their new post-crisis normal: occupancy transition and a shift in transaction profiles. While homeownership and occupancy trends are easy to trace at the national level—and are in some cases qualitatively similar—legacy city regional changes have been more pronounced, and the implications more troubling, because of the interrelated legacies playing out. Additionally, the impacts of occupancy changes have not been evenly distributed across the space or the populace (Shlay 2015), an issue that takes on an even greater relevance given the interplay of race, segregation, and foreclosures (see, for example, Hall et al. 2015). Changing transaction profiles, on the other hand, are more elusive, and are typically examined at the city level (see, for example, Center for Community Progress 2015). These too, however, have regional impacts that reach beyond homeownership to leave their impact on the surrounding environments.

In this research, occupancy transition and transaction profiles are investigated using data for the Cuyahoga County housing market (comprised of Cleveland and fifty-seven suburbs) from 1990 to 2015. While these transitions were certainly in motion long before the time under study, the housing/financial crisis acted as an accelerant on a steady, but slow-burning, fire.

The first transition is the changing composition of residential property occupancy. While the national homeownership rate has been steadily falling since its 2004 peak, there is spatial variation to this trend, particularly in declining regions. Traditionally, in areas where homeownership was declining, the primary focus of discussion was rentals. The discussion of housing trends was an "owning versus renting" discussion almost exclusively. Fast-forward to 2010 and vacancy is a major player in many metropolitan neighborhoods. The balance between owner, renter, and vacant is analyzed at the tract level between 1990 and 2010, and neighborhoods with distinct housing consumption patterns emerge—essentially neighborhood "types" based on their housing consumption structure. These neighborhood types are quite familiar for the 1990 data, and quite telling in the 2010 data.

A feeder into this occupancy transition is a fundamental change in the transaction profile for residential properties. Traditionally, individuals made up both sides of the transaction—one individual (or household) as the buyer and another as the seller. This, however, is no longer universally the case. In many neighborhoods, a substantial portion of all sales involves nonhouseholds. This includes a mix of banks, land banks, nonprofits, governments, investors, rehabbers, flippers, and others. Collectively labeled *institutional* in this analysis, they play a much larger role, particularly, though not exclusively, in city and inner suburban markets. Individual and institutional markets also typically operate at different price points and among different properties, since they are acting within the market to meet different objectives. The underlying volume and price characteristics of the different transaction profiles are driving neighborhood and community change.

The planning, policy, and governance implications of these changes are far-reaching, impacting not only the many facets of cities' residential landscapes but also their financial and economic vitality. Communities find themselves in a bit of a holding pattern, relative to their housing markets. Are the changes they are undergoing part of a prolonged market shock that will eventually dissipate and leave markets structurally similar to their pre-crisis days? Is each norm-challenging day of legacy city housing markets another step toward a new reality? Have legacy city markets found their new equilibrium? Whether legacy city planners and policymakers embrace a new future, potentially a smaller one (Hollander et al. 2009), or reject that fate in hopes of reversing recent trend lines (Piiparinen 2017), they have to manage their present reality—a reality that more prominently features renter occupancy and vacancy while in some neighborhoods witnessing a substantial transformation in who is buying and selling homes.

THE CUYAHOGA COUNTY MARKET: PRICE, VOLUME, AND INSTABILITY

Causes and implications of the housing crisis for legacy cities and their regions are not understudied topics. One research stream focuses on impacts. For example, Gabe and Florida (2013) focus on Great Recession employment impacts relative to regional housing characteristics. Jones and Pridemore (2016) analyze the relationship between crime and vacancy, while Ding (2014) studies the impact of lending information asymmetries. The role of regional land banks is detailed by Keating (2013), while the post-crisis future of homeownership is covered by Shlay (2015). At the same time, many studies empirically focus on how a process is playing out in a particular place: St. Louis (Gordon 2013), Cleveland (Whitaker and Fitzpatrick 2013), Buffalo (Silverman, Yin, and Patterson 2013), and Detroit (Ding 2014). As complex and far-reaching as the housing crisis and its impacts were and are, a traditional set of housing indicators can serve as an effective and quick introduction to the nature, severity, and duration of the problem in Cuyahoga County.

First is perhaps the most widely used—median sales price. Increasing sales prices are reflective of a healthy market, where adequate demand of a limited (short-run) supply of physical housing stock pushes prices, even modestly, upward. Increasing prices can yield equity for owners and incentives for both owner-occupiers and owner-managers to reinvest in housing. Figure 10.1 shows the trend of unadjusted median sales price in Cuyahoga County for the years 1995–2015.

A slow, steady increase in values characterized the aggregate market through the mid-2000s. Gains reflected the housing demand of a stable regional market, fueled more by outward growth from the core than demand that was new from outside the region. The market withstood a multiyear price slide that began after 2005, and although the region has experienced modest gains in recent years, prices have yet to return to their 2005 pre-crisis levels.

Concurrent to the stalling of aggregate prices in the early 2000s was a spike in sheriff sales, representing the transfer of properties at the conclusion of the foreclosure process. Shown in figure 10.1 as a percent of all transactions, sheriff sales were long a small part of the region's housing economy. Lower-value properties were purchased out of the foreclosure process, and generally returned to productive use, either after a subsequent sale to a homeowner, or as a rental. Either scenario might have involved rehabilitation—discounted sheriff sale prices combined with the slow but steady appreciation in housing prices allowed for meaningful (re)investment. The escalation of sheriff sales activity, starting in 2004, reached a point where the market could not absorb these sales as easily. The lower prices garnered at sheriff sale, for this increasing slice of the market, amongst other market ills, served to pull down aggregate market activity, both in terms of price and overall sales volume (also shown on the left-hand axis of figure 10.1). While it is not the goal here to explore the causal factors of market changes related to the foreclosure crisis, it is noteworthy that none of these three

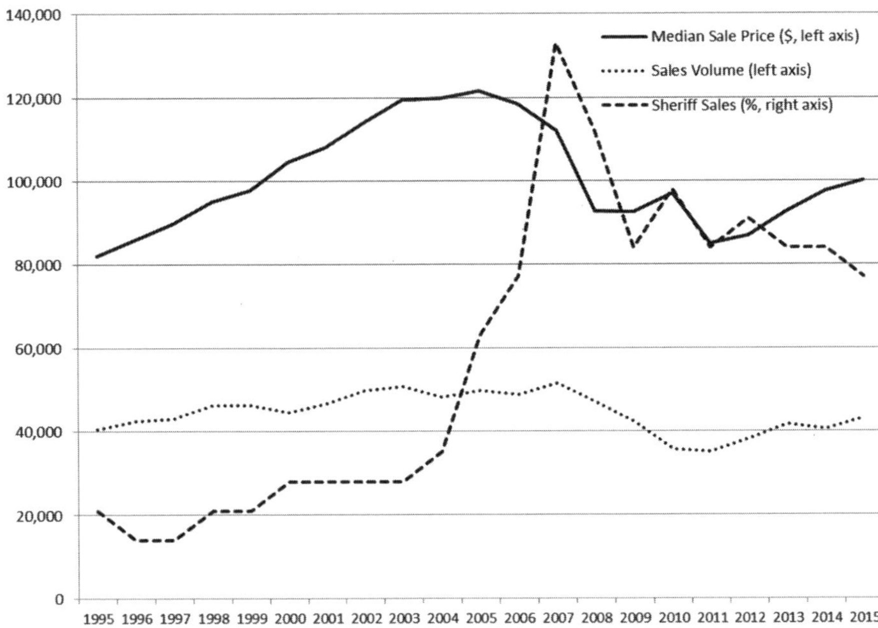

FIGURE 10.1: Cuyahoga County housing market indicators, 1995–2015

mainstay indicators—price, volume, or sheriff sales—have returned to their pre–housing crisis levels.

Where did these trends of increased foreclosure sales with declining prices and volume leave the regional market? Certainly, buyers were less drawn to an asset that was declining in value, and with prices down, owners who could afford not to move were less apt to—perhaps thinking that they would wait out the market. This further depressed sales volume. The declines in value put many recent purchasers, especially those who took advantage of low-money-down opportunities, underwater on their mortgage. Additionally, some new owners signed for low introductory rates and/or payments that were not sustainable for the long term. In sum, market uncertainty skyrocketed.

One way of quantifying this uncertainty is by comparing sold house prices to their county assessor estimated market value. From 1995 through 2006 the ratio of sales price to assessor's value steadily increased, with some fluctuation, from 1.1 to 1.4. This certainly reflects the run-up in prices while values remained relatively stable. The ratio dropped precipitously in 2007 and reached its low of 0.6 in 2009. Even though the mean ratio had recovered to 1.0 by 2015, there was still increased uncertainty in the market. For example, the 95 percent confidence interval around the mean ratio was 0.01 in 1995. In 2014 and 2015 it was 0.43 and 0.26, respectively.

What impact are these trends of decline and instability having on the market? Two are investigated. First is the degree to which decline and instability are influencing the way housing is being consumed. Then, the changing mix of buyers and sellers is brought to the forefront.

THE CHANGING STRUCTURE OF OCCUPANCY

The first fundamental change impacting legacy city housing markets is the way in which housing is, and is not, being consumed. To explore, data from the 1990 through 2010 decennial censuses are aligned into 2010 tract boundaries. The focus here is on the bookends of the time period and the following variables: the percent of housing units that are owner-occupied, renter-occupied, and vacant. For both 1990 and 2010, separately, a clustering procedure is used to identify the distinct types of housing consumption patterns in each year, for each of the census tracts in Cuyahoga County. Relying on a clustering procedure as an exploratory tool takes advantage of the natural groupings/patterns in the three variables, rather than deciding on an arbitrary number of groupings, and then imposing arbitrary membership rules for each group (for example, 75 percent owner-occupied, no more than 5 percent vacant).

Working with data from two time periods yields several sources of information. For each year, the method produces a specific number of clusters, and these are not restricted to be the same in number or context from year to year. For example, there might be three types of neighborhoods based on their housing consumption patterns in one year, but only two in another. For each year, the characteristics of each cluster will be of interest. How are they similar to or different from the other neighborhood clusters in that year? Finally, comparisons between years will shed light on neighborhoods that have changed their housing consumption patterns over the two decades.

The results of the clustering procedure are telling, and detailed in table 10.1. In 1990 there were but two types of neighborhood housing consumption—*owner* neighborhoods and *renter* neighborhoods. Eight out of every ten units in *owner* neighborhoods were owner-occupied. There was a low rental rate (16 percent) and vacancy was limited (< 4 percent). *Renter* neighborhoods were only slightly more than half renter-occupied units (53 percent), 37 percent owner-occupied, and roughly one in ten units were vacant. The county's neighborhoods were divided roughly evenly among *owner* and *renter* neighborhood types in 1990.

These neighborhood types, however, were not randomly scattered across the landscape in 1990. As one might expect, there is a clear core bias of renter neighborhoods. The central city and many of its contiguous inner-ring

TABLE 10.1: Housing consumption clusters, 1990 and 2010

Table 10.1a: Cluster characteristics

	1990			
Cluster	n	Percent owner-occupied	Percent renter-occupied	Percent vacant
Owner	212	81.0%	15.8%	3.2%
Owner-renter mix		120	50.4%	38.0%
Renter	231	36.7%	52.8%	10.5%
Balance		89	29.2%	41.9%
County total	443	57.9%	35.1%	7.0%
	2010			
Cluster	n	Percent owner-occupied	Percent renter-occupied	Percent vacant
Owner	161	79.3%	14.7%	6.0%
Owner-renter mix	11.6%			
Renter	73	19.2%	65.2%	15.6%
Balance	28.8%			
County total	443	51.5%	34.8%	13.7%

Table 10.2b: Transitions from 1990 to 2010

		2010 cluster				Total
		Owner	Owner-renter mix	Balance	Renter	
1990 cluster	Owner	159	53	0	0	212
	Renter	2	67	89	73	231
Total		161	120	89	73	443

suburbs are either entirely (East Cleveland, Linndale, Cuyahoga Heights, and Newburgh Heights) or substantially (Brooklyn, Cleveland Heights, Fairview Park, Lakewood) comprised of renter neighborhoods. Renter neighborhoods are not the exclusive domain of the city and inner ring, however. They are also dispersed throughout the county, although their pattern seems more dispersed on the west side, and more clustered on its east side. Similarly, while owner-occupied neighborhoods were the norm farther from the core, that was not their exclusive domain either. The city of Cleveland and most of its inner-ring neighbors, circa 1990, had swaths of owner-occupied neighborhoods within their boundaries.

The picture that emerges from the 1990 housing consumption patterns is a fairly traditional one. Renter neighborhoods were more typical of core areas and owner neighborhoods more typical of the periphery, with notable and spatially patterned exceptions to both. The structure and consumption patterns for 2010 become more nuanced, also shown in table 10.1.

The neighborhoods that were classified as owner-occupied in 1990 (n = 212) are represented by two neighborhood types by 2010. Roughly three-quarters of these neighborhoods are grouped in 2010's owner-neighborhood cluster, which is quite similar to its 1990 counterpart. It has high owner-occupancy (79 percent in 2010 vs. 81 percent in 1990), low rental occupancy (15 percent vs. 16 percent), and comparatively low vacancy, although at 6 percent, it is nearly three percentage points higher. The remaining quarter of the 1990 owner neighborhoods are 2010 members of the owner-renter mix cluster. These fifty-three previously owner neighborhoods join with sixty-seven 1990 renter neighborhoods to form this new owner-renter mix cluster in 2010. Its owner-renter-vacant profile of 50 percent/38 percent/12 percent represents a middle ground for its member neighborhoods. For previously owner members, average owner occupancy fell by 30 percent, renter occupancy more than doubled, and vacancy more than tripled. For previously renter members, vacancy was relatively stable while occupancy shifted from renter (-15 percent) to owner (+14 percent).

Nearly a third of 1990 renter neighborhoods remained predominantly renter neighborhoods in 2010 (n = 73). The renter cluster has the highest renter-occupancy (65 percent) and the lowest owner-occupancy (19 percent). Compared to its 1990 counterpart, the 2010 renter cluster is far more renter-oriented (+12 percent) and has a higher vacancy rate (+5 percent), coming at the expense of owner-occupancy (-18 percent).

It is a telling result, and not a favorable one, that most 1990 renter neighborhoods (89 of 231) transitioned to 2010 balance neighborhoods, the final 2010 cluster type. Its profile features the second highest rental occupancy rate (42 percent), and a near balance between owner-occupancy and vacancy (29 percent each). With the highest vacancy rate of any cluster across both years of study, it would seem that these neighborhoods are, on average, in danger of having their vacant homes outnumber their owner-occupied homes.

The spatial arrangement of the four housing consumption types in 2010 further refines the core-periphery patterns established in the 1990 data. The 2010 owner neighborhoods again dominate the periphery but make more limited appearances closer to the core in 2010. Several trajectories emanating from the downtown characterize the 2010 renter neighborhood locations. There are two clusters connected to the downtown and bordering Cleveland's industrial corridor both to the east and the west. While their 2010 housing value and demographic profiles are distinct, their housing consumption patterns find them in the same cluster. A trajectory extends from downtown to the east along one of the city's primary transportation routes (Euclid Avenue) to the city's cultural and secondary economic

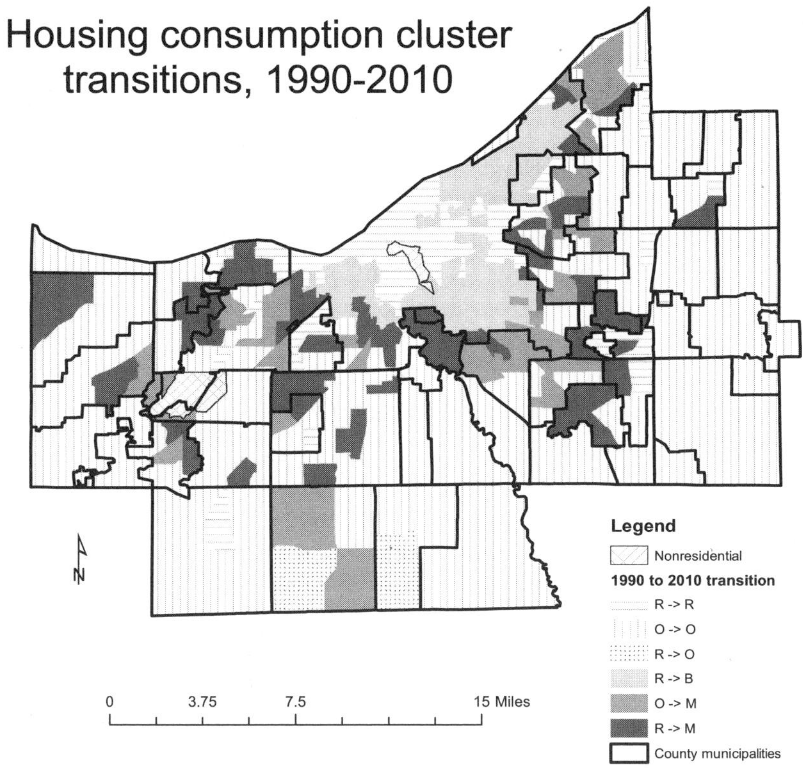

FIGURE 10.2: Housing consumption cluster transitions, 1990–2010

hub, University Circle. To the west, the renter trajectory extends along the shoreline neighborhoods into the inner-ring suburb of Lakewood. There are also isolated renter neighborhoods in the periphery of the county, likely dominated by multiunit rental developments. Beyond the centrally located renter trajectories, generally, are balance neighborhoods, followed by mix neighborhoods that occupy Cleveland's edges, as well as many inner-ring suburbs, before yielding to owner neighborhoods of the more distant suburbs.

The neighborhood transitions between 1990 and 2010 (shown in table 10.1) were not spatially random, as shown in figure 10.2. First, note the horizontal (primarily in the core) and vertical (primarily in the periphery) fill, showing renter and owner neighborhood persistence, respectively.

Renter neighborhoods of 1990 that did not remain so in 2010 most commonly became balance neighborhoods—this happened primarily in three separate locations in Cleveland and one contiguous area in neighboring East Cleveland.[1] The loss of both owner and renter households, and the resultant skyrocketing vacancy was not a crisis uniformly distributed across the market. Rather, it was concentrated in three of the region's most struggling neighborhood areas. It is notable that in a county housing market whose crisis ills were not limited to the central city, the neighborhood profile with the most pronounced role of vacancy (29 percent) resides only in Cleveland and East Cleveland.

Owner neighborhoods of 1990 that did not remain so in 2010 (most did), transitioned exclusively to mix neighborhoods. Similarly, sixty-seven (1990) renter neighborhoods also became mix neighborhoods. Taken together, their spatial pattern is largely a story of what is occurring within inner-ring suburban housing markets. Nearly forming a border around Cleveland, but also notably in some of the city's more peripheral neighborhoods, a dynamic and likely still evolving drama of renters, owners, and vacancies is playing out.

It is worth reiterating that there certainly is variation within the entire neighborhood housing-consumption profile clusters. But even while employing a clustering procedure aimed at reducing complexity, several important lessons are evident. First, housing-consumption profiles were simpler in 1990. Countywide vacancy was 7 percent. It was 11 percent in renter neighborhoods, where we would perhaps anticipate higher vacancies as part of the process of higher turnover of rental households. By 2010 vacancy was a major competitor for units in clusters representing over a third of the county's neighborhoods (balance and renter). Nearly 70 percent of all neighborhoods belonged to a cluster where, on average, more than one in ten units were vacant—that translates roughly into either a vacant house next door, or next to a direct neighbor. In the highest vacancy balance cluster, both owners (-8 percent) and renters (-11 percent) yielded to vacancy. Finally, these transitions did not happen in a spatially dispersed fashion whereby the associated gains and losses were distributed among the county's many fragmented local government units. Rather, the housing-consumption patterns are arranged in ways that unevenly distribute challenges, and inequitably draw on limited resources to address them.

WHO'S BUYING AND SELLING? CHANGES IN THE TRANSACTION PROFILE

Are these consumption patterns representative of the new normal for legacy city housing markets? Or is this a blip, albeit a prolonged blip, on the region's housing radar? If all the market actors were the same, it would be tempting to think that indicators will return to normal—prices, volume, the role of homeownership, vacancy levels, etc. However, the players have changed. The county's transaction profile has shifted so dramatically away from individuals and toward institutional buyers and sellers that our traditional market metrics might not soon be helpful again.

To demonstrate, institutional involvement in the housing market was estimated from 1995 through 2015. To determine if a transaction had an institution as a buyer or seller, the buyer and seller fields of residential property transaction records were filtered for phrases commonly found in institutions' names, such as *LLC*, *Inc.*, *develop*, *housing*, *invest*, etc. These buyers and sellers could include small or large redevelopment and investment companies, local or nonlocal flippers, banks taking back the deed as part of the foreclosure process, and so forth. In all, forty search terms were used as flags to indicate an institutional transaction. While the search set could certainly have contained additional terms, and while there is certainly potential for a degree of misclassification, this process serves its purpose—to show a market transformed from what it was roughly twenty years ago.

Two components of this transformation are particularly relevant: discount rate and market share. The discount rate is the ratio of the median sale price involving an institution as the buyer, the seller, or both, to the median sale price between individuals for each year in the data. At the beginning of the time period, the median institution-involved transaction price was 56 percent that of the median transaction not involving an institution. At its trough in 2008, the value was just 22 percent, and it took until 2015 to again reach above 30 percent. That is not quite half the price point at which this portion of the market was operating two decades ago, and a near 70 percent off sale, compared to the individual, arms-length market. While this comparison is likely not apples to apples (there may well be systematic differences in structure, location, and/or neighborhood characteristics between the two submarkets), it does illustrate the disparity, and the persistence in that disparity, between the two submarkets over time.

These disparities would not be so deeply concerning if the institutional submarket was a small percentage of an otherwise normally functioning regional housing market. Unfortunately, this is not the case. It is notable, and troublesome, that institutional involvement, as a share of the total residential market, started its steady rise in the late 1990s, from roughly a 10 percent market share. As households filter up the housing ladder, and housing units filter down, institutions play an increasing role in markets where regional population growth does not generate sustained housing demand, particularly in the core. Even though the percent market share has been on the decline since its countywide peak of over 60 percent in 2008, institutional transactions are still near 40 percent of the total residential market.

This combination of deeply discounted prices and substantial institutional market share would be a heavy burden for a regional housing market to carry, even if that burden were evenly distributed throughout the region's neighborhoods. Of course, it is not. Figure 10.3 shows the 2015 distribution of institutional market share across the county's census tracts. While market share in some neighborhoods are at countywide pre-crisis levels, many suburban neighborhoods, perhaps surprisingly, are facing institutional sales rates of at least one in five. Meanwhile, many city and some inner-ring suburban neighborhoods are experiencing even more extreme institutional market share concentration, exceeding 50 percent, or even 70 percent.

These numbers are trajectory-altering for many neighborhoods. When between one-quarter and three-quarters of all sales in a neighborhood are deeply discounted sales, the traditional market for arms-length sales can erode quickly. The discounted prices, once viewed as the ill that was dragging down the neighborhood market, simply becomes the chief characteristic of the neighborhood market. Arms-length sales prices are depressed and individual demand for residential properties all but disappears. This puts additional downward pressure on prices and reinforces the transition from a private to an institutionally dominated housing market.

DISCUSSION: WHAT IS THE PATH FORWARD FOR LEGACY CITY HOUSING MARKETS?

Putting these trends together creates a murky operating space for planning and policy in legacy cities. They impact not only the many facets of cities' residential landscapes but also their financial and economic viability. They demonstrate how legacy cities' legacies are in many cases inseparable. Are they inescapable?

Vacancy, for example, comes together at the nexus of economic restructuring and population decline to devastate the fabric of many city neighborhoods. Without an economic motivation, how is a region to attract financially viable households to repopulate—and rehabilitate—its (aging) housing stock? In a region that is not growing, fragmented jurisdictions might compete in a legacy city housing version of musical chairs, where the same—or even declining—population shifts about. In this version of the game, unfortunately, there are always too many chairs. Vacancy plays twice the role in neighborhood housing markets in 2010 as it did in 1990. In the county's eighty-nine balance neighborhoods, vacancy is—on average—less than a percentage point away from being as prevalent as owner-occupancy. That level of vacancy erodes a neighborhood's buying power, making it more difficult to sustain the local economic activity serving these areas. This increases the likelihood of commercial vacancies, and when combined with the housing vacancies, serves as a strong and negative signal as to the

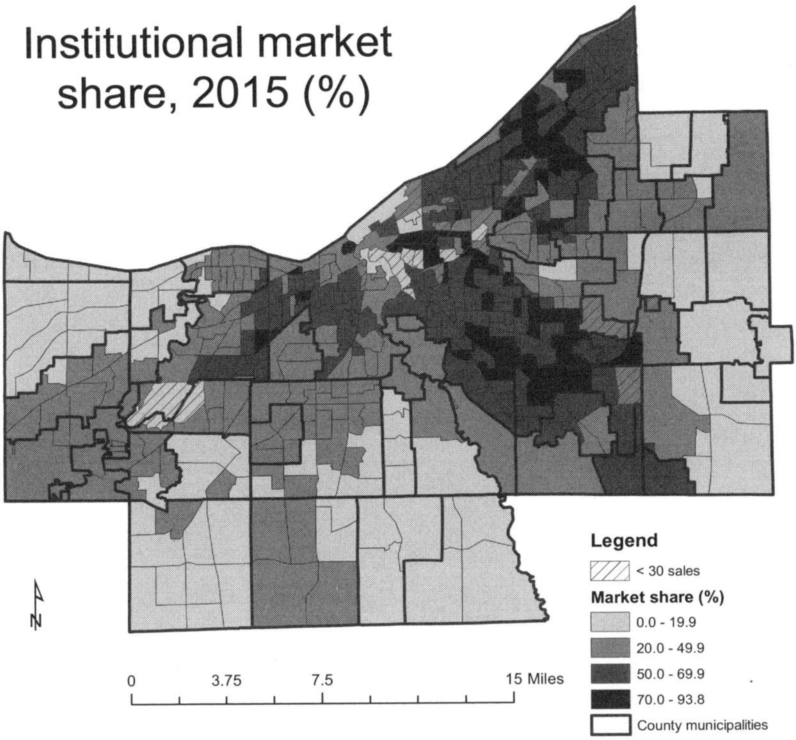

FIGURE 10.3: Institutional market share, 2015 (%)

trajectory of the neighborhood, encouraging further flight and disinvestment.

Increased out-migration and decreased investment directly impact the built environment left in the wake of these changes. The degree to which sales prices can recover in such a context is an open question. Reduced demand in high-vacancy neighborhoods limits traditional market demand and opens the door to institutional demand (figure 10.3), which further drives down prices (figure 10.1). Very low prices in neighborhoods with low demand and high institutional purchases increase the difficulty of obtaining traditional financing, further increasing the challenge of owner-occupancy and reinvestment in these neighborhoods and their housing stock, as described by Hatch in chapter 5.

This makes it imperative that cities are prepared as their housing stock, and potentially their neighborhoods, transition to higher levels of renter-occupancy and vacancy. In other words, the policy focus will be on the mix and balance neighborhoods. In 1990 and 2010 cities had neighborhoods where owners and renters played the lead role—this is not new territory. On the contrary, mix and balance neighborhoods present new challenges. It is good news that many cities have policies in place to ease these neighborhood transitions. These include proactive code enforcement, point-of-sale inspections, rental registrations, rental inspections, vacant property registration programs, and foreclosure bond requirements, to name a few.

Unfortunately, it has often been the case that the success and impact of these efforts relied on owners voluntarily registering, or were complaint-driven. With the data that are increasingly available, this no longer need be the case. For example, institutional purchasers are unlikely to be owner-occupiers, meaning that their properties are likely candidates for a city's permitting process (if the property is being rehabilitated), its rental or vacant property registration program, depending on its occupancy plans, or its point-of-sale process, if it is to be resold. Upon identifying an institutional purchaser, via something as straightforward as an Excel filter on a downloaded spreadsheet of monthly or quarterly real estate transfers, the city could initiate contact.

This contact, however, should not assume that all new owners are looking to profit at their new neighbors' and city's expense. Cities could not have a larger stake in the success of all of their property owners—not just the owner-occupiers. Just as they have traditionally served as a resource for owner-occupiers, they must make sure they are serving that same role for all of their owners and residents. The persistent efforts at initiating and maintaining contact with new owners will signal to existing stakeholders of all varieties that the city is aware of the changes that are occurring in their neighborhoods, and that they are being proactive in maintaining the city's quality of life.

This highlights the fact that cities' path forward should be one that invests in the collection and analysis of actionable data. These need not be "big data" investments or initiatives for cities with scarce resources. The analyses presented here, for example, are based upon data that are publicly available at regular intervals. These data revealed critical shifts and emerging crises in neighborhood housing markets, but there remain many avenues to explore, even with these data. For example, the analyses presented here aggregated all institutional actors into one category when many are possible. For example, post–foreclosure transactions may well differ from that of a local nonprofit. Or large-scale purchasers would be easily identifiable in the data. Similarly, the analysis here considered both sides of the transaction at once—the buyer and the seller. Separating those into distinct efforts could shed additional light on the dynamics of legacy city markets.

However, policy or practice reactions to changes in the housing market are not costless to undertake. And as prices decline, or even if they were stagnant, the cost of providing the vast array of city services continues to rise, putting cities composed of struggling neighborhoods at further disadvantage as they try to maintain quality municipal services in a cost and revenue context that is steadily shifting out of their favor.

The final message is not new, but it is also not widely received. Suburban leaders in fragmented regions may look at the housing consumption transition patterns (figure 10.2; primarily owner neighborhood persistence) and the 2015 market share (figure 10.3; largely in the lower two categories) and think they are nearly back to their normal state of affairs. Even if that were to be true now, the outward moving process of legacy cities foretells that their new normal might not be normal for long. Longer than their council or mayoral terms? Probably. But subsequent council members and mayors will watch these patterns repeat themselves farther and farther from the urban core for as long as the region struggles to attract new residents and new investment while it deals with the consequences of an overbuilt region.

Searching for a new equilibrium based on a right-sized regional housing supply is a slow and untidy process. The interplay of occupancy vs. vacancy, ownership vs. rental, and institutional vs. individual purchasing and ownership contribute to a residential landscape that is vastly different from that of the recent past. It impacts the residential mix, and their current and future needs, demands, and resources. It impacts city and school services and budgets. It drives the patterns of residential (re)location and preference. Identifying, understanding, and responding to these housing market realities and their implications will be a critical step if legacy city stakeholders hope to discover and thrive within their new normal.

NOTES

This chapter would not have been possible without Charlie Post's and Megan Hornyak's valuable assistance. The author thanks the editors for valuable feedback on earlier versions.

1. The two tracts that transitioned from renter to owner are highway-proximate neighborhoods in the outer suburbs that likely transitioned due to new single-family residential development.

REFERENCES

Center for Community Progress. 2015. "Laying the Foundation for Strong Neighborhoods in Trenton, NJ: A Market-Oriented Assessment." ttps://www.communityprogress.net/filebin/Trenton_Report_Full_Final_Copy.pdf.

Ding, Lei. 2014. "Information Externalities and Residential Mortgage Lending in the Hardest Hit Housing Market: The Case of Detroit." *Cityscape: A Journal of Policy Development & Research* 16, no. 1: 233.

Gabe, Todd M., and Richard Florida. 2013. "Effects of the Housing Boom and Bust on US Metro Employment." *Growth and Change* 44, no. 3: 391–414.

Gordon, Colin. 2013. "St. Louis Blues: The Urban Crisis in the Gateway City." *St. Louis University Public Law Review* 33, no. 1: 81–91.

Hall, Matthew, Kyle Crowder, and Amy Spring. 2015. "Neighborhood Foreclosures, Racial/Ethnic Transitions, and Residential Segregation." *American Sociological Review* 3: 526.

Hollander, Justin B., Karina Pallagst, Terry Schwarz, and Frank Popper. 2009. "Planning Shrinking Cities." *Progress in Planning* 72, no. 4: 223–32.

Jones, Roderick W., and William Alex Pridemore. 2016. "A Longitudinal Study of the Impact of Home Vacancy on Robbery and Burglary Rates during the U.S. Housing Crisis, 2005–2009." *Crime & Delinquency* 62, no. 9: 1159–79.

Keating, W. Dennis. 2013. "Urban Land Banks and the Housing Foreclosure and Abandonment Crisis." *St. Louis University Public Law Review* 33, no. 1: 93–107.

Piiparinen, Ritchie. 2017. "'Smart Decline' Doesn't Work. Why Do Cities Keep Trying It Anyway?" CityLab. https://www.citylab.com/housing/2017/03/smart-decline-is-dumb/518640/.

Shlay, Anne. B. 2015. "Life and Liberty in the Pursuit of Housing: Rethinking Renting and Owning in Post-Crisis America." *Housing Studies* 30, no. 4: 560–79.

Silverman, Robert, Li Yin, and Kelly L. Patterson. 2013. "Dawn of the Dead City: An Exploratory Analysis of Vacant Addresses in Buffalo, NY 2008–2010." *Journal of Urban Affairs* 35, no. 2: 131–52.

Whitaker, Stephen, and Thomas. J. Fitzpatrick IV. 2013. "Deconstructing Distressed-Property Spillovers: The Effects of Vacant, Tax-Delinquent, and Foreclosed Properties in Housing Submarkets." *Journal of Housing Economics* 22, no. 2: 79–91.

PART THREE

STRATEGIES FOR MITIGATING DECLINE IN CLEVELAND

11

Re-Imagining Cleveland and the Desire for a Collective Generosity

HELEN LIGGETT

Cleveland is a legacy city hard hit by economic restructuring and the 2008 financial crisis, while also characterized by strong anchor institutions, a rich philanthropic tradition, and a history of community activism. If presented in terms of conventional demographic and economic indicators, Cleveland appears as a paradigmatic case of urban decline. Yet Cleveland is also the site of ongoing nationally recognized initiatives that nurture urban life and are emulated elsewhere.

This seeming paradox is the backdrop for interpreting Re-Imagining Cleveland, a vacant land initiative, as it evolved from 2008 to 2016. I analyze how heterogeneous forces influenced both its successes and its weaknesses and link Re-Imagining garden projects to legacies of aesthetic and cultural practices in Cleveland.

Rancière's notion of "the distribution of the sensible" and the related ideas of "dissensus," the "presumption of equality," and "the politics of aesthetics" frame the analysis. First, I look at the administrative level of Re-Imagining Cleveland, analyzing the regime of ongoing negotiation in terms of which it operates. Secondly, I examine Re-Imagining Cleveland from the project level. This raises issues of value and visibility in the institutionalized cartographies of urban space. If put in the context of historic civic art and agrarian traditions in Cleveland, Re-Imagining Cleveland gardens represent a grounded civic art, part of a cultural infrastructure as fundamental to urban life as physical infrastructure.

URBAN CARTOGRAPHY AND "THE DISTRIBUTION OF THE SENSIBLE": A FRAMEWORK FOR ANALYSIS

The statistics are familiar, but still startling: In the 1950s Cleveland's population was 918,000; in 2017 it is just over 396,800. There are roughly 20,000 vacant lots, over 3,500 acres, in variously sized parcels unevenly distributed throughout the city (Zautner 2012). After years of stereotypical images of inner cities as dense, tight places, a drive through town reveals suburban and even rural land use patterns. Wyly and Ponder et al. (2012) argue that loose regulatory frameworks and local structures of inequality worked in conjunction with national and transnational investment practices to produce this blankness. In their cartography, Ohio appears as part of a NE cluster where state restrictions are weak; there is a higher subprime market penetration, and a subprime profile oriented toward highly leveraged, low-credit borrowers (Wyly and Ponder 2012).

In 2008 Neighborhood Progress, Inc. (now Cleveland Neighborhood Progress), a respected local community development intermediary, and Kent State University's Cleveland Urban Design Collaborative created Re-Imagining Cleveland for the purpose of addressing the vacant land crisis. Other founding partners include the city of Cleveland Planning Department, and ParkWorks, Inc. (now LAND studio). Work began with a systematic study of Cleveland funded by the Surdna Foundation and involving over thirty local government and nonprofit agencies with expertise in land use, environmental planning, stormwater management, parks, agriculture, brown fields and economic development. Land bank parcels and green spaces in the city were identified and mapped. The City Planning Department developed a land use decision matrix as a tool for evaluating proposed reuse of vacant land, using economic variables, sustainability goals and quality of life factors as criteria. The results of the studies were made available to the public with the goal of enhancing general understanding of existing and potential land use patterns. This report and subsequent publications are analyzed in this chapter as representations of the play of values and patterns of visibility within Re-Imagining Cleveland.

The framework for this analysis is based on Jacques Rancière's work interpreting systems of meaning within which public action occurs. Professional practices in planning and urban design are examples of "distributions of the sensible" that set up what appear to be "self-evident facts," as the basis for operating and for recognizing types of membership (Rancière 2004, 12). Distributions of the sensible actively configure "a particular sphere of experience" for various recognized members while excluding others from membership (Rancière 2007, 24). Dikec (2007) argues that within distributions of the sensible urban policy does not merely regulate spatial patterns, it constitutes them. Planning and public policy function by making and maintaining urban cartographies that produce realms of what is possible as well as the subjects who can or cannot inhabit them. He says in this regard: "Urban policy constitutes its spaces of intervention as part of the policy process, rather than by acting on given spaces" (5).

Rancière's foundational idea of generative frameworks in terms of which policy is produced is indebted to Michel Foucault. Foucault's thought, particularly his early work, was criticized for being too rigid; for not allowing for agency nor being able to explain change. Rancière addresses both problems by extending Foucault's thought in two directions that are particularly useful for interpreting urban policy and design initiatives. First, Rancière's model is not totalizing. He argues that even within the most authoritarian system there are germs of what he calls "dissensus." Distributions of the sensible contain the potential for alteration, no matter how well policed they are. The presence of "positive contradictions" (Rancière 2006, 8) can lead to challenges out of which new modes of intelligibility, new experiences, new rules for membership, and new forms of visibility can emerge (Rancière 2010). Rancière begins with the assumption of heterogeneous potential within distributions of the sensible.

Secondly, Rancière's investigations begin from the perspective of those who are the least visible within any distribution of the sensible. This is illustrated by his intellectual history. The traditional Marxist activist seeks to educate workers about their limitations and train them to better themselves. Rancière takes the position that workers are not limited and do not need to be educated. He bases this position on his research into the writings and letters of nineteenth-century workers. He found them to be aware of their situation and able to articulate it as well as to reflect on life, art, and nature at abstract levels. As a result, he argues that investigation should begin with the recognition that subjects have capacities that go beyond what is assumed within dominant distributions of the sensible (Rancière 1991). In addition to approaching analysis at the level of the distribution of sensible, the researcher should also work from the presumption of equality. It is not that equality is actualized under current operating conditions—it is that one investigates from that perspective. For Rancière, equality is real even if it is not realized.

The interwoven dynamics of the distribution of the sensible, and dissensus within it frame the analysis in part 1 of this chapter, which examines Re-Imagining Cleveland at the administrative level. I discuss how a regime of ongoing negotiation both enables and limits the scope of activities. In part 2 Re-Imagining Cleveland garden projects are given the visibility that the presumption of equality would confer. They are examined in relation to the legacies of aesthetic and cultural practices in Cleveland. I argue that taking the view from the garden allows these small projects to be recognized as *grounded civic art.* I then briefly discuss characteristics of urban design practices oriented towards nurturing cultural infrastructure.

THE TRAJECTORY OF RE-IMAGINING CLEVELAND WITHIN A REGIME OF ONGOING NEGOTIATIONS

Cleveland Neighborhood Progress plays an intermediary role among funders, such as the Cleveland Foundation, Gund Foundation, and other entities, such as community development corporations and citizen grantees, which are directly involved in community development projects. This mode of urban governance is increasingly common. Instead of a stable structure of elected officials and administrative departments with explicit rules of accountability, a complex mix of public and private agents in formal and informal relationships participate in planning and implementation. Ronald Richard, CEO of the Cleveland Foundation, notes that legacy cities such as Cleveland no longer have the resources to provide what used to be thought of as basic governmental functions (Richard 2014). Joel Ratner, president and CEO of Cleveland Neighborhood Progress expresses the generally held belief "that non-profit groups can assemble land, work privately with developers to nurture projects and conduct real estate negotiations in ways that are more agile and flexible than government" (Litt 2013). Community foundations also understand themselves as "reducing the impact of politics" (Krumholz 1997; Litt 2013; Mazany and Perry 2014).

Within this distribution of the sensible, roles are divided into roughly three interlocking levels: (1) executive funders, (2) intermediary administration, and (3) project-level operations. Public-sector agencies are involved, as are "stakeholder groups" at all three levels. Others with situation specific interests, funding capabilities and areas of expertise participate on an ad hoc basis. Authority is also distributed horizontally at each level, with interwoven differences and varying ideas about how best to proceed. Contradictions that inevitably appear are worked out or, just as frequently, allowed to stand. Fluid continuing agonistic relations are characteristic of urban initiatives where formulation and implementation are distributed among a number of public and private agents. Re-Imagining Cleveland was organized and proceeded as an active collaboration among unequal, divergent, and highly resourceful partners. This form of the distribution of the sensible for planning and urban design I call *regimes of ongoing negotiation.* Below I describe how Re-Imagining Cleveland's working group operated as a regime of ongoing negotiation.

The Cleveland City Planning Commission adopted the strategies to address vacant land developed by Re-Imagining Cleveland in December 2008. Cleveland Neighborhood Progress funded the publication of *Re-Imagining a More Sustainable Cleveland: Citywide Strategies for the Reuse of Vacant Land*, designed by the Cleveland Urban Design Collaborative and published by Kent State University Press. This publication explained the approaches to vacant land developed by the working group and presented relevant physical and social data from the supporting studies.

The regime of ongoing negotiation established by Re-Imagining Cleveland was both traditional and innovative. *Re-Imagining a More Sustainable Cleveland* maps this combination. Positive contradictions visible in this document influenced planning as the initiative adapted to shifting circumstances. The basic spatial logic is based on two categories: "conventional real estate development" and "alternative land use strategies." Together they are seen as beneficial for the city within a range of goals including productive use, public benefit, ecosystem function, and remediation. The "Core Development Areas" identified by the city in *Connecting Cleveland 2020 Citywide Plan* define and map areas of the city in traditional economic development terms. The rest of the city is presented in terms of definitions of alternative valuable goals, such as sustainability, and links to the core—that is, the potential to make economic development more likely. The primary criteria for considering whether a parcel of vacant land is appropriate for a particular reuse is how it relates to the core development areas. For example, in the decision tree developed for determining whether land should be reserved to contribute to building a "green infrastructure" how a parcel ranks in terms of economic development potential is a higher priority than the physical characteristics of the space. At the same time Re-Imagining Cleveland articulated new spatial possibilities and moved the city toward recognizing sustainable practices, it operated within a distribution of the sensible that reinforced economic productivity as a central measure of value for urban space.

Using this framework, Re-Imagining Cleveland negotiated among funding contingencies, the agendas of multiple players and horizontal and vertical layers of operation. All these enabled, while also inhibiting, the level of practice. I focus here on the shifting meanings given to individual projects, particularly community gardens. Gardens began as the most common project type, then took on meaning as inspirational symbols of Re-Imagining Cleveland and then served as examples of successful implementation in campaigns for funding—while resources supporting gardens all but disappeared.

At the operational level, Re-Imagining Cleveland began with six privately funded pilot projects in 2008. Because of the enthusiasm with which these projects were received, a citywide call for proposals that would use parcels in the Cleveland Land Bank was distributed that summer. A second publication, *Re-Imagining Cleveland: Vacant Land Re-Use Pattern Book* (*The Pattern Book*), directed toward potential applicants, presented specific ideas for vacant land reuse and also provided detailed information about plans, costs of component parts, and the potential benefits to the community. While *Re-Imagining a More Sustainable Cleveland* was data-based, *The Pattern Book* presented targeted, practical information.

Individuals, schools, social service and educational organizations (including existing groups and groups created for the purpose of applying) applied to the first round of Re-Imagining Cleveland. Roughly half were selected, bringing the first round to fifty-six sites. Funds for implementation came from a variety of sources. Neighborhood Stabilization Funds from the Department of Housing and Urban Development given through the Cleveland Community Development Department accounted for $500,000. Cleveland Neighborhood Progress raised additional funding and in-kind services from the Environmental Protection Agency, the Ohio State University Extension, the Trust for Public Land, Cleveland State University, and the City of Cleveland Neighborhood Stabilization Program.

First-round grantees were given stewardship of a vacant parcel for five years and received financial, technical, and in-kind support for the first year. There were a number of project types, including phytoremediation, passive and pocket parks, native plantings, orchards, vineyards, and market and community gardens. Gardens were the most popular form and tended to be developed early. Cleveland Neighborhood Progress began orientation and training sessions in 2009. An interactive website for participants and a documentation process, including oral interviews and photographs, also began in the fall of 2009. These were sponsored by the Center for Digital Humanities and the Maxine Goodman Levin College of Urban Affairs at Cleveland State University. The photo documentation is available on the Cleveland Neighborhood Progress' website. A third publication, *Re-Imagining Cleveland: Ideas to Action Resource Book* (*Ideas to Action*), appeared in 2011. *Ideas to Action* was more specific then *The Pattern Book*, moving away from discussion of potential uses of vacant land to present concrete descriptions and photographs of successful projects and advice by first-round grantees based on their experiences. In *Ideas to Action* the grantees became visible participants in the movement to restore vacant land.

The operation of Re-Imagining's first round was characterized by vertical integration. The combination of the administrative working group's organizational skills, of immediately available public monies, the openness of the public sector to multiple potential uses for vacant land and something that might be called the impulse to garden were woven together. The commitments to linking vacant land reuse to development potential and sustainability at a citywide level remained constant; however, these were not rigidly defined. Staff and volunteers who worked directly with grantees were deeply committed to helping make the projects successful in the grantees' terms. Re-Imagining empowered citizens committed to transforming vacant land and in return they created useable space, often market and community gardens.

The successful interweaving of priorities that constituted Re-Imagining's start-up years led to widespread recognition albeit within different narratives. Local media attention tended to focus on the human-interest aspects of individual projects and their connection to healthy food. At the national level, Re-Imagining Cleveland was awarded a 2012 National Planning Excellence Award for Innovation in Sustainable Places (Davidson 2012). Re-Imagining Cleveland was discussed in *Urban Agriculture: Growing Healthy Sustainable Places*, published by the American Planning Association in the context of challenges of farming in past industrial cities. (Hodgson, Campbell, and Bailkey 2011). *Smithsonian* magazine printed a feature article about a Re-Imagining vineyard project, focusing on potential job creation. Re-Imagining administrators made presentations in other cities interested in similar projects. Photographs of projects sites appeared on websites concerned with community gardening, vacant land issues, greening interest groups, and others. The images of community and market gardens became symbols of how creativity and community commitment can meaningfully address the vacant land crisis.

Because of their interest with creating sustainability at the citywide level, "bringing the program to scale" became a concern at the administrative level of Re-Imagining Cleveland after the initial round. However, changes instituted during round two of Re-Imagining Cleveland were largely dictated by funding contingencies rather the aspirations of the organization. Because of limitations tied to HUD monies that funded the second round, round two projects were limited to urban agriculture (thirty-three projects from the first round) and greening projects (ninety-one projects). Greening projects were dominated by pocket parks (twenty-eight projects) and new side-yard expansions (fifty-five projects). In addition to more limited formats, round two projects were also characterized by less direct initiative at the citizen level. Community development corporations had responsibility for selecting income-qualified participants. Professional contractors, chosen through a bidding system administered by the city, were required to construct fencing for the lots.

Vertical negotiations were central to round three and planning for round four. Without permanent public funding, the administrators of Re-Imagining Cleveland had to seek out and negotiate with potential funders. The working group necessarily became more sensitive to the preferences of community foundations. Richard, CEO of the Cleveland Foundation, a funder of Cleveland Neighborhood Progress, argues that in addition to making social investments in areas where governments can no longer afford to do so, foundations also have greater latitude to innovate (2014). Although by law they cannot engage in political activities, within regimes of ongoing negotiation funders are in fact intimately involved in what Rancière refers to as policing the common. They innovate in their terms. In addition, "charitable funding is increasingly being experienced as calculative" (Hinchhilff 2007, 266). That is, funders require measurable results. These dynamics mean that intermediaries, such as Re-Imagining Cleveland, must develop the fine art of negotiating among their desires and funders' demands. Having to negotiate with funders' priorities and ways of measuring success to weave together beneficial programs puts intermediaries in the position of having to win standing. So, while at the operational level grantees are more likely to think in terms of continuity, professionals working within regimes of ongoing negotiation must develop shifting horizontal strategies at the administrative level to weave together the next iteration of the possible.

Round three of Re-Imagining Cleveland was funded with monies from Wells Fargo Bank's settlement with the federal government stemming from alleged predatory lending practices. Combining lessons learned from the first rounds with an eye toward how to best manage projects and secure future funding, applications were required to be sponsored and administered by community development corporations. Among other things, applicants had to explain their capacity to complete the proposed project, provide evidence of their collaboration with other public and private groups, and explain how they would measure success. Nine new projects were accepted, including greening improvements at two rapid transit sites, side-yard improvements in two neighborhoods, community green spaces, and neighborhood pathways.

While round three projects were in process, work began to secure funding for the following round. Re-Imagining Cleveland had sought out opportunities while continuing to meet with partners about current issues. These included the considerable efforts of active committees to develop online tools for vacant land and address ongoing operational issues. *Re-Imagining Cleveland: Field Manual for Vacant Land Reuse Projects* for use by citizens interested creating vacant land projects was published in 2015.

Because of the innovative nature of Re-Imagining Cleveland and the timing of the availability of public monies, a systematic form of evaluation was not developed for the early rounds, although there was photo documentation of each project. This documentation was used in meetings with Wells Fargo to win future support. Cleveland Neighborhood Progress also sponsored a bus tour of Re-Imagining Cleveland sites for Wells Fargo officials. The projects on the tour were not the third round Re-Imagining Cleveland sites Wells Fargo was currently funding as these were still underway. Instead, community and market gardens sites from round one were visited, and grantees spoke about their projects. This occurred in a context in which Wells Fargo was asking for calculable measures of success, defined as rising property values. The City Planning Department continued to focus on enhancement of land for development as major criteria for measuring the value of vacant land projects, while at the same time listing round one projects as one of their successes in vacant land reuse. The role of the gardens and gardeners had shifted from direct involvement in determining and implementing vacant land reuse to providing support to Re-Imagining Cleveland as a successful and evolving initiative. Within the distribution of the sensible that sees measurable outcomes in terms of property values, gardens and gardeners became less visible, becoming, in Rancière's terms, the part outside of the common.

Re-Imagining Cleveland secured funding for technical assistance in gathering data about projects in calculable terms, with the hope that this would demonstrate visible success. The results were disappointing. The final report, *The Reimagining Cleveland Vacant Lot Greening Program: Evaluating Economic Development and Public Safety Outcomes*, did not differentiate among types of projects, nor did it involve participants at the operational level. Data from the limited study areas on such measures as property values, tax delinquencies, and crimes rates led the authors to conclude that, "For the most part the analysis found no significant impact" (Center for Community Progress 2016, 6). In terms of articulating the value of Re-Imagining Cleveland projects, the report is helpful only insofar as one is: (1) in agreement with how success was measured, and/or (2) interested in building on previous studies in other cities using the same measures.

Re-Imagining Cleveland has also responded to increased interest among foundations in addressing the effects of climate change in vulnerable neighborhoods, weaving together a successful narrative for funding. Work is currently underway in targeted neighborhoods.

The potential to create and implement innovative civic projects exists within regimes of ongoing negotiation *but only within constraints*. Projects are tied to funding and other contingencies beyond the control of initiating groups. In the case of Re-Imagining Cleveland, internal and external inconsistencies and the separation among levels of administration and levels of implementation created positive contradictions that made room for play within existing constraints. Masterful ongoing negotiation at the administration level produced positive change in thinking about and acting on vacant land issues. At the project level a range of improvements, including gardens, came into being, and continue to enhance the city.

THE PRESUMPTION OF EQUALITY AND THE LEGACY OF CLEVELAND'S GARDENS

In the previous section I analyzed the shifting functions of community gardens and their decreasing visibility within Re-Imagining Cleveland. In this section I consider gardens from the viewpoint of the presumption of equality, putting them at the center of the discussion. I explore two legacies of urban gardening in Cleveland: gardening as an aesthetic practice and gardening as a cultural practice.

Rancière argues that what constitutes aesthetic practice shifts over time. Two ways of defining art are common in Cleveland. In "representative regimes of art," only specific media such as painting, sculpture, architecture, and landscape architecture are recognized. Art requires craft, and artists are thought to possess special talents. Most art is displayed in museums where the visitors who understand the work share the higher sensitivities of artists. In this way, representative regimes of art reinforce hierarchical structures of society. However, dissensus and positive contradictions within representative regimes can undercut them leading to what Rancière calls the "aesthetic regime of art." In aesthetic regimes of art, strict criteria for approved media, themes, craft, and venues are superseded. Art may use a range of media, address any issue, and appear outside museums. For Rancière the defining feature of aesthetic regimes of art is their relationship to the larger society. Instead of reinforcing hierarchy, aesthetic practices within the aesthetic regimes present challenges to conventional categories.

The dynamics Rancière outlines in the shift from representative regimes of art to aesthetic regimes of art are reflected in Cleveland's civic art and have direct bearing on the understanding the value of gardens. The Fine Arts Garden at the Cleveland Museum of Art, designed by the Olmsted brothers, is an example of an urban garden in the mode of representative regimes of art. Frederick Law Olmsted studied England's picturesque gardens, which were seen as high art in contrast to the economically productive spaces they were often designed to mask (Bermingham 1986; Daniels 2014). Gardeners were lowly paid, although often highly skilled workers who remained invisible (Hoyles 2005). Olmsted altered this approach in ways that reflect American sensibilities. His urban gardens do emulate nature and offer refuge from economically productive spaces. The gardens were distinct from the rest of the city, offering physical and psychological experiences that the city could not. But Olmsted also introduced dissensus and heterogeneity into the art of gardening by challenging social hierarchy. His urban gardens were meant to improve the well-being of all citizens, regardless of class (Roger 2001; Lange 2012). Just as Rancière discovered that nineteenth-century workers already had aesthetic sensibility, Olmsted argued that citizens of all classes in New York City had the ability to benefit from visiting Central Park (Olmsted 1870).

The Cleveland Museum of Art has exemplified this kind of heterogeneity since its opening in 1916. The founders were prominent citizens committed to the city's cultural advancement as represented by the City Beautiful tradition (Robinson 1903). They defined civic art in terms of the representative regime of art and held paternalistic views of the role the arts play in the city (Turner 1991). At the same time, the motto of the museum has always been "For the benefit of all the people forever," and the founders insisted on free admission, a policy that continues today. Frederic Allen Whiting, the Cleveland Museum of Art's first director, initiated educational programs and argued that the collections should reflect Cleveland as an industrial center (Whiting 1914).

Today, the inclusive components of the founders' vision have been reconfigured to increase participation and involvement in the city. "All the people forever" is now used as a major identifier by the museum. Programming includes art in many media made and presented inside and outside the museum. Recognition now extends to other gardening practices in addition to the museum's Fine Arts Garden. For example, from March to October 2016 the Cleveland Museum of Art sponsored an exhibit, *Painting the Modern Garden: Monet to Matisse*, which was connected to a workshop in University Circle featuring local community gardeners. Other University Circle institutions—including the Cleveland Botanical Garden, Case Western Reserve University, and the Natural History Museum—sponsor off-site greening and gardening projects.

Community gardens, including Re-Imagining Cleveland gardens, can lay claim to the legacy of civic art in the mode of the aesthetic regime of art. Because they are the result of direct labor on the land, they have an aura that the ready-made, clichéd element of modern life lack. When you stand in a garden you see the hand of an artist and encounter commitment to a particular locality. Gardens are civic art not because they are part of a grand tradition one can aspire to but because they make the city ours by amending urban space as a field of experience. Urban designers and policymakers could take up the challenge to conventional hierarchies that gardens represent and create urban cartographies that promote closer relations between the experience of living in a city and active civic art.

The second legacy of gardening in Cleveland is cultural—that is, gardening is part of citizens' shared heritage. This extends back to and beyond the victory gardens of World Wars I and II. The Cleveland School Gardens Program existed from 1904 to 1977, when public schools had gardens that were woven into the curriculum. Some school gardens still exist and are being expanded—for example, the Ben Franklin Elementary garden. In 2008 Re-Imagining Cleveland data showed over two hundred community gardens in the city. Today, the number is thought to be closer to four hundred. It is not surprising that gardening projects were the first choice among the original Re-Imagining Cleveland grantees.

Documentation of Re-Imagining Cleveland gardens included frequent discussions about parents and grandparents who grew up gardening either in Cleveland or down south. In a series of interviews with African American gardeners in Cleveland, Fiskio (2016) found they were connected to a legacy of activism and mutual support that stretched back before the Great Migration. The gardeners described the value of what they do in terms of hospitality, empowerment, and giving back. Alice Walker taps into this tradition in her book *In Search of Our Mothers' Gardens* (2003), in which gardening is celebrated as a paradigmatic example of women's art set against the forces that oppressed them, suggesting a gentle, yet potent dissensus based on resilience and memory. Urban designers can honor this heritage by acknowledging its physical manifestations.

The dual legacy of gardens as aesthetic practice and cultural heritage introduces positive contradictions into cartographies of the city organized around economic development potential. The question of how to articulate the value of gardens comes to the fore. Blomley's (2004) study of Vancouver found that residents value public spaces, including community gardens, as "belonging" to them but not in the limited sense of private property with market value. Belonging is based on their care of the spaces they improve. Degen et al. (2006) found that deeply felt connections developed among gardeners and the land they work, as a result of their direct interaction. Moulin-Doos (2013) describes interaction created in German intercultural community gardens she studied as "respect." Hinchliffe and Kearnes (2007) describe the passion and commitment necessary to making immigrant garden projects successful and argue that it goes far beyond the calculable requirements of funders.

These studies suggest that gardens have value beyond temporary spaces that only become visible to planners in terms of their economic development potential (Bishop and Williams 2012; Colomb 2012). Alternative patterns of valuation emerge from the legacies of civic art and cultural heritage and current research discussed above. Gardens affect how people circulate in urban space and they expand the terms in which citizens can encounter each other. Gardeners participate in the production of meaning in urban space. Gardens make space, not only for display but also for living in. As such they are examples of what Lefebvre (1996) calls the right to the city: valorizing citizens in making space at the level of everyday life and promoting noninstrumental encounters as a basic component of civic life. Gardens should be mapped as a component of cultural infrastructure as integral to urbanism as transportation infrastructures, media networks, or green infrastructure (Corner 2006; Brenner 2013).

CONCLUSIONS

Institutionalized cartographies are distributions of the sensible that only appear to be self-evident. So it only seems obvious to evaluate Re-Imagining Cleveland projects in terms used in other studies of vacant land projects and in conjunction with the land use goals of the city. But from another point of view, interrogating how projects are valued should be logically prior to evaluating them. If our approach to defining value were reconfigured based on the presumption of equality, participation in the production of meaning at sites of encounter would become the basis for considering their worth.

The challenge for planning and urban design is to harness positive contradictions that enable programs such as Re-Imagining Cleveland and create self-conscious cartographic practices grounded in the past and present lived experience of the city. Rather than denying political involvement, regimes of ongoing negotiation could become centers of practice based on the political philosophy that undergirds the presumption of equality: the "desire to create a collective generosity" (Massumi 2015, 9).

REFERENCES

Bermingham, Ann. 1986. *Landscape and Ideology: The English Rustic Tradition, 1740–1860*. Berkeley: University of California Press.

Bishop, Peter, and Lesley Williams. 2012. *The Temporary City*. London: Routledge.

Blomley, Nicholas. 2004. "Un-Real Estate: Proprietary Space and Public Gardening." *Antipode* 36, no. 4: 614–41.

Brenner, Neil. 2013. "Theses on Urbanization." *Public Culture* 23, no. 1: 85–114.

Colomb, Claire. 2012. "Pushing the Urban Frontier: Temporary Uses of Space, City Marketing, and the Creative City Discourse in 2000s Berlin." *Journal of Urban Affairs* 34, no. 2: 131–52.

Conan, Michel, and Wangheng Chen. 2008. *Gardens, City Life and Culture*. Washington, DC: Dumbarton Oaks Research Library and Collection and Spacemaker Press.

Corner, James. 2006. "Terra Fluxus." In *The Landscape Urbanism Reader*, edited by Charles Waldheim, 21–34. New York: Princeton Architectural Press.

Daniels, Stephen. 2014. "Moveable Views: Repton's Composite Art of Landscape Gardening." In *Composite Landscapes: Photomontage and Landscape Architecture*, edited by Charles Waldheim and Ann Hansen. Boston: Isabella Stewart Gardner Museum.

Degen Monica, Sarah Whatmore, Steve Hinchliffe, and M. B. Kearnes, 2006. "Greenfingers, Greenspaces: Passionate Involvements with Urban Natures." www.Ibrarian.net/Greenfingers_Greenspaces_Passionate_Involvements.

Dikec, Mustafa. 2007. *Badlands of the Republic: Space, Politics, and Urban Policy*. Oxford: Blackwell Publishing.

Fiskio, Janet. 2016. "Cultivating Community: Black Agrarianism in Cleveland, Ohio." *Gastronomica* 16, no. 2: 18–30.

Hoyles, Martin. 2005. "The Garden and the Division of Labour." In *Vista: The Culture and Politics of Gardens*, edited by Tim Richardson and Noel Kingsbury, 21–38. London: Frances Lincoln.

Hodgson, Kimberly, Marcia Caton Campbell, and Martin Bailkey. 2011. *Urban Agriculture: Growing Healthy, Sustainable Places*. Chicago: American Planning Association.

Hinchliffe, Steve, Matthew B. Kearnes, Monica Degen, and Sarah Whatmore. 2007. "Ecologies and Economics of Action: Sustainability, Calculations, and Other Things." *Environment and Planning* 39: 260–82.

Krumholz, Norm. 1997. "The Provision of Affordable Housing in Cleveland: Patterns of Organizational and Financial Support." In *Affordable Housing and Urban Redevelopment in the United States*, edited by Willem Van Vliet, 52–72. Thousand Oaks, CA: SAGE.

Lange, Alexandra. 2012. *Writing about Architecture*. New York: Princeton Architectural Press.

Lawson, Laura. 2005. *City Bountiful: A Century of Community Gardening in American*. Berkeley: University of California Press.

Lefebvre, Henri. 1996. "The Right to the City." In *Writings on Cities*, edited by Eleonore Kofman and Elizabeth Lebas, 147–59. Oxford: Blackwell.

Litt, Steven. 2013. "Neighborhood Progress Inc. Merges with Two Other Organizations to Improve Community Revitalization in Cleveland." www.cleveland.com/architecture/index.ssf.2013/neighborhood_progress-inc.merge.

Mader, Joel. 2010. *Cleveland School Gardens*. Chicago: Arcadia Publishing.

Massumi, Brian. 2015. *Politics of Affect*. Cambridge: Polity Press.

Moulin-Doos, Claire. 2013. "Intercultural Gardens: The Use of Space by Migrants and the Practice of Respect." *Journal of Urban Affairs* 36, no. 2: 197–206.

Mazany, Terry, and David C. Perry, eds. 2014. *Here for Good: Community Foundations and the Challenges of the 21st Century*. London: M. E. Sharpe.

Olmsted, Frederick Law. 1870 (2012). "Public Parks and the Enlargement of Towns." In *Writing about Architecture*, edited A. Lange, 121–33. Reprint, New York: Princeton Architectural Press.

Rancière, Jacques. 1991. *The Ignorant Schoolmaster: Five Lessons in Intellectual Emancipation*. Stanford, CA: Stanford University Press.

Rancière, Jacques. 2004. *The Politics of Aesthetics: The Distribution of the Sensible*. London: Continuum.

Rancière, Jacques. 2006. *Film Fables*. Oxford: Berg.

Rancière, Jacques. 2007a. *Aesthetics and Its Discontents*. Cambridge: Polity Press.

Rancière, Jacques. 2007b. *The Future of the Image*. London: Verso.

Rancière, Jacques. 2009. *The Emancipated Spectator*. London: Verso.

Rancière, Jacques. 2010. *Dissensus: On Politics and Aesthetics*. London: Bloomsbury.

Richard, Ronald B. 2014. "A Mandate to Innovate." In *Here for Good: Community Foundations and the Challenges of the 21st Century*, edited by Terry Mazany and David C. Perry. London: M. E. Sharpe.

Robinson, Charles Muford. 1903. *Modern Civic Art: Or The City Made Beautiful*. New York: Putnam's Sons.

Rogers, Elizabeth Barlow. 2001. "Expanding Cities and New Social Institutions: The Democratization of Landscape Design." In *Landscape Design: A Cultural and Architectural History*, 311–56. New York: Harry N. Abrams.

Turner, Evan. 1991. *Objects Lessons: Cleveland Creates an Art Museum*. Cleveland: Cleveland Museum of Art.

Walker, Alice. 2003. *In Search of Our Mothers' Gardens*. New York: Mariner Books.

Whiting, Frederic Allen. 1914. Letter to the board of directors of the Cleveland Museum of Art, January 6, 1914.

Wyly, Elvin, C. S. Ponder, Pierson Nettling, Bosco Ho, Sophie Ellen Fung, Zachary Liebowitz, and Dan Hammel. 2012. "New Racial Meanings in Housing in America." *American Quarterly* 64, no. 3: 571–604.

Zautner, Lilah. 2008. *Re-Imagining a More Sustainable Cleveland: Citywide Strategies for Reuse of Vacant Land*. Cleveland: Cleveland Land Lab, Cleveland Urban Design Collaborative, and Kent State University Press.

Zautner, Lilah. 2009. *Re-Imagining Cleveland: Vacant Land Re-Use Pattern Book*. Cleveland: Kent State University's Cleveland Urban Design Collaborative with the assistance of McKnight Associates.

Zautner, Lilah. 2010. SustainLane. http://www.sustainlane.com/us-city-rankings/categories/local-food-agriculture.

Zautner, Lilah. 2011. *Re-Imagining Cleveland: Ideas to Action Resource Book*. Cleveland: Kent State University's Cleveland Urban Design Collaborative and Neighborhood Progress, Inc., in collaboration with the City of Cleveland.

Zautner, Lilah. 2012a. *2012 Summer Sprout Community Garden Report*. Cuyahoga County: Ohio State University Extension.

Zautner, Lilah. 2012b. "Re-Imagining Cleveland: Transforming Vacant Spaces into Vibrant Places." Paper presented at the Reclaiming Vacant Properties Conference, New Orleans, LA, June 20–22, 2012.

Zautner, Lilah. 2015. *Re-Imagining Cleveland: Field Manual for Vacant Land Reuse Projects*. Cleveland: Kent State University's Cleveland Urban Design Collaborative.

Zautner, Lilah. 2016. *The Reimagining Cleveland Vacant Lot Greening Program: Evaluating Economic Development and Public Safety Outcomes*. Washington, DC: Center for Community Progress.

12

The Arts as a Catalyst for Neighborhood Revitalization

DENNIS KEATING

The arts and culture play important roles in American cities. Cultural institutions like theaters, museums, and art galleries have a long history in the life of these cities. Even those cities in decline, including legacy cities, often still have major arts and cultural institutions that remain viable and often serve as anchors. In recent history, a prominent example was the Detroit Institute of Arts (DIA) and the successful and unprecedented effort of many funders amidst the city's financial crisis and bankruptcy to save its arts collection from being sold to help reduce the city's debt. Legacy cities like Detroit retain their cultural institutions even while suffering severe population and economic declines.

Distressed neighborhoods in these cities have been hit hard with poverty, crime, and blighted and abandoned housing as discussed by Hatch in chapter 5, Krumholz in chapter 7, and Mikelbank in chapter 10. The combination of local government, community development corporations (CDCs), and philanthropic foundations have promoted neighborhood revitalization. One avenue has been the use of the arts as a catalyst for redevelopment. Often, it has been artists who have found a haven in these distressed neighborhoods.

A famous example in Detroit is the artist Tyree Guyton and his Heidelberg Project. Beginning in 1986 Guyton transformed a few blocks in his blighted east side neighborhood by decorating vacant houses on city-owned land with artistic themes using everyday products. Despite threats from the city to close down his art installations, the controversial project not only survived but expanded. Guyton won the support of foundations and his project has drawn enormous numbers of visitors, becoming a Detroit landmark. But in recent years a wave of unsolved arsons destroyed several of the houses. In 2016 Guyton announced that the project would be partially disassembled and relocated to become more of a permanent installation (Stryker 2016).

Guyton's Heidelberg Project inspired others to see Detroit neighborhoods differently and to undertake redevelopment projects, including those that are art-related. There is now a Detroit neighborhood art project with the goal of transforming five of Detroit's neighborhood business districts into destinations for the arts. The Knight Foundation has funded numerous arts projects in Detroit's neighborhoods through its Arts Challenge Detroit program. Rip Rapson, CEO of the Kresge Foundation, has noted that Detroit's Future City framework provided the opportunity for neighborhood residents and organizations to employ art as a tool of neighborhood redevelopment. The 2012 Detroit Future City Strategic Framework Plan promoted art in Live+Make neighborhoods. The Kresge Foundation sponsors artist fellowships in greater Detroit. Rapson has been a leader in promoting creative placemaking and in the creation of ArtPlace (Axel-Lute and Simon 2017). ArtPlace is a ten-year collaboration among a number of foundations, federal agencies, and financial institutions that works to position arts and culture as a core sector of comprehensive community planning and development in order to help strengthen the social, physical, and economic fabric of communities. It has a national grants program, and in 2015 created a special community development investments program that funded six nonprofit organizations over three years to develop creative placemaking.

PLACEMAKING: ARTS AND URBAN NEIGHBORHOOD REVITALIZATION

There has long been a debate over whether to attempt to revitalize distressed urban neighborhoods or instead to focus on their residents, including relocating them to better neighborhoods, offering opportunities for improved lives. In 1968 the Kerner Commission addressed this in the context of inner-city poverty in predominantly African American neighborhoods and the predominantly white suburbs surrounding the central cities. While *gilding the ghetto* was a term for revitalizing neglected inner-city neighborhoods, this presidential commission investigating the urban riots of the 1960s also advocated dispersing the minority populations of these neighborhoods to racially segregated suburbs.

Some progress has been made in racially diversifying the inner suburbs. While poverty rates have risen in some of these suburbs, a majority of the poor still reside in central cities, as Krumholz discussed in chapter 7. With the rise of the community development movement, efforts have continued over the past several decades to pursue the redevelopment of distressed central city neighborhoods.

The term *placemaking* has been applied to remake some of these communities. It is a term long used by the Project for Public Spaces and by arts promoters to signify the process of using arts-based projects for community development. A leading organization promoting creative placemaking is ArtPlace America.

Legacy cities like Detroit have turned to the arts as one mechanism to help to revive neglected neighborhoods. In May 2008 a conference titled "From Rust Belt to Artist Belt: Challenges and Opportunities in Rust Belt Cities" was held in Cleveland to inform local lenders, community developers, real estate companies, commercial and residential developers, elected and appointed officials, and civic leaders about best practices that could integrate artists into Rust Belt community development. Cleveland is an example of a legacy city where this has been happening over an extended period, as Ryberg-Webster and Tighe discussed in the introduction to this volume.

This chapter focuses on several Cleveland neighborhoods and the incorporation of the arts into community redevelopment by community development corporations. It will explore the impact of the arts as a catalyst for the revitalization of these neighborhoods. This encompasses the impact of the arts on residents, businesses, and the neighborhood's image. Indicators of the impact of the arts include investment in the neighborhood reflected in new businesses (including art galleries), visitors to the neighborhood attracted by arts-related attractions, and physical improvements in the neighborhood.

CLEVELAND'S ARTS AND CULTURE LEGACY

Cleveland has a legacy of major cultural institutions. They have long existed and generally have significant endowments dating from the period of Cleveland's ascent as an industrial powerhouse. Many of these cultural institutions are located in the University Circle district, including the Cleveland Museum of Art, the Cleveland Institute of Art, the Museum of Contemporary Art, the Cleveland Orchestra, the Music Settlement, the Cleveland History Center, and the Cleveland Museum of Natural History. University Circle is also the location of Case Western Reserve University, the main campuses of two major hospital systems—the Cleveland Clinic and University Hospital—and the Cleveland Botanical Gardens.

Following World War I, five theaters opened in 1921–1922 in downtown Cleveland in a district known as Playhouse Square. These were venues for vaudeville, silent films, and drama, and later movie theaters. With the decline of downtown Cleveland and increasing suburbanization—including the growth of malls with multiplex movie theaters—four of the five theaters closed in 1968–1969. They were slated for demolition as outmoded entertainment facilities. However, Ray Shepardson became their savior, creating the Playhouse Square Association, with the aim of preserving the theaters. In 1973 the Playhouse Square Foundation was created to oversee the restoration and operation of the theaters. In 1978 they were placed on the National Register of Historic Places. Funding was raised locally and nationally, and in 1982 and 1984 two of the restored theaters were reopened. Eventually, the other theaters were also restored and reopened (Litt 2014). One has become the home of the Great Lakes Theater and, more recently, the Cleveland Playhouse moved to Playhouse Square. The Playhouse Square Foundation has reported that on average more than one million visitors attend events at the theaters in Playhouse Square annually. With a significant economic impact, Playhouse Square has been heralded as a major cultural success and downtown anchor: "In a newspaper poll, civic leaders hailed 'the saving of Playhouse Square' as the leading triumph on a list of the top 10 successes in Cleveland history" (Playhouse Square Foundation 2017).

In addition to individual private donors, several Cleveland philanthropic foundations have provided major and continuing supports for the arts and cultural organizations. Foremost among them is the Cleveland Foundation. In 1997 the Cleveland Foundation and the Gund Foundation commissioned a regional strategic cultural plan. Out of this came the Community Partnership for Arts and Culture (CPAC), which produced the Northeast Ohio Arts and Culture Plan in May 2000. It has since issued numerous reports on the arts in the region. CPAC facilitates an occasional arts and culture roundtable.

In 2006 Cuyahoga County voters voted to create the Cuyahoga Arts & Culture (CAC) district and funded it through a cigarette sales tax to provide support to arts organizations and artists, primarily through competitive grant programs. This followed an unsuccessful campaign in 2004 to support the arts in the county through a property tax levy, which was narrowly rejected by voters. Between 2007 and 2015, CAC distributed $136 million in grants to art organizations and artists. In November 2015 voters extended the cigarette tax for another decade to support CAC. In 2016 CAC funded 152 arts organizations with $1,651,624 through its Project Support grant program. Some of this funding has gone to neighborhood-based arts projects and organizations, including some of those in selected Cleveland neighborhoods.

CLEVELAND NEIGHBORHOOD CASE STUDIES

Across the United States, the rise of creative placemaking emphasizing the arts has grown in the field of community development. This has been reported by *Shelterforce* magazine (2016–2017). This chapter illustrates this trend by profiling three primary examples of neighborhoods and CDCs in Cleveland that have used the arts as a key element in promoting revitalization. They represent major success stories. They are among a number of such examples, of which two others will also be mentioned.

The Tremont, Detroit Shoreway, and North Collinwood neighborhoods grew and prospered as Cleveland industrialized and had large populations of European immigrants working in their factories. All saw steep declines in their population and employment with the decline of industry and manufacturing in Cleveland over the past several decades. All three have predominantly white populations and have experienced the same high rates of poverty as the overall rate in Cleveland, second only to Detroit among major cities. Their decline and more recent revitalization efforts are fueled, in part, by their promotion of the arts.

TREMONT

Tremont is a small (approximately 2.5 square miles) old neighborhood bordering the Industrial Valley (known as the Flats) along the Cuyahoga River (Keating 2016). It became a magnet in the late nineteenth century for European immigrants seeking work in the factories in the nearby Flats. They brought with them their cultures and religions. During this time more than twenty Christian churches were built in Tremont. Tremont suffered from deindustrialization and the construction of two freeways that bisected parts of the neighborhood, drastically reducing its population. From a peak historic population of about thirty-five thousand, by 2015 it had only about one-fourth of this total. In the 1970s, as Tremont's reduced population became poorer, some landlords began to burn down their buildings for the insurance money. Tremont was called the "White South Bronx" because of this destructive wave of arson.

In this same decade, artists began arriving in Tremont, attracted by its cheap housing (Hartshorn 2016). This eventually led in 1993 to the beginning of a monthly art walk organized by an attorney who also established an art gallery in her Tremont law office. This art walk was modeled after one previously begun in Cleveland's Little Italy. Local artists' work was featured in Tremont galleries and also in bars and restaurants. This brought recognition and visitors to a neighborhood that had experienced difficult economic and social problems. In 2016 the art walk was transformed into "Walkabout

Tremont," intended to provide a broader appeal than just the arts. However, the arts had become a critical factor in Tremont's revitalization. Other arts programs were established. These have included Arts Renaissance Tremont, the Tremont Arts and Cultural Festival, and Arts in August. In 2016–2017, a resident artist involved numerous residents in a ceramic art project at the gazebo in Lincoln Park. Related to these burgeoning arts activities, Tremont became the site for destination restaurants like Michael Symons's Lola, and new housing that is far more expensive than that of the existing stock. In addition to traditional church festivals, a midsummer Taste of Tremont festival and other activities draw tens of thousands of visitors to the neighborhood.

The Tremont West Development Corporation (TWDC), formed in 1979 through Merrick House, has played an important role in promoting the arts in Tremont as part of its redevelopment mission. It promotes these events and is also involved in managing some of them. Over the past twenty-five years there is no doubt that the arts have played a very important role in revitalizing the Tremont neighborhood. The arts helped to establish Tremont as a destination for visitors and new residents, contributing to new housing and businesses in a previously depressed neighborhood. However, in 2014 the poverty rate was 37.5 percent. Tremont remains a predominantly white (72 percent) neighborhood, but with significant African American (19 percent) and Hispanic (19 percent) minority populations.

Often, this kind of phenomenon has led to the displacement of artists and art galleries as gentrification caused housing and real estate prices to considerably increase. While some artists have left Tremont and some galleries have closed in the face of the arrival of newcomers with much higher incomes than those of older residents, there is no evidence yet of any significant displacement of longtime residents (including artists) or arts-related businesses. On the whole, the arts have had a very positive influence on Tremont.

DETROIT SHOREWAY AND GORDON SQUARE

Detroit Shoreway is another west side Cleveland neighborhood, bordering Lake Erie to the north. Like Tremont, deindustrialization and suburbanization resulted in high levels of resident and job losses. Like Tremont, part of this neighborhood was also lost to a freeway.

In 1973 the priest at a local Italian Catholic church took the initiative to address substandard housing and other signs of decline by forming the Detroit Shoreway Community Development Organization (DSCDO). In 1979 the fledgling community development corporation bought the Gordon Square Arcade, a landmark anchor building in blighted condition. It contained the old Capitol Theatre, built in the same era as the downtown Playhouse Square theaters. While much of the DSCDO's efforts were dedicated to providing affordable housing for poor residents, the organization also hoped to save the theater. However, it closed due to falling attendance and its deteriorating condition.

In the 1980s the Cleveland Public Theater moved from downtown Cleveland to a former Irish dance hall across the street from the Gordon Square Arcade. The theater's owner, James Levin, later bought an adjoining theater and a desanctified Romanian Orthodox church. Meanwhile, the Near West Theater, a community theater located in a church in a nearby neighborhood, was looking for a new home and decided to move to Gordon Square. Levin sowed the seeds for a collaborative effort of the two theaters and the DSCDO. In 2002 these three entities formed the Gordon Square Arts District (GSAD) to jointly seek $30 million in capital funding to help to expand the Cleveland Public Theater, restore and reopen the Capitol Theatre (which reopened in 2009), and build a new theater to house the Near West Theater (Keating 2014; Krumholz and Roller 2012). In tandem with this campaign, the city of Cleveland funded a new art-oriented streetscape in Gordon Square.

In 2015 the GSAD celebrated the success of its capital campaign and the opening of the Near West Theater in its new groundbreaking building in Gordon Square. Many artists occupy the 78th Street studios nearby in a former warehouse. They attract many visitors during a monthly third Thursday open house. Since its inception, the GSAD has staged an annual Hip2BSquare event to highlight the arts in Gordon Square. Among its 2015 visitors were the heads of the National Endowment for the Arts and the Ohio Arts Council. The success of the emergence of this arts partnership contributed to the revitalization of the Detroit Shoreway neighborhood. According to the DSCDO, many new businesses (ninety since 2006 and fourteen in 2016) have opened in Detroit Shoreway, attracted in part by the three theaters. It should be noted that the Capitol Theater has struggled to meet its attendance goal in order to pay off a loan from the city of Cleveland. While it has drawn around sixty thousand moviegoers annually, it had to negotiate a postponement of repayment of a city loan for the fifth time in 2016 (Attassi 2016). In its 2015–2017 strategic plan, the DSCDO stated: "Feedback from the planning process suggests that many feel the [Gordon Square Arts] district needs to push more aggressively toward delivering on the arts concept and recruiting more complementary businesses. DSCDO will partner with GSAD to catalyze and recruit new retail and arts organizations that fit within the concept of the arts district and help burnish the destination. DSCDO will also position the neighborhood to those in search of studio, maker, and creative spaces, building upon the success of places such as the 78th Street Studios and Cleveland Cycleworks" (18).

The Detroit Shoreway neighborhood has a population of about ten thousand people (almost two-thirds are white), and it still has a large number of poor residents and a poverty rate of 41 percent. Even as the housing market has increasingly prospered since the foreclosure crisis, the DSCDO remains committed to having a diverse neighborhood. It has been involved in the development and management of around one thousand units of affordable housing, but in 2014 almost half of neighborhood households lived in unaffordable housing (paying more than 30 percent of their income on housing). At the same time new market-rate housing projects are being built not far from Gordon Square. In its 2015–2017 strategic plan, the DSCDO stated: "DSCDO's service area has been named by some as the hottest housing market in Northeast Ohio . . . But amidst this, DSCDO remains committed to maintaining the character of the neighborhood as a mixed income, diverse community, ensuring that those of limited means are not marginalized or excluded" (13).

NORTH COLLINWOOD AND WATERLOO

This east side Cleveland neighborhood also borders Lake Erie. The larger Collinwood neighborhood was bisected by a freeway. In its heyday many of its residents worked in the railyards once located there. That kind of industrial work has largely disappeared. The population has declined and, like Tremont and Detroit Shoreway, the North Collinwood neighborhood also has a high poverty rate and is predominantly white (as opposed to the predominantly African American South Collinwood neighborhood).

In 2000 two entrepreneurs opened a music club in the former Croatian Liberty Home on Waterloo Road (Barber 2004). The Beachland Ballroom and Tavern initially became a popular but rather isolated music venue. It has since gained a national reputation with a diverse offering of bands. In 2002 a group of artists and neighborhood residents organized an art show and subsequently formed Waterloo Arts (originally called Arts Collinwood). In 2004 Waterloo Arts moved into a former tavern at Waterloo Road and East 156th Street.

The Northeast Shores Development Corporation (NESDC) began to see the arts as a way to promote the revitalization of North Collinwood (CPAC and NESDC 2014). In 2011 it partnered with the CPAC of Cuyahoga County to start an artist in residence program with a two-year grant of $500,000. These funds helped the NESDC to obtain vacant foreclosed homes and then sell them to artists at a modest price—initially $6,500—on the condition that they occupy and bring them up to code standards, usually as live/work homes and studios. This drew a few dozen artists to move into houses in North Collinwood. The NESDC also has created an earned equity program that allows tenants, including artists, in its Glencove building, to build equity with the hope that they will use it in the future as a down payment for the purchase of a home in the neighborhood.

In 2012 the NESDC received another $500,000 grant, this time in a national competition from ArtPlace America for its Collinwood Rising initiative. In 2013 Waterloo Arts launched the Zoetic Wall project, which involved local artists in painting twenty murals throughout North Collinwood. The two organizations have sponsored the monthly Walk All over Waterloo with art galleries and other open businesses, and they sponsor the Waterloo Arts Festival. In 2015 the NESDC won another competitive grant from ArtPlace America. This $200,000 Ballot Box Project was used for nine art projects, which were decided among thirty proposals by a vote of neighborhood residents in March 2016. The NESDC's former director saw these projects as a lab space for arts-based community development.

As with Gordon Square, the city of Cleveland redid Waterloo Road's streetscape with an arts focus. It reopened in 2015, and has spurred the opening of several art galleries and arts businesses and a microbrewery (Martens 2016). Without the pioneering Beachland Ballroom and Tavern, Waterloo Arts, and the arts projects of the NESDC, it is highly unlikely that the Waterloo district would have been transformed. The NESDC has since turned its attention to the rebirth of the vacant LaSalle Theater in the 185th Street commercial district. The goal is to have the theater become a video and music production center along with housing, retail, and a number of different events, including multimedia art exhibitions and music and theatrical performances.

These three examples are among the strongest and most successful Cleveland neighborhoods in which CDCs have used the arts as a catalyst for revitalization. However, there are other neighborhoods which are pursuing a similar strategy. Two of these are St. Clair Superior and Slavic Village.

ST. CLAIR SUPERIOR

The east side St. Clair Superior neighborhood, like Detroit Shoreway, is separated from Lake Erie by a rail line and a highway. Once an industrial area and home to a concentration of Slovenian immigrants, it also became home to the center of Cleveland's Asian groups (known now as Asia Town). Beginning in 2006 the St. Clair Superior Development Corporation (SCSDC) began an annual practice of holding public art campaigns to celebrate the Chinese New Year by commissioning for sale and display fiberglass sculptures of the animal of the year. These sculptures are seen throughout the neighborhood.

With funding from ArtPlace America and the Kresge Foundation, in 2014 the SCSDC launched its Upcycle Parts Shop. It promotes the transformation of unwanted materials into products with creative reinterpretation. Neighborhood residents, including artists, have participated in this program. The SCSDC has also used pop-up art murals to call attention to its revitalization efforts. Additionally, the SCSDC has promoted several major events to draw visitors—an annual Asia Town festival, the Cleveland Flea Market, and Asian Night Markets.

SLAVIC VILLAGE AND BROADWAY

This southeastern Cleveland neighborhood bordering the Flats attracted European immigrants as they came to work in the Industrial Valley. Like the other Cleveland neighborhoods previously profiled, this neighborhood also has experienced a major loss of population (almost two-thirds of its peak population) and jobs over the past several decades. Its poverty rate has soared to 46 percent, and the African American percentage of the much-reduced population has risen to a slight majority.

Slavic Village gained national (and international) notoriety as the epicenter of the foreclosure crisis (Kotlowitz 2009). Predatory lending, including illegal practices, led to high vacancy rates and the abandonment of foreclosed homes, which later became nuisance properties. This has required the demolition of about 1,500 blighted houses, leaving empty lots behind. Slavic Village Development (SVD) has initiated recovery programs to stabilize the neighborhood in the wake of this disaster.

Those SVD initiatives include arts-related projects. Its 2010 Slavic Village Neighborhood Summit focused on the arts. Arts projects have included a mural along a bike trail on an abandoned rail right-of-way, art benches in a park, and the *Cycle of Arches* exhibition placed at an entry to the neighborhood. The Broadway School of Music and the Arts has been a neighborhood fixture, and in 2015 the Cleveland Orchestra at Home had a Broadway Slavic Village residency with performances in various venues. City Music has also been a partner in the neighborhood. A mixed-use art gallery has located on Fleet Avenue, a rebuilt multimodal major street. In the past four years SVD has organized *Rooms to Let*, an art exhibition in which artists transform condemned vacant houses scheduled for demolition into temporary venues for artistic displays. All of these arts-related activities are seen as an important element in changing the image of Slavic Village as a blighted area into a desirable neighborhood attractive to newcomers.

CONCLUSION

These aforementioned examples in Cleveland typify what has happened in many other US cities. While arts-related activities and programs may not rank as important as addressing other issues in poor neighborhoods like the need for affordable housing and jobs, crime, and education, it has been seen as a very helpful element to positively change the image of these neighborhoods. They have attracted visitors and also have been a factor in increasing investment in these neighborhoods. While arts-related investment is not necessarily quantified, the successful capital campaign for the theaters in Gordon Square and the ArtPlace America grants in the North Collinwood and St. Clair Superior neighborhoods attest to the belief that the arts can be a very positive factor in neighborhood revitalization. According to Karen Chapple and Shannon Jackson (2010): "Where an emerging literature in urban studies and planning embraces artists as agents is in neighborhoods where arts and culture plant the seeds of local empowerment. This work is showing how smaller arts venues and cultural activities based in low-income neighborhoods-including a host of non-arts amenities that allow for cultural participation and creative expression, such as community centers, churches, and parks-can serve as catalysts for gradual change while benefitting the existing community" (481).

It should be noted that while the CDCs in these neighborhoods have been critically important to the planning and promotion of the arts, their efforts and those of the arts organizations involved are heavily dependent upon external funders—both public and private. Not all of their major redevelopment projects are entirely successful, of course. One example is the attendance shortfall of the restored Capitol Theatre in Detroit Shoreway, which presents a potentially difficult financial problem for the DSCDO.

With success in creative placemaking for the arts in some of these urban neighborhoods, there has been concern about the changes that result in gentrification and displacement of existing residents and businesses (Grodach, Foster, and Murdoch 2014). Artists have often been the so-called pioneers in beginning to see the potential of older neighborhoods. According to Maria Rosario Jackson (2012): "Without question, affordability of space is a feature that attracts many artists to live and/or work in moderate and low-income communities. But there are other important factors that draw artists to marginalized neighborhoods. Some reasons are pragmatic; others are philosophical. The overriding theme, however, is that where many people see only blight and deficiency, artists can see assets. Artists often recognize and are inspired by both the assets and challenges of marginalized communities, and many are eager to participate in problem-solving using arts and creativity" (5).

With gentrification artists may then find themselves priced out the neighborhoods that they helped to revive. In the Cleveland examples of this process, there has not yet been gentrification to the extent that displacement has been a significant issue. CDCs such as the DSCDO and NESDC have shown their commitment to developing and protecting affordable housing for residents, including artists, and having a diverse population in their neighborhoods. This policy should help to prevent displacement from gentrification should it threaten poorer residents.

CDCs have also sought to involve neighborhood residents in arts-related projects. Examples in these Cleveland neighborhoods include the ceramic tile project in Tremont, the Ballot Box Project in North Collinwood, and the Upcycle Parts Shop in St. Clair Superior. Funders like ArtPlace America have emphasized the need to involve neighborhood residents in order to avoid conflicts because of a possible fear that artists and arts-related activities may lead to an undesirable change in the neighborhood.

Recognizing that creative placemaking can be a very positive influence in neighborhood revitalization while there also be possible conflicts, cities have embraced this element of redevelopment. The Cleveland case studies include the arts-related streetscapes provided by the city in the Gordon Square district in Detroit Shoreway and the Waterloo Road district in North Collinwood. In its Connecting Cleveland 2020 plan the Cleveland Planning Commission (1990) includes a section on arts and culture. It notes the important contributions of the arts and arts institutions and organizations to the economy. In its section on policies and strategies, the plan promotes the establishment of arts districts, live-work districts, and neighborhood placemaking. The plan sees the arts as a catalyst for neighborhood development, and states that it is necessary to "encourage arts organizations to expand their outreach and publicity to the city's neighborhoods" (8a), and "encourage partnerships among community groups, arts and cultural organizations and the city" (8b).

As these Cleveland examples demonstrate, the combination of community organizations like the five CDCs profiled in this chapter, Cleveland's planning department, arts organizations like the GSAD and Waterloo Arts, and funders like CAC and philanthropic foundations can result in creative placemaking and successful art-related projects and programs that do act as a catalyst for neighborhood revitalization. By supporting arts in neighborhood revitalization, legacy cities are building on their legacy of strong arts and cultural institutions and creating an expanded arts landscape beyond their past experience. While not all neighborhoods in these cities may be suitable for creative arts placemaking, in those neighborhoods where CDCs embrace this as a catalyst for revitalization and involve the residents, cities should provide what support that they can to promote the arts.

REFERENCES

Barber, Cindy. 2004. "Culture Can Be a Catalyst for Neighborhoods Too." *Plain Dealer* (Cleveland, OH), November 28, 2004.

Chapple, Karen, and Shannon Jackson. 2010."Commentary: Arts, Neighborhoods, and Social Practices: Towards an Integrated Epistemology of Community Arts." *Journal of Planning Education and Research* 29, no. 4: 478–90.

Cleveland Planning Commission. 1990. "Connecting Cleveland 2020 Citywide Plan." http://planning.city.cleveland.oh.us/cwp/planIntro.php.

CPAC and NESDC. 2014. "When Artists Break Ground: Lessons from a Cleveland Neighborhood Partnership." https://artscleveland.org/Reference-Desk/Research-Library/neighborhoods/When-Artists-Break-Ground.

Detroit Shoreway Community Development Organization (DSCDO). 2015. "Strategic Vision 2015–2017."

Grodach, Carl, Nicole Foster, and James Murdoch. 2014. "Gentrification and the Artistic Dividend: The Role of the Arts in Neighborhood Change." *Journal of the American Planning Association* 80, no. 1: 21–35.

Hartshorn, Robert. 2016. "Art and Artists Live in Tremont." CAN Journal. http://canjournal.org/2016/11/art-artists-live-tremont/.

Jackson, Maria Rosario. 2012. *Developing Artist-Driven Spaces in Marginalized Communities: Reflections and Implications for the Field.* Washington, DC: Urban Institute.

Keating, W. Dennis. 2014. "The Gordon Square Arts District in Cleveland's Detroit Shoreway Neighborhood." Maxine Goodman Levin College of Urban Affairs, Cleveland State University, Cleveland, OH.

Keating, W. Dennis. 2016. *A Brief History of Tremont: Cleveland's Neighborhood on a Hill.* Charleston, SC: History Press.

Kotlowitz, Alex. 2009. "All Boarded Up." *New York Times Magazine*, March 4, 2009. https://www.nytimes.com/2009/03/08/magazine/08Foreclosure-t.html.

Krumholz, Norman, and Joy Roller. 2012. "Here Comes the Neighborhood: A Cleveland Success Story." *Planning* 80, no. 3: 35–38.

Litt, Steven. 2014. "The Miracle of Cleveland's Playhouse Square: How a Performing Arts Complex Helped Save Downtown and Launch a National Revival of Historic Theaters." *Plain Dealer* (Cleveland, OH), April 25, 2014.

Martens, Benno. 2016. "A Walk Through North Collinwood." *Belt Magazine*, February 24, 2016.

Playhouse Square Foundation. n.d. http://www.playhousesquare.org/about-playhouse square-main/history.

Shelterforce. 2016–2017. "Art, Culture, and Community Development." (Winter): 6–45.

Stryker, Mark. 2016. "The End, and a New Beginning for Detroit's Iconic Heidelberg Project." *Detroit Free Press*, August 14, 2016.

13

Back to the Beginning

THE RESURGENCE OF THE CUYAHOGA RIVER AND CLEVELAND

ARITREE SAMANTA AND WENDY KELLOGG

> You know I think the best cities, and the best places in the best cities, are very comfortable with their origin stories. And it is really a little bit unsettling to think that for a very long time the place from which this city grew, for most people, was not only a place which they had never visited, or participated in, or been on or in or through. And it is something that if we just recognize its uniqueness and honor its authenticity, and appreciate its origin, and not just protect it but also lift it up and tell people how wonderful it is—the good is just going to keep happening.
>
> **Local ward official, Cleveland**

In the Great Lakes region, the growth of cities is intimately linked to the many rivers that flow into the lakes. These rivers provided ecosystem resources that led to dense urban development and industrial production. Emblematic of the industrial and urban legacy of the United States, water resources were exploited to such an extent that their ecosystem services were threatened and lost (Fitzhugh and Richter 2004). River systems were altered, becoming virtual sewers for industrial discharges, and eventually Great Lakes cities turned away from these river systems, forgetting their history and relinquishing the range of ecosystem services the rivers had provided. Beginning in the 1950s, much of the Northeast and Midwest regions of the United States, including Cleveland, underwent severe deindustrialization followed by a steep urban decline, as discussed by Stephanie Ryberg-Webster and J. Rosie Tighe in the introduction to this volume. The decline reshaped people's perceptions about the environmental crisis and the ensuing environment movement (Stradling and Stradling 2008). Using rivers as industrial sewers was no longer the only benefit they sought. In this chapter we present the case of how the rebirth of the Cuyahoga River through a focus on revival of the river's legacy has supported revitalization of Cleveland. We argue that intentional transformation of the narrative of loss to an asset-based narrative was key. Based on the origin story and legacy of the river, the city, and the region, this narrative provided a novel and sustainable organizing policy and governance framework for restoration and revitalization efforts.

During the late nineteenth and early to mid-twentieth century, Cleveland, which was settled and grew along the Cuyahoga River, experienced phases of upsurge, decline, and rebirth. Through the early twentieth century, Cleveland made significant contributions to industrial America. Factories, warehouses, and docks claimed the river waterfront during the years of industrial and economic growth. Railroads crisscrossed the neighborhoods flanking the river. The rapid development of the city and the industries and commercial businesses reshaped the river through dredging, straightening, and widening. The Cuyahoga River's legacy of sustained pollution from the oil and steel industries along its banks over the course of a century often led to fires on the water, including the 1969 fire that caught the attention of the national media. Cleveland, a city known for its prosperity and industrial might, came to be associated with the burning river and, consequently, with the nation's environmental crisis and urban decline. In *Where the River Burned*, David and Richard Stradling (2015) chronicle the Cuyahoga River's long, troubled, and interwoven relationship with the city that it helped create: "In the 1960s, Cleveland suffered through racial violence, spiking crime rates, and a shrinking tax base, as the city lost jobs and population...When the Cuyahoga River caught fire in the summer of 1969, the city was at its nadir, polluted and impoverished, struggling to set a new course. The burning river became the emblem of all that was wrong with the urban environment in Cleveland and in all of industrial America."

The Cuyahoga River also became emblematic of water policy to restore rivers in the United States. The 1969 fire was a catalyst for the ongoing environmental movement and stimulated passage of the 1972 Clean Water Act (CWA). More recently, the shift in larger economic and social forces—including new competition for capital investment in service industries such as banking, insurance, education, and health care—has shaped the landscape of economic production along the Cuyahoga River (Stradling and Stradling 2015). Over time, the closure of industrial facilities reduced ongoing pollution. Deindustrialization—coupled with the regulation of direct discharges from manufacturing plants, factories, pipes, and municipal sewage plants through National Pollutant Discharge Elimination System (NPDES), a permit system for regulating point sources of pollution under the CWA—reduced river pollution. While the Cuyahoga River's condition has dramatically improved, problems remaining today include contaminated sediments and combined sewer overflows (CSOs) in the lower section of the river, continued soil erosion and nonpoint source pollution from upstream development, and habitat loss and degradation in the main stem of the river and the tributary watersheds. These issues continue to affect the ecological integrity of the watershed and have a substantial impact on the quality of life and economic redevelopment opportunities in the area. Driven by citizens that demanded better recreational, housing, public access, and clean water opportunities, the city is reclaiming its waterfront, creating opportunities for a mixed-used district that connects to multiple uses of the river. How was this trajectory shaped?

Restoring the health of the river watershed over the past five decades has resulted not only from top-down policy efforts and implementation of federal mandates but also through concerted local action. Governance of a complex urban watershed like the Cuyahoga River has required intentional shifts in practice, requiring coordinated action by a range of stakeholders including local, state, and federal government agencies, nonprofit organizations, private businesses, community leaders, and civic groups. Our research focuses on these stakeholders' experiences and the meaning of everyday practice of governance. During in-depth interviews these stakeholders shared stories about their work on the Cuyahoga River, relating personal experiences with organizational roles, policies, and decision-making, perceptions about the river, and the innovative ideas they introduced through their work that shifted the public narrative about the river. We use the metaphors that the actors use to describe the Cuyahoga River to reveal shifts in intentions, actions, and practice (Yanow 2000), and the critical ideas that were transformational to their understanding of the river. Their stories shed light on the slow and intentional transformation of governance of the Cuyahoga River watershed and Cleveland.

The Cuyahoga River watershed is a social-ecological system (SES)—an integrated and interdependent system of ecosystems and human society, functioning with reciprocal feedbacks. SESs provide ecosystem services, "the benefits human populations derive, directly or indirectly, from ecosystem functions" (Costanza et al. 1997, 253). Just as with any other SES, provision of ecosystem services is fundamental to urban watersheds, as urban areas depend on their watershed ecosystems and their components to sustain long-term conditions for ecological and human well-being (Gómez-

Baggethun and Barton 2013). Human intentionality and agency (visioning, planning, and action) play a critical role in transforming an SES if past or existing ecological, sociopolitical, and economic conditions have reduced ecosystem services to make the system untenable. We discovered that a shift in governance, based on intentional choices and novel ideas of key actors, was necessary to restore a broad range of ecosystem services and transform the Cuyahoga River SES. Using the key idea of connecting to the river as a place, actors linked the active envisioning of the revitalization of the watershed communities to the efforts to restore vital ecosystem services through the restoration of the river: "Once it gave us our identity, fueled our economy and helped launch America's industrial revolution. Then it became our burden, a symbol of environmental neglect, of a city so dysfunctional its river burned. Today, the heavily industrialized northern section of the Cuyahoga Valley and the river that runs through it could be the engine that drives the next Cleveland renaissance . . . A rebirth is in its first tentative stages, spurred by planners, environmentalists and neighborhood activists. Their numbers are small, but their fervor is unmistakable" (Litt 2000).

The aforementioned excerpt is from a five-part series—"The Forgotten Valley"—published in the *Plain Dealer*. It presents a narrative about the Cuyahoga River valley as a place, and the symbolic meaning that people and communities associate with this place, creating a regional identity or image. This image also reflects concrete realties (Shibley, Schneekloth, and Hovey 2003). For decades the deterioration of the Cuyahoga River and its watershed paralleled the surge of industrialization, followed by deindustrialization and disinvestment, in the Rust Belt. Due to the negative imagery associated with the Cuyahoga as an industrial, polluted, and burning river, and because private property flanked large areas along the riverbanks, making them inaccessible for public access, residents and communities in the area had little or no sense of belonging to the river.

In the seventeen years since the *Plain Dealer* exposé was published, the Cuyahoga River and Cleveland have undergone a major transformation. History has served as the basis for an alternative future. Key actors, including planners at the Cuyahoga County Planning Commission, officials at the Cuyahoga Valley National Park (CVNP) and Cleveland Metroparks, and advocates for the Ohio & Erie (O&E) Canalway Towpath Trail, recognized the importance of history and started reshaping the narrative, paying homage to the natural history and legacy of the Cuyahoga River and its watershed. Over time these efforts, through repetition and resonance, created a new image of the watershed and the region.

FIGURE 13.1: The Cuyahoga River watershed in northeast Ohio

HISTORICAL EVOLUTION OF THE CUYAHOGA RIVER

CUYAHOGA RIVER AND CLEVELAND: AN INTRICATE INTERCONNECTION

The Cuyahoga River has shaped the ecology, economy, and sociopolitical landscape of northeast Ohio for centuries. The lower section of the river traverses the cities of Cleveland and Akron, with the last 5.6-mile stretch of the river, a designated federal navigation channel, flowing through downtown Cleveland before draining into Lake Erie (figure 13.1). The Cuyahoga Valley National Park encompasses twenty-two miles of the river between Akron and Cleveland. While the watershed makes up less than 2 percent of Ohio's total land area, the urban areas comprising 6 percent of the watershed support 15 percent of the state's total population. Most of this population resides in the lower section of the river from Akron to Cleveland (NPS 2016).

The Cuyahoga River has a rich history. Paleo-Indian hunters became the first people of the valley thirteen thousand years ago, followed by Native American tribes that used the river for fishing and hunting, living space, and transportation for close to two thousand years. Early white settlers from Europe arrived in the valley in the 1700s as fur traders. By the turn of the nineteenth century, the Cuyahoga River was the official western boundary of the United States as part of the Northwest Territory. The area around the Cuyahoga River became part of the Connecticut Western Reserve, owned and managed by the state of Connecticut in the years after the American Revolution (Hatcher 1949). European settlers drove away the Native Americans, replacing their settlements with new villages, towns, and cities (NPS 2014; CRR 2016).

The natural drop of the river (395 feet in 38 miles) in the Cuyahoga Valley made it unsuitable for transportation. To provide a reliable system of transport, the Ohio and Erie Canal was built between 1825 and 1832, filled with water diverted from the Cuyahoga River (CCPC 1999). The Ohio and Erie Canal allowed the passage of cargo between Lake Erie and the Ohio River and connected Cleveland with the Midwest, increasing the region's prosperity by opening up new agricultural markets and trade. The completion of the railroads in the Cuyahoga Valley in 1850 further encouraged industrial development and the growth of an economy centered on trade and commerce. Population in communities along the Cuyahoga River and in Cleveland grew rapidly as the use of the river intensified. Over the nineteenth and twentieth centuries, with its access to Lake Erie, shipping, railroads, and the canal, and the growth of manufacturing facilities, the Cuyahoga River was turned into a polluted sewer.

ECOSYSTEM SERVICES OVER DECADES: A SLOW DISCONNECT WITH THE RIVER

As an SES, the Cuyahoga River provided a variety of ecosystem services that co-evolved over time with changes caused by human settlement, influence, and domination (WRI 2005). The river's four distinct life phases—Native American pre-settlement era, European settlers era, industrial era, and post-industrial era—reshaped the river's ecosystem services (see table 13.1).

Native Americans used the Cuyahoga River valley and its forested lands as provisions for food and dwelling. The densely forested areas also performed key regulating functions such as erosion control and supported a wide variety of habitats. Culturally, the river served as a connector and a trade route between the native populations and other regions.

The advent of the European settlements initiated profound changes in the Cuyahoga River watershed. The settlers originally settled in the Flats—the flat bottomland and coastal wetlands near the mouth of the river (where it enters Lake Erie), but eventually moved to higher grounds, using the Cuyahoga River and the Flats chiefly for agricultural purposes. Extensive wetlands along the main stem of the river in the Flats and in the tributary watersheds performed regulatory functions of erosion and flood control.

TABLE 13.1: Ecosystem services provided by the Cuyahoga River watershed

	Pre-settlement era	European settlers era	Industrial era	Post-industrial era
Provisioning services (food, fresh-water, wood, willow)	Fish for consumption, wildlife habitat for hunting, wood for dwelling	Animals for fur, large game, mills and dams harnessing river flow, diversion of water for Ohio and Erie Canal, agricultural use of the flats	Drinking water storage reservoirs, conduit for wastewater discharges, channelization for transportation	Native plants providing habitat for local and migratory birds, improved water quality for fishing
Regulating services (erosion and flood control, water purification, climate regulation)	Dense beech, sugar maple, hemlock forests prevented erosion and maintained water quality and supported habitat	Extensive wetlands in the flats and tributary watersheds for flood and erosion control	Development and building on wetlands and floodplains, dredging, industrial and municipal sewage pollution, erosion issues	Restoration of floodplains and wetlands, stream bank restoration, riparian buffer leading to less erosion and better flood control
Supporting and habitat services	Fish and aquatic habitat supported by healthy water, riparian areas, and forested lands	Fish and aquatic habitat supported by healthy water, riparian areas, and forested lands	Emergence of dead zones, adverse impact on fish and aquatic life, degraded terrestrial wildlife habitat	Exceptional warmwater habitat in main stem and tributaries, cold-water habitat in tributaries, return of fish, aquatic life, and native birds
Cultural services (recreation, tourism, spiritual)	Connector to other regions and tribes	Transportation resource for agriculture and trade	Transportation resource for commerce and industries, degraded aesthetics and impairments to recreation	CVNP, local and state parks, towpath trail, and river water for recreational and cultural opportunities

The topography of the valley offered opportunities for building dams to harness the power of water for sawmills and gristmills and transport of raw materials and finished products for a thriving agricultural economy via the Ohio and Erie Canal. Although the river supported provisioning services such as food, wood, and transportation, the settlers in the valley never used it as a source of drinking water. The upstream areas of the river, however, before it enters steep ravines and gorges, were designated as a public drinking water source in 1911 for the city of Akron. Construction of the mills, canal water diversions, dams, drinking water storage reservoirs, and growing population affected the flow and volume of water in the Cuyahoga River, changing its ecology and ecosystem functions over time.

The building of the railroads in 1850s supported industrialization in the Cuyahoga Valley and northeastern Ohio, leading to the demise of the canal era and the agricultural economy. To maintain smooth trade operations, the lower stretch of the oxbow river was channelized to flow straight into Lake Erie and this 5.6-mile stretch flowing through downtown Cleveland functioned as a shipping channel to the steel mills and other heavy industries. Industrialization and urban development degraded the ecosystem and ecosystem functions of the river, some of which continue to this day. Industries discharged heavy metals, oils, solvents, polychlorinated biphenyls (PCBs), and other pollutants, causing adverse impacts to aquatic life. Municipal sewers and sewage treatment plants along the river discharged high levels of biochemical oxygen demanding substances (BODs), untreated sewage, solids, ammonia, and phosphorus, resulting in the loss of the river's natural nutrient-cycling functions, the lack of dissolved oxygen in parts of the river, and an increase in algal growth in Lake Erie. A portion of the river between Akron and Cleveland was even designated as a "dead zone" due to poor water quality and the complete lack of aquatic habitat (CCPC 1999).

The channelization, annual dredging of the navigation channel, construction of steel bulkheads along the riverbanks for commercial shipping, and the total lack of riparian buffer adversely impacted the lower river habitat (CCPC 1999). Additionally, urban development on the Cuyahoga River's one-hundred-year floodplains reduced its ability to mitigate flood impacts. As suburbanization increased, development upstream increased water runoff into the tributaries. Sedimentation caused by upstream construction activities, riverbank erosion due to lack of riparian buffers and forested areas along the river, and CSOs that increase pollutants and bacteria into the river continued to affect the watershed. As a result of these actions, the river lost most of its provisioning, regulating, habitat-supporting, and cultural ecosystem functions.

By the mid-twentieth century the Cuyahoga River was highly polluted and caught on fire several times. However, cleanup of the river at the local level had started in the 1960s when local industry and municipal leaders formed the Cuyahoga River Basin Water Quality Committee and started mobilizing funds for addressing the river's pollution (Adler 2004). Some of the most notable changes resulted from passage of the Clean Water Act in 1972 and the river's designation as one of the forty-three Great Lakes Areas of Concern under the 1972 Great Lakes Water Quality Agreement between the United States and Canada. In 1974 the Cuyahoga Valley was designated a national recreation area, and later a national park (CVNP).

Several key changes—environmental regulations and their implementation, the demise of industries, and local stewardship efforts—have improved the health of the river watershed and also restored some of its ecosystem functions over the past several decades. The Cuyahoga River, though no longer a source of essential provisioning services such as food or timber, has regained some of its regulating, habitat-supporting, and cultural functions. Inclusion of native plants and grasses in replanting and restoration projects in vacant properties and along the river have led to higher quality habitats for local bird population and migratory birds, and an influx of animals to the now improved ecosystem (CCPC 1999). Within the Cuyahoga Valley National Park, the Cuyahoga River and its tributaries, creeks, and wetlands provide habitat to approximately seventy species of native fish. The national park helped in preserving numerous forested tributary watersheds, open grassy plateaus, townships, and rural communities. The upper Cuyahoga Valley is still home to small, privately owned agricultural lands that supply food to local communities and markets in the area (NPS 2013). Current and future restoration projects are planned to connect the river to the floodplains in the downstream areas and restore wetlands to minimize sedimentation and erosion effects and restore the regulating functions of the Cuyahoga River (CRR 2016).

The local movement in the greater Cleveland area to reconnect people with their natural resources played a significant role in shaping river restoration and recovery actions. Access to the river via the Towpath Trail, the natural, historic, cultural, and recreational opportunities provided by the CVNP, and the collection of city and county parks around the river and its tributaries, shifted the identity of the Cuyahoga Valley from industrial wasteland to a resource benefitting the quality of life for the residents. The extension of biking and hiking paths along the navigational section of the Cuyahoga River, resurgence of paddling and canoeing activities in the shipping channel and further upstream, and renewed birding and fishing opportunities have reshaped the landscape of the valley in recent times.

CREATING A SENSE OF PLACE AND A LOCAL IDENTITY

During the interviews, stakeholder narratives emphasized connecting with the resource, experiencing it firsthand, reflecting about what was and how it had changed over the years. An underlying theme across the various narratives was to sustainably revitalize Cleveland by restoring watershed-based ecosystem services and connecting people to place. Most of the actors concurred with one observation that "it's the element that ties our whole region together . . . and the history of where it was and where it has come is really sort of important to Cleveland and who we are."

CONNECTING DISPARATE GEOGRAPHIES AND A DISJOINTED HISTORY

For much of the past two centuries, Cuyahoga Valley residents faced a "disconnect" with the river. Stakeholders suggested that the original reason for this disconnect was that the Cuyahoga River was never a source of drinking water for the communities that flank the river, so these communities didn't particularly pay much attention to the water quality in the river or dedicate efforts toward preserving and/or restoring it. Historically, Cuyahoga Valley residents had used ponds and trucked-in water and, more recently, like the rest of Cleveland, received drinking water from Lake Erie. Since the times of the earliest settlers, the Cuyahoga River's primary use was for trade and transportation, and later for industrial purposes when it was turned into a conduit for carrying industrial waste. During the height of the industrial era in Cleveland, communities were settled along the river to get easy access to the factories, but the river itself was used almost exclusively for industrial purposes, tucked in the Cuyahoga Valley, and out of sight (Stradling and Stradling 2015). The Cuyahoga Valley was walled off with railroads and highways, landfills and garbage dumps filled creeks and ravines, and the river was treated almost as a drainage ditch (Litt 2000). A longtime watershed steward described the community attitude toward the Cuyahoga River at the time: "the Cuyahoga was just so degraded that in a sense people just gave up on it. It was kind of written off as an industrial wasteland and it was like—why even clean this thing up? People couldn't even envision the value."

This is one of the chief reasons that municipalities along the river, while involved with the management of the CVNP, were not involved with managing the Cuyahoga River itself, which flowed through the heart of the National Park. A retired National Park superintendent observed, "the municipalities, if you think about it, are sort of strangely silent about the river. They didn't in any sense *own* the river." State and federal environmental protection agencies (Ohio EPA and the federal EPA) focused their attention on the river but, by and large, general public interest was missing. The communities in the post-industrial Cuyahoga Valley were battling through poverty, struggling school systems, and high unemployment. A relationship with the natural environment wasn't really a priority; at least not at the grassroots level. This was a key policy and planning action to consider—generating public interest around the river and the valley—and the leadership at several Cleveland-area institutions did exactly that. They leveraged the notion that bringing about a transformation in perception was most important—that is, using history as a lens to look at places differently and envision what those places, and the river, could become.

Two key local events in the late 1980s–early 1990s started shaping broad changes in the Cuyahoga Valley. First was a change in the leadership of the Cuyahoga Valley National Park. The new National Park superintendent deliberately sought to consolidate the patchwork of pieces and parcels of land that were owned by the park in the valley. The now-retired CVNP superintendent gave an account of his efforts to evoke public interest about the river: "I made the statement to the Akron Beacon Journal that the Cuyahoga River is a river that had no friends, and I did that purposely. It was intended to be a provocative statement. It had exactly the right effect, because there were people that read that article . . . and the people stepped up and said that the river does have friends."

The second key event was the initiative to support and fund the Towpath Trail along the old Ohio and Erie Canal. Proponents of the Towpath Trail saw it as a way to address the "geographic amnesia" of the communities and to focus attention to the natural armature of the Cuyahoga River and Valley around which Cleveland had grown. Along with the community leaders, staff at the CVNP and the Cuyahoga County Planning Commission (CCPC) also advocated for the creation of the Towpath Trail. The Towpath Trail would serve as a physical connector between the Cuyahoga Valley National Park and downtown Cleveland, and a metaphorical and cultural connector between the current public awareness (or lack thereof) to the history of the valley. As the Towpath Trail developed, people went from having no access to a very intimate access to the Cuyahoga River. Though the river wasn't swimmable yet (due to biological impairments), people could access and view it from the Towpath Trail.

Planners at the CCPC, a regional planning entity, coined the concept of the North Cuyahoga Valley Corridor in a study that first framed the valley as a unified entity. A retired CCPC deputy director recalled: "Well, I said it really makes a lot of sense because right now [in the late 1980s] there is really no destination. It [the National Park] was National Recreation Area then, it was heavily visited, but mostly people drove through it. . . . The valley was always some place to cross, so we tried to make it a destination . . . to create a much bigger destination than just a National Park."

Over the past two decades Cleveland Metroparks, a regional special district, has played a key role in providing access to the Cuyahoga River and increasing recreational opportunities in and around it. Dam removals in the middle section of the river have not only improved water quality but have also extended canoeing opportunities on a longer stretch of the river.

Cleveland Metroparks created a new park along the riverbank in the Flats, offering canoe and kayak rentals in partnership with a local rowing club. More recently, local leadership and community efforts facilitated other revitalization efforts, including entertainment and residential development in the Flats. A key local government official involved in these efforts attributed the difference in the recent revitalization efforts compared with the previous history of development in the Flats to a fundamental shift in the stakeholders' understanding—that a place should be appreciated for what it is. That the "messy vitality" and "chaos" of the Flats shouldn't be controlled, but appreciated, and revitalization efforts should be geared around it. A retired CCPC planner summarizes the various actions assumed under the placemaking efforts in the Cuyahoga Valley as: "You know all these things are coming together in a much more sustainable way. The improvement of the river as a destination, Metropark's commitment to Rivergate and Wendy Park, and Scranton Flats; these are public spaces we never had before. There was no access to the river whatsoever, and now there is. Now people can fish and row, they can't swim, but they can do these other things . . . people can use trails, they can use water taxis, and it is going to be awesome."

CREATING A NEW PARTICIPATORY GOVERNANCE ENVIRONMENT

The Cuyahoga River Flats had been dominated by industrial and commercial land uses for 150 years. In terms of residential use, Irish laborers who built the Ohio and Erie Canal had settled the banks, and a few areas of public housing were built during the Great Depression. In the 1990s, after decades of primarily industrial land use, the Flats saw a brief period of development as an entertainment district that included clubs, pubs, and restaurants. During these brief periods of development the area still lacked a critical mass of residents needed to sustain a thriving city neighborhood. A local ward official describes this period: "In some ways it was considered to be too dirty or too dangerous that the only uses that would have been appropriate were alcohol establishments or places like adult entertainment . . . You know it is kind of almost like a human dumping ground with what society doesn't consider being important. And yet those liquor establishments eventually closed."

Eventually, stakeholders realized that the traditional institutional form of governance was limiting the scope of management actions required to revitalize downtown Cleveland. A local elected official explained the difficulty in transforming the function of the Flats because the traditional institutional set up in the area had "artificially instigate[d] one sector [industry] over another," reducing the diversity and the related benefits that might accrue to the area. The institutional set up in the Flats consisted of the Flats Oxbow Community Development Corporation (Flats Oxbow CDC). CDCs are nonprofit community-based organizations whose typical role is to revitalize low-income, underserved neighborhoods. CDCs in Cleveland, by the nature of their constitution, history of work, and continued public investment (funded by the mayor and the city council) exert significant influence. The Flats Oxbow CDC was formed with predominant representation from industrial and commercial entities on its organizational board. Its purpose was to orient the management of the Flats to support industrial interests, and for years Flats Oxbow CDC members discouraged the presence of housing and recreational activities in the Flats. Such a singular view of the use of the river and the Flats was seen as inherently unsustainable to stakeholders focusing on long-term sustainability of the Cuyahoga River and Cleveland. To overcome this institutional barrier, key government agency, political, and nonprofit leadership proactively engaged in designing a fundamentally different and innovative governance form. The slow transformation of the Flats into a thriving multiuse region in recent times can be attributed to this transformation in governance of the Flats, one that adopted expansion of the vision of placemaking and revitalization based on a broader set of restored ecosystem services.

The local ward leadership, backed up with support from local communities and agencies such as the Cuyahoga County Planning Commission, embarked on an "intentional process" to create an entirely different governance form. They lobbied Cleveland's mayor and city council to defund the Flats Oxbow CDC organization. Their main argument was that improving the river and the Flats hinged on changing the framing of the use of the Cuyahoga River and the Flats from single to multiple, and creating an institutional entity that would facilitate such uses. A ward official explained: "we started changing the direction of the neighborhood by not just making it a place where people did their industrial work, but a place where people wanted to enjoy, they wanted to walk through, they wanted to run through, they wanted to row through."

In contrast to the operation of the Flats Oxbow CDC, which had sustained a nonparticipatory "community development" process, the key actors now focused on a grounds-up democratic process in a collaborative format. The ward officials conducted public meetings and received overwhelming participation and support from local community members, and input from a broader range of stakeholders, including local neighborhood residents, navigation channel rowers, bicyclists, commercial truck drivers, salt mine workers, industrial workers, restaurant owners, and other new and potential businesses. Based on the input from these stakeholders, in

2012 Flats Forward was formed as the new nonprofit CDC for the area. Representatives from commercial, residential, recreational, industrial, maritime, and entertainment formed the organization's board. The mission of Flats Forward is to facilitate collaboration among various stakeholders and interest groups, for which the organization provides coordination support—an example of the type of collaboration that Rubado described in chapter 1.

Transforming the governance through such an intentional intervention emerged from two critical shifts in understanding among the key political leadership. The first was honoring the authenticity of the place, and leveraging that for watershed and regional planning and management. A local elected leader described this as:

> [A] critical mistake that people make in thinking that the craziness, the chaos, the disorder, the complete diversity of uses in the Flats—are things that we want to control—[rather] it is what makes people want to go there. When I go on those trails, and I hear the train and I hear those ships, and there is the heron, and the trucks are going by, and there are people living there. That is why people want to be there. They do not want to be in a gated community in some ex-urban complex . . . on a land that used to be a farm, living in a McMansion and watching TV. The Flats are the opposite of that.

The second critical shift was in the form of recognition within the political leadership that building human capital is key for transformation. Offering forums for good communication helps build human capital so that people can assist each other's work and collaborate. Circumstances change, but nurturing diversity and facilitating partnerships between various groups to enhance human and social capacity is critical for building governance capacity.

URBAN RESURGENCE: CONNECTING PEOPLE WITH ORIGIN STORIES AND A WAY FORWARD

An analysis of the metaphorical language used by the actors revealed the critical ideas that were transformational, including changing the narrative associated with the Cuyahoga River and its watershed. Actors used the metaphor of "controlled chaos" rather than "controlling the craziness, chaos, and disorder" to describe the desired state for the Flats. Confronting commonly accepted interpretations of events, places, people, and culture deepened knowledge and understanding of the river's context; uncovering potential pathways and strategies for recognizing what could be different (Schneekloth and Shibley 2005). Stakeholders reframed the Cuyahoga River as a regional asset, creating the image of the Cuyahoga Valley as a unified entity and a destination, while designing programs and initiatives to facilitate public access and raise public awareness about the resource, and designing a new governance mechanism to leverage the inherent vitality of the river and its flats. This narrative and response honors the authenticity of the river as a place, connecting the river to the city and its history.

There are broader implications to the shift in narrative. By focusing on the Cuyahoga River as a place, the stakeholders have created a more holistic view of the river and of the city, intertwining stories of the built form, natural resources, and governance. While not using the language, people in Cleveland now think of the Cuyahoga River as an SES—a complex system of human and natural elements that draws on the legacy of the city to support a different future. The multiple perspectives have embedded multiple uses that will serve as the basis of continued redevelopment on land and continued improvements to the river itself.

Deliberately reshaping the narrative of the river changed the way management has been carried out. The metaphors of the stakeholders shaped the way they understood how local-, state-, and federal-level policies and programs could be used to change the river and its ecosystem services and who or what organizations were most appropriate to create and lead implementation of those policies. As we have described, the shift in governance of the Cuyahoga River watershed occurred because policies meant many things to many actors, each based on their sometimes overlapping, and sometimes distinct interpretations. It is this mix that ultimately supports adaptation of governance over time to match and respond to the complexity of the river ecosystem.

On any given summer evening, rowers and kayakers dot the Cuyahoga River, accommodating the movement of lake freighters on their way to the steel mills and other manufacturing areas upstream, both serving as inspiration for the patrons at many restaurants now lining the river and the residents who can now come down to the river to play. Each year more people connect to the Cuyahoga River and the land along its banks, creating the way forward for collaborative governance that will continue to restore the river and its ecosystem services.

REFERENCES

Adler, Jonathan H. 2004. "Fable of Federal Environmental Regulation: Reconsidering the Federal Role in Environment Protection." *Case Western Reserve Law Review* 55, no. 1: 93–113.

Costanza, Robert, et al. 1997. "The Value of the World's Ecosystem Services and Natural Capital." *Nature* 387, no. 6630: 253–60.

Cuyahoga County Planning Commission (CCPC). 1999. "Linking the Corridor: A

Plan for the Towpath Trail in the North Cuyahoga Valley." http://publicworks.cuyahogacounty.us/pdf_engineer/en-US/towpath/LinkingCorridor.pdf.

Cuyahoga River Restoration (CRR). 2016. http://www.cuyahogariver.org/.

Ellis, William D. 1985. *The Cuyahoga*. Dayton, OH: Landfall Press.

Fitzhugh, Thomas W., and Brian D. Richter. 2004. "Quenching Urban Thirst: Growing Cities and Their Impacts on Freshwater Ecosystems." *Bioscience* 54, no. 8: 741–54.

Gómez-Baggethun, Erik, and David N. Barton. 2013. "Classifying and Valuing Ecosystem Services for Urban Planning." *Ecological Economics* 86: 235–45.

National Park Service (NPS). 2013. "Foundation Document: Cuyahoga Valley National Park, Ohio." https://www.nps.gov/cuva/learn/management/upload/Foundation-Document-CUVA-July-2013-for-web.pdf.

National Park Service (NPS). 2014. "Cuyahoga River Recovers." https://www.nps.gov/cuva/planyourvisit/upload/CuyahogaRiver6 percent20final.pdf.

National Park Service (NPS). 2016. "Cuyahoga Valley: Watersheds." https://www.nps.gov/cuva/learn/nature/watersheds.htm.

Schneekloth, Lynda H., and Robert G. Shibley. 2005. "Imagine Niagara." *Journal of Canadian Studies* 39, no. 3: 105–20.

Shibley, Robert G., Lynda H. Schneekloth, and Bradshaw Hovey. 2003. "Constituting the Public Realm of a Region: Placemaking in the Bi-National Niagaras." *Journal of Architectural Education* 57, no. 1: 28–42.

Stradling, David, and Richard Stradling. 2008. "Perceptions of the Burning River: Deindustrialization and Cleveland's Cuyahoga River." *Environmental History* 13, no. 3: 515–35.

Stradling, David, and Richard Stradling. 2015. *Where the River Burned: Carl Stokes and the Struggle to Save Cleveland*. Ithaca, NY: Cornell University Press.

World Resources Institute (WRI). 2005. *Millennium Ecosystem Assessment: Ecosystems and Human Well-being: Synthesis*. Washington, DC: Island Press.

Yanow, Dvora. 2000. *Conducting Interpretive Policy Analysis*. Thousand Oaks, CA: SAGE.

14

Legacy Cities and Their Regions

HUNTER MORRISON AND MARK SALLING

Legacy cities do not stand alone. They each exist within the context of their metropolitan region and its economy. Their assets and liabilities cannot be seen as separate and apart from those of their region and of the adjacent suburbs, small towns, and rural townships which, taken together, we define as their *hinterland*.

The important connection between legacy cities and their metropolitan areas is well recognized. By definition, they have "a high degree of social and economic integration among their parts" (US Census 2017). Scholars of legacy cities have noted the importance of understanding the nature of the social and economic connections between these cities and their metropolitan regions. Several have developed metric typologies to better describe and analyze that relationship (Katz 2006; Vey 2007; Todorovich and Hagler 2009; Hill et al. 2012, 2013).

Hill et al. have written that long-term metropolitan growth rates are strongly associated with the demographic and economic trajectories of their central city: "If the entire region is experiencing economic decline, then the region's core city is virtually certain to be doing so, and the city population is likely to decline as well" (Hill et al. 2012, 39).

Likewise, Mallach and Brachman (2013) have noted both the importance and the complexity of legacy city/metro relationships: "Experts have recognized that there is a symbiotic relationship between legacy cities and their regions, but it is particularly complex in places where the urban/suburban economic imbalance exists and the vehicles for fostering regionalism are unclear or ineffective" (3).

Katz (2006) emphasizes the importance of understanding the reciprocal nature of the relationship between a legacy city and its region and argues that population and economic decline at the metropolitan scale exacerbates the economic challenges faced by legacy cities, stating that "a strong city depends on a strong metropolitan region and the ability to capture a critical share of the metro economy." He identified fifty-nine "weak market cities," a categorization roughly similar, although not identical, to legacy cities, and found that two-thirds (thirty-nine) were located in weak-market metropolitan areas. Other research characterizing legacy cities has generally found a similar pattern (Vey 2007; Todorovich and Hagler 2009).

Understanding the symbiotic relationship between individual legacy cities and their respective metropolitan areas is critical to developing effective tools and strategies for these cities. In order to better understand this relationship, we rely on the list of forty-eight legacy cities identified by the Legacy Cities Partnership as "cities [that] have lost between 20–70% of residents since their mid-century population peak, but are still vibrant, mid-sized cities home to around 50,000 to 1.5 million people each" (Legacy Cities Partnership 2017). The Legacy Cities Partnership identified these cities using data current as of 2010. We add 2015 population estimates to this analysis and exclude two from the list—Louisville, Kentucky, and Macon, Georgia—because they merged with their counties since the 2010 US Census, resulting in very substantial population growth.[1] We assign each of the remaining forty-six legacy cities to their respective metropolitan statistical area (MSA) and label these MSAs *legacy metros*.

Legacy cities are concentrated in the Northeast and Great Lakes "megaregions"—two large geographic regions delineated by America 2050, a partnership established by the Lincoln Institute of Land Policy and the Regional Plan Association to study the nation's long-term settlement patterns (Regional Plan Association 2017).[2] Forty-three (93 percent) of the nation's legacy cities can be found in these two megaregions.

We note that there are significant differences in the demographic trajectories of the Northeast and Great Lakes legacy cities and argue that these differences call for the development of tools and strategies that take more fully into account the unique trajectories of the legacy cities and metros found in each megaregion. Simply put, what works in Philadelphia, Providence, or Camden may not be equally effective in Cleveland, Youngstown, or Flint.

Overall, sixteen states and the District of Columbia have legacy cities. Over half (twenty-four of forty-six) are found in four historically industrial states: New York (seven), Ohio (seven), Pennsylvania (five), and Michigan (five). Legacy cities, as a group, experienced population decline between 1950 and 2000. Between 2000 and 2015 sixteen legacy cities, most of which are concentrated in the Northeast, experienced population growth.[3] The decline in aggregate population of the forty-six legacy cities was most precipitous between 1970 and 1980 (15.4 percent). The rate of decline moderated between 1980 and 2010 and ranged between 6.2 percent and 7.6 percent during those decades. Most legacy cities continued to decline in population between 2010 and 2015. Due to economic recovery in a handful of legacy cities concentrated in the Northeast, the collective population of the forty-six cities grew slightly, by 1.4 percent, from 2010 to 2015.

A similar pattern emerges when we examine the population of legacy cities in relation to their larger metropolitan areas. As a group, legacy cities constituted a smaller percentage of their metropolitan area's population in 2015 than they did in the forty-five years prior. In 1970 the forty-six legacy cities, taken together, constituted almost 15 percent of total legacy metro population; by 2015 they constituted less than 9 percent. Even legacy cities that have experienced recent population growth continue to lose demographic market share to their faster growing suburban hinterlands. The long-term demographic decline of legacy cities relative to their hinterlands suggests that these cities have lost much of their regional preeminence, both economic and political, within their respective regions, and face an increasingly difficult challenge of competing with neighboring communities for state and federal funds to meet their needs.

Figure 14.1 shows how the population of legacy cities in these two megaregions compares over the last forty-five years (1970–2015). It also shows how legacy cities in each megaregion have fared relative to their respective MSAs. Legacy metros in both of these megaregions began to experience population decline between 1970 and 1980. Since 1980, however, the trajectories of the legacy metros in these two megaregions have diverged. Northeast legacy metros, as a group, have experienced decade-on-decade population growth since 1980. Great Lakes legacy metros, in contrast, continued to experience population decline between 1980 and 1990, experienced a modest increase between 1990 and 2000, and then stagnated.

Both Northeast and Great Lakes legacy cities have declined in importance relative to their metros and, though both show some stabilization in recent years, the rate of population decline has been steeper in the Great Lakes than in the Northeast megaregion. While legacy cities, as a group, are no longer seeing the rapid suburbanization that occurred between 1970 and 1990, they will continue to experience its lasting impact at they face relentless competition with their hinterland communities for jobs, households, tax revenues, and funding from state and federal sources.

The pattern of divergent trajectories holds true when we look at the lega-

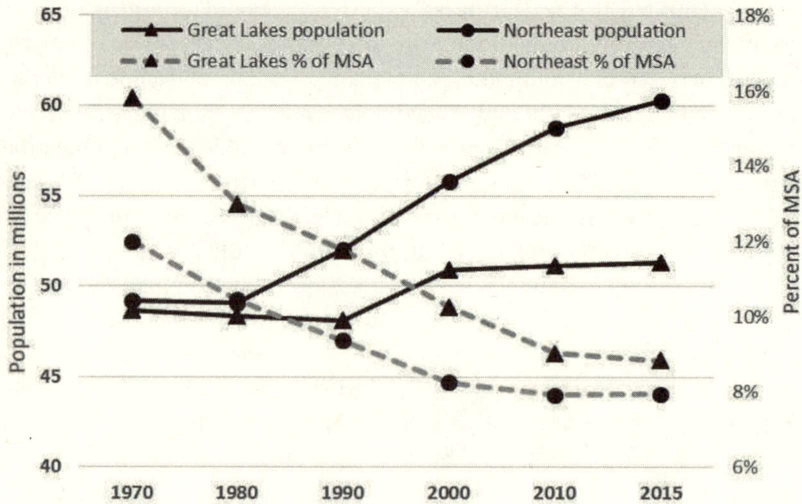

FIGURE 14.1: Legacy city population and legacy city percentage of MSA population by megaregion

cy cities in each megaregion: most of the legacy cities that experienced continued population loss are located in the Great Lakes megaregion. Northeast legacy cities as a whole are faring better demographically than inland cities. Except for Minneapolis and Milwaukee, all of the legacy cities that have experienced multi-decade population growth are found in the Northeast megaregion.

These findings sound a cautionary note for those seeking to develop planning and policy strategies to address the needs of America's legacy cities: legacy city regeneration strategies that rely on improving a city's "ability to capture a critical share of the metro economy" (Katz 2006) may not be appropriate for cities located in legacy metros that are experiencing little or no growth. For legacy cities located in these metros, the "zero-sum game" described by Tighe and Ryberg-Webster in the introduction to this volume is stark. These cities do not have the opportunity to compete for a larger market share of a growing metropolitan pool of jobs and households. They must, instead, fight with their neighbors for a market share in a metropolitan market that is growing modestly, if at all.

USING SCENARIO PLANNING TO OVERCOME JURISDICTIONAL FRAGMENTATION

There is broad consensus among scholars on the importance of the legacy city/legacy metro relationship (Katz 2006; Vey 2007, Mallach and Brachman 2012). There is far less consensus on the appropriate means to strengthen that relationship. As Mallach and Brachman (2013) note: "While practitioners and policy makers agree that bolstering regions is critical to any economic revitalization strategy, there is less agreement over how to carry out a successful regional strategy" (3). Some authors have emphasized the need for states to remove "the artificial barriers that too often set cities and suburbs in opposition to one another and, instead, work toward bolstering opportunities in, and the marketability of their regions as a whole" (Vey 2007, 67). Some have emphasized action at the local level, stressing the importance of fostering intergovernmental collaboration (see chap. 1) and fostering public/private partnerships (Voinovich 2017). Finally, others have identified specific policies that legacy cities and their metros can put in place to improve intergovernmental collaboration and operational efficiency (Mallach and Brachman 2013).

Regardless of whether the nexus of policymaking is local, state, or federal, legacy city revitalization strategies must confront the challenge of implementing these policies in the complex, fragmented, and often competitive world of multijurisdictional local government. Collaboration between legacy cities and the communities in their hinterland is made immensely more difficult by the political challenge of achieving consensus between elected officials representing the cacophonous ensemble of counties, municipalities, townships, school districts, and special taxing districts that compete with each other for jobs, population and tax revenues within a single regional economy. Finally, well-intentioned efforts to encourage regional collaboration may be frustrated by long-standing suspicion or animosity between officials representing the interests of legacy cities and those representing the interests of hinterland communities. As Rubado noted in chapter 1: "Citizens and leaders in suburban municipalities and counties often see the struggling central city as a liability and fear the potential effects of inter-municipal partnerships with struggling cities or more dramatic government reorganization, such as city-county consolidations or mergers." Jurisdictional fragmentation is one of the six "legacies of legacy cities" identified by Tighe and Ryberg-Webster in the introduction to this volume. They note that: "Legacy cities, and their associated metropolitan regions, suffer from a high degree of jurisdictional fragmentation and suburban sprawl without overall growth . . . resulting in high infrastructure and other costs relative to population size and dwindling revenues to support maintenance and service provision."

Confronting the reality of jurisdictional fragmentation is critical to the success of any effort intended to reverse the decades-long decline of the nation's legacy cities. This is nowhere truer than in the Great Lakes metro areas, where employment and population have been stagnant or declining for several decades, and where hinterlands are increasingly facing their own fiscal challenges and may be less inclined to share strategies for mutual survival with their central cities unless they come to see and understand their interconnectedness.

Great Lakes legacy cities, unlike their northeastern counterparts, cannot rely upon growing metropolitan economies to support their recovery. The anemic metropolitan growth rates found in most Great Lakes legacy metros translates to anemic growth in infrastructure dollars and other tax-supported resources available to meet the needs of the established legacy cities, adjacent suburbs at the center, and the newly developed communities at the periphery of these metros. This scarcity of regional resources reinforces the zero-sum game that Tighe and Ryberg-Webster describe in the introduction to this volume.

Successfully navigating the complex and often adversarial relationships between a legacy city and its suburban hinterlands requires the application of tools that will enable elected and appointed officials from all segments of the metropolitan region to visualize the urban/suburban codependences at work within the larger regional economy, and to more accurately measure the impact of alternative development policies on both the legacy city and its hinterland communities. Such tools should support the efforts of officials to collaborate across jurisdictional boundaries and, over time, replace zero-sum thinking with win-win policies and practices that benefit city and suburb alike.

GIS-based visualization and scenario planning is one such tool. The use of geographic information systems (GIS) for scenario planning in the context of regional or metropolitan planning provides a data-driven decision support system for the analysis and evaluation of different assumptions and goals concerning regional and local development. It is a tool for articulating the likely outcomes of implementing public policies and funding priorities.

The use of scenario planning in rapidly growing regions demonstrates the power of this tool and its ability to enable decision-makers at the local and state level to analyze current conditions, evaluate alternative development scenarios, and visualize the impact of each scenario on both the physical environment and the fiscal health of their region including its multiplicity of local jurisdictions. After examining regional planning processes used to develop framework plans for Portland, Salt Lake City, Sacramento, Denver, Chicago, and Washington, DC, Knapp and Lewis (2011) concluded that: "The critical role of GIS cannot be overstated. While plan maps for metropolitan areas have been produced since the 1930s, the ability of GIS to conduct analysis at the metropolitan scale and to illustrate the results of such analyses substantially increased the planners' ability to engage the public" (204).

While scenario planning is a well-established and highly regarded planning tool for use in high-growth metropolitan regions, its use in slow growth legacy metropolitan regions is rare. By modifying this tool to accurately model the economic and demographic trends found in legacy cities and metros, scenario planning can help these cities and their regions overcome jurisdictional fragmentation and collaborate more effectively in the identification of win-win strategies for investing limited tax dollars.

Increasingly powerful GIS-based scenario planning systems, both open-source and proprietary, offer an alternative to traditional governance-based analysis of city/metro relationships. Through the manipulation of large sets of parcel-based land information and community-based fiscal and environmental data, these tools can be used to identify multiple alternative development scenarios and evaluate their impact on a community's environmental quality of life and fiscal health.

Operating in or near real time, scenario visualization combined with fiscal impact analysis can give local public officials a clearer understanding of their community's relationship to the metropolitan region and the consequences, both environmental and financial, of alternative regional development patterns and policies. Such information is critical if legacy cities are to make the political case to other communities within their metros that regional collaboration will have community-specific benefits sufficient to overcome substantial obstacles of past practice and existing governmental structures.

The use of GIS in planning is not new, but its importance and use has accelerated since the development of several technological advances—relatively inexpensive and powerful computing of stand-alone personal computer and multiuser enterprise systems; the development of large, publicly available databases, together with the much reduced cost of data storage; the progression of more powerful and functional software for managing and using geographic information; the rapid growth in academic and business education and training of GIS specialists and professionals; and, of course, the growth of the internet and the accommodation of software and data providers to this data- and application-sharing vehicle. Interactive GIS software can also facilitate the process of public participation in the planning exercise.

Historically, GIS-based scenario planning can be traced to the land-use suitability analyses initiated after Ian McHarg's landmark book, *Design with Nature* (1969), together with the advances seen in computing in the 1980s and 1990s. The use of computers to assist in selectively overlaying and combining attributes of different transportation, environmental, demographic, land use, and socioeconomic geographic distributions, given assumptions about economic and demographic change and exiting constraints and policies, enabled prediction of future land development. When alternative policy is introduced, geographically new predictions of the future are possible.

Not only has GIS software added functionalities and become easier to use at the same time, there are more highly customized applications built on top of (as extension to) standard GIS software systems. Some are shared in the public domain and others are proprietary products developed and/or used by consultants. For example, the Federal Highway Administration offers the Tool Kit for Integrating Land Use and Transportation Decision-Making, which provides guidelines and case studies using several software platforms that help assess the relationship between transportation, land use, and economic development to assist metropolitan planning organizations (MPOs) in their transportation planning (US Department of Transportation 2017). GIS-based scenario-planning systems also help assess factors such as land consumption, water and sewer demands, and public expenditures. Each such system of tools is designed to address a specific set of questions and issues, and use specific sets of data and assumptions.

There are several time-tested GIS-based scenario-planning systems available for use by legacy cities and their metros. Regardless of which system is selected, these tools offer a new approach to regional planning, one that takes into account the codependent relationships among central cities and their hinterlands and allows for spatial variation in assets, liabilities, and applied policies to change the physical, socioeconomic, and political environments in a region and its constituent communities.

THE APPLICATION OF SCENARIO PLANNING IN NORTHEAST OHIO LEGACY CITIES AND METROS

Vibrant NEO 2040, a regional vision and policy framework for northeast Ohio, offers a robust case study of GIS-based scenario planning and its use in the planning of legacy cities and metros. Developed by the Northeast Ohio Sustainable Communities Consortium (NEOSCC), Vibrant NEO 2040 provides a framework for long-range planning in a highly fragmented, jurisdictionally complex region that is roughly the physical size and population of the state of Connecticut (Northeast Ohio Sustainable Communities Consortium 2017).

The NEOSCC is a nonprofit partnership established by northeast Ohio's five intergovernmental planning agencies to address the long-term (twenty-five-year) future of the twelve-county region within which they are collectively responsible for long-range transportation, environmental, and economic development planning.[4] The NEOSCC received a $4.25 million Sustainable Communities Regional Planning Grant in fiscal year 2010 from the federal Partnership for Sustainable Communities to develop a "regional sustainability plan" for northeast Ohio (US Department of Housing and Urban Development 2017). This federal funding was matched by local cash and in-kind services, totaling over $3 million. The Partnership is a multiyear collaboration between the US Department of Housing and Urban Development, the US Department of Transportation, and the US Environmental Protection Agency.[5]

Developing a long-range regional vision for northeast Ohio required that the Consortium confront the "wicked problem" of achieving broad consensus about the shared future of a shrinking urbanized region with five intergovernmental planning agencies, four legacy cities (Cleveland, Akron, Canton, and Youngstown), twelve counties, and over seven hundred municipalities, townships, and other taxing districts. To identify a win-win policy framework for the region, the NEOSCC used a free and open-source GIS-based scenario-planning tool called Envision Tomorrow (ET), which links spreadsheets with Esri's ArcGIS software platform. Envision Tomorrow "allows users to analyze how their community's current growth pattern and future decisions impacting growth will impact a range of measures from public health, fiscal resiliency and environmental sustainability" (Fregonese Associates 2017). It includes both scenario design and fiscal analysis tools. The analysis tools help to analyze aspects of the current community using commonly accessible GIS data, such as tax assessor parcel and census data.

The NEOSCC and its consulting team modified Envision Tomorrow to address the conditions of modest long-term job and population growth found in northeast Ohio.[6] The team developed a spreadsheet of region-specific building types and their physical and financial attributes, and another spreadsheet of twenty-five development types, falling into categories such as residential, office/industrial, retail, mixed-use, institutional/public, protected open space, abandoned/vacant, and residential.

Geospatial datasets included: (1) a parcel-level database with characteristics of the properties, including land use, zoning, and tax and assessment values; (2) census blocks, block groups, and tracts with associated population and socioeconomic data; (3) existing and planned transportation and utility infrastructure layers; (4) environmental layers, including slope, water features, parks and open space, FEMA one-hundred-year floodplains, soil quality, and brownfields; and (5) miscellaneous other layers. Some of these data were used as development constraints or to determine risk of abandonment, conservation attractiveness, and housing demand. Others were used to describe existing development patterns. The four legacy cities in the planning region were identified as a discrete "place type," along with the region's first- and second-ring suburbs, outer-ring suburbs, established cities and towns, and rural townships.

The scenario-painting tool calls on users to interactively "paint" alternative future development scenarios on the landscape. The spreadsheets and the inputs from painting various development types are dynamically linked to the map and GIS data, and alternative scenarios are compared in real time using outcome measures. Thus, the impacts of policies, development decisions, and current growth trends were evaluated, and the system was applied at a variety of geographic scales, including metropolitan and larger regions, such as northeast Ohio.

Metric outcomes in charts and graphs were generated automatically from these alternative visions of future landscapes so that the participants could evaluate the impacts of their inputs. The ET outputs included land conservation, employment and population, housing vacancy and abandonment, and building permits. The ET fiscal-impact tool projected local government revenues and expenditures and estimated infrastructure capital and maintenance costs. The resulting GIS maps showed areas of abandonment and new development based on the existing development trends and three alternative development scenarios.

Public participation was solicited from concerned citizens and local experts in meetings at several locations around the region. Participants were asked to help paint different development types into a scenario layer in the first round of meetings; evaluate the results of comparing the existing trend with the three alternative development scenarios in second round; and review draft policy recommendations in the third. Additional input was solicited though statistically based telephone surveys and the development of an innovative interactive planning game, *Imagine MY NEO*, a web-based open-source engagement tool based on the Crowd Gauge platform. *Imagine MY NEO* enabled users to participate in the planning process online or at the public meetings convened throughout the region. Over six thousand people—representing proportionally each of the twelve counties—participated actively in developing Vibrant NEO 2040.

Four alternate development scenarios were identified and analyzed (figure 14.2):

- *Trend*: The region's population grows at its current rate and the region maintains its outward-oriented land development patterns;
- *Grow the Same*: The region's population grows at the national rate and the region maintains its current land development patterns;

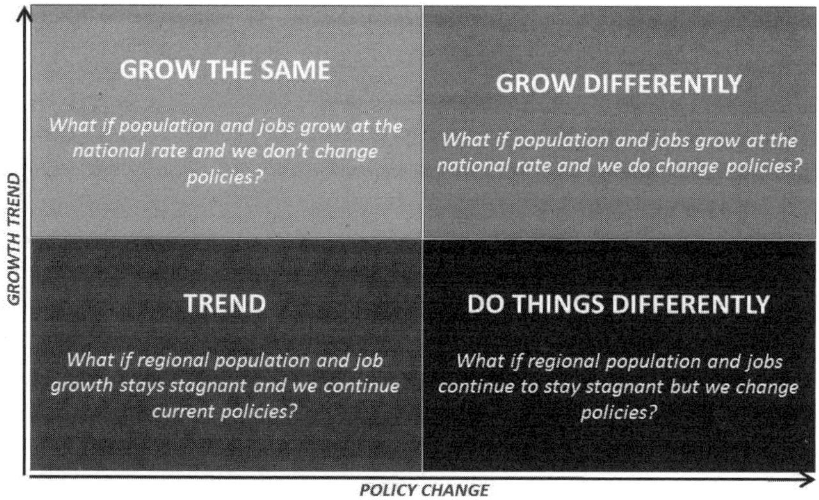

FIGURE 14.2: Alternative development scenarios

- *Do Things Differently*: The region's population grows at its current rate and the region adopts policies that favor development on sites with established infrastructure networks; and
- *Grow Differently*: The region's population grows at the national rate and the region adopts policies that favor development on sites with established infrastructure networks.

Forecasts for 2040 population, employment, and households were developed for each scenario. The impacts of each scenario on the region's housing market, transportation network, and environment were determined as was the impact of each scenario on the fiscal health of the region as a whole and of each of the region's twelve counties and their constituent municipalities, townships, and other taxing districts.

While the scenarios demonstrated a range of impacts, the starkest and most powerful contrast was found in the difference in fiscal impacts of the two low-growth scenarios: *trend* and *do things differently*. The *trend* analysis suggested that the twelve-county region and each of its counties will experience significant and persistent fiscal stress if the region's current pattern of outward development continues. In contrast, *do things differently* suggests that the region as a whole and all of its counties will benefit fiscally from a regional development pattern that emphasizes investment in established communities and limits outward expansion of the region's infrastructure networks. The twelve-county region experienced a 44 percent improvement in the ratio of revenues to expenditures, while its individual counties experienced improvements ranging from 8.8 percent to 78.6 percent. No county was worse off fiscally by "doing things differently."

Community-level development and abandonment trends were mapped for each of the four scenarios and the communities that are likely to experience significant change during the plan period were identified. These communities were aggreaged into three discrete "areas," and policy recommendations were developed for each:

- *Asset Risk Areas*: These neighborhoods and communities experienced high rates of vacancy and extensive abandonment between 1990 and 2010. *Asset risk areas* are principally located in the region's legacy cities. The *trend* scenario suggests that, in the absence of significant reinvestsment, these areas are likely to continue to experience widespread abandonment, placing further fiscal stress on these cities.
- *Strategic Investment Areas*: These neighborhoods and communities showed increasing rates of vacancy and abandonment between 1990 and 2010. *Strategic investment areas* are principally located in the newest neighborhoods and oldest suburbs of the region's legacy cities. Though threatended by growing vacancy and abandonment, these cities and neighborhoods retain assets with which they can compete within their metros for firms and households. The *Trend* scenario suggests that, in the absence of effective code enforcement and carefully targeted reinvestment, many *strategic investment areas* are likely to transition to *asset risk areas* in the future.
- *Cost Risk Area*: These areas are typically undeveloped properties located at the edges of the region's urbanized areas. These are likely to be developed at a low density, requiring the extension of existing infrastructure networks—the construction of schools, libraries, and retail centers—and the provision of police, fire, and other public sevices. The *trend* scenario suggests that, in the absence of changes in local development practices to constrain the impacts of outward expansion, *Cost risk areas* are likely to continue to expand, placing fiscal stress on the communities experiencing this additional low-density development.

Information was presented for each metro and county as well as for the region as a whole. This disaggregation of information allowed public officials in each metro and county to see the impacts of each alternative scenario on their community within the context of the larger region.

Unprecedented in its scope and the breadth of its analysis, Vibrant NEO

2040's scenario plans give northeast Ohio's legacy cities a data-driven and visually engaging way to understand the dynamic nature of the relationship between legacy cities and their metros. It supports collaboration between legacy cities and their hinterland communities by enabling them to identify win-win solutions to their mutual challenges. By rigorously modeling the impacts of alternative development scenarios, Vibrant NEO 2040 scenario planning makes a compelling case for the region to invest in its established communities and in the existing infrastructure networks that support them.

SUMMARY AND CONCLUSIONS

Vibrant NEO 2040 is a pioneering application of GIS-based scenario planning to legacy cities and their respective metropolitan regions, and offers lessons to other legacy cities and metropolitan regions faced with the challenge of managing change without growth. The resulting regional sustainability plan was completed and adopted in 2014 by northeast Ohio's five intergovernmental planning agencies to guide their long-range transportation and environmental planning. In 2015 the NEOSCC received the Daniel Burnham Award for comprehensive planning from the American Planning Association for Vibrant NEO 2040.

Vibrant NEO 2040 used GIS-based scenario planning to enable policymakers in northeast Ohio the ability to understand long-term (2015–2040) regional trends at work in their region, identify and evaluate alternative development scenarios, and understand the region-wide beneficial impacts of investing in northeast Ohio's legacy cities and first suburbs. It demonstrated that continuing the region's current development patterns (the *trend*) is a lose-lose scenario for the region, its four legacy cities, and the communities in each of its twelve counties. This scenario is likely to result in a pattern of continued exurban expansion combined with continued abandonment of large sections of the region's legacy cities and first suburbs. This pattern of regional development is likely to exacerbate the impacts of jurisdictional fragmentation and perpetuate the zero-sum game that has long frustrated efforts to encourage regional collaboration.

Vibrant NEO 2040 introduced GIS-based scenario planning to the region's five intergovernmental planning agencies. One of them, the Northeast Ohio Areawide Coordinating Agency (NOACA), has used the findings to frame its vision statement and its regional strategic plan, Going Forward Together (NOACA 2015), and to support its long-range transportation and water quality plans. It furthered the agency's effort to advance regional cohesion as a strategic policy goal and provided a policy rationale for grant programs supporting multimodal transportation investments in the established communities in its five-county service area. The other intergovernmental agencies have more limited staff and technical resources and have been slower to apply scenario planning in the development of their long-range plans.

While to date the application of Vibrant NEO 2040 by northeast Ohio's intergovernmental planning agencies has been modest, we believe that scenario planning offers a powerful tool for long-range economic and physical planning in legacy cities and their regions. Regional scenario planning enables local policymakers to overcome the impact of jurisdictional fragmentation on their efforts to collaborate with other communities in their region. By analyzing and visualizing change at multiple scales, local policymakers can place their community in the broader regional context and to systematically evaluate the impacts on their community's budget and physical environment of alternative development scenarios and policy interventions. Regardless of which GIS-based scenario planning system is selected, this tool offers the opportunity for legacy cities to collaborate more effectively with the communities in their metropolitan hinterland to identify and implement win-win approaches to their regeneration and restored prosperity.

NOTES

1. Louisville merged with Jefferson County in 2003. Macon consolidated with Bibb County in 2014.

2. The Northeast megaregion is popularly known as the Boston-Washington Corridor, and includes the coastal metropolitan areas of Maine, New Hampshire, Massachusetts, Connecticut, Rhode Island, New York, Pennsylvania, Maryland, Delaware, and Virginia. The Great Lakes megaregion consists of the metropolitan areas found in the Great Lakes, Ohio River, and Upper Mississippi watersheds and includes portions of Ohio, Michigan, Indiana, Illinois, Wisconsin, Minnesota, western Pennsylvania, and upstate New York.

3. Most notable population increases occurred in Washington, DC (11.7 percent), Richmond (7.9 percent), Minneapolis (7.4 percent), and Philadelphia (2.7 percent). New Orleans, recovering from the impact of Hurricane Katrina in 2005, grew by 13.3 percent from 2010 to 2015.

4. The Northeast Ohio Areawide Coordinating Agency—NOACA; the Akron Metropolitan Area Transportation Study—AMTS; the Stark County Area Transportation Study—SCATS; the Northeast Ohio Four County Regional Planning and Development Organization—NEFCO; and the Eastgate Regional Council of Governments—Eastgate

5. Two other regions anchored by legacy cities received regional planning grants: the seven-county bistate St. Louis region, which prepared OneSTL (East West Gateway Council of Governments, 2013), and the two-county Buffalo Niagara region, which prepared One Region Forward. One Region Forward, the latest of the three plans to be completed, made extensive use of GIS-based scenario planning in developing its regional vision and policy framework.

6. Sasaki Associates and City Architecture were engaged by the NEOSCC to apply ET to northeast Ohio.

REFERENCES

Fregonese Associates. "Geodesign Redesigned. Envision Tomorrow: A Suite of Urban and Regional Planning Tools." n.d. http://envisiontomorrow.org/.

Fregonese, John, and C. J. Gabbe. 2011. "Engaging the Public and Communicating Successfully in Regional Planning." In *Regional Planning in America: Practice and Prospect*, edited by Ethan Seltzer and Armondo Carbonell, 222–42. Cambridge, MA: Lincoln Institute of Land Policy.

Hill, Edward W., Harold L. Wolman, Katherine Kowalczyk, and Travis St. Clair. 2012. "Forces Affecting City Population Growth or Decline: The Effects of Interregional and Inter-Municipal Competition." In *Rebuilding America's Legacy Cities: New Directions for the Industrial Heartland*, edited by Alan Mallach, 31–79. New York: American Assembly.

Katz, Bruce, ed. 2000. *Reflections on Regionalism*. Washington, DC: Brookings Institution Press.

Katz, Bruce. 2006. "Revitalizing Weak Market Cities in the U.S." Presentation made to the Council on Foundations, March 8, 2006. https://www.brookings.edu/wp-content/uploads/2016/06/20060508_WeakMarketCities.pdf.

Katz, Bruce, and Jennifer Bradley. 2013. *The Metropolitan Revolution*. Washington DC: Brookings Institution Press.

Knapp, Gerrit-Jan, and Rebecca Lewis. 2011. "Regional Planning for Sustainability and Hegemony of Metropolitan Regionalism." In *Regional Planning in America: Practice and Prospect*, edited by Ethan Seltzer and Armando Carbonell, 176–211. Cambridge, MA: Lincoln Institute of Land Policy

Lang, Robert E., and Arthur C. Nelson. 2009. "Metropolitan America: Defining and Applying a New Geography." In *Megaregions: Planning for Global Competitiveness*, edited by Catherine L. Ross, 107–26. Washington, DC: Island Press.

Legacy Cities Partnership. n.d. "Legacy City Partnership: Working Together to Empower America's Legacy Cities." www.legacycities.org.

Mallach, Alan, and Lavea Brachman. 2013. *Regenerating America's Legacy Cities*. Cambridge, MA: Lincoln Institute of Land Policy

McHarg, Ian L. 1969. *Design with Nature*. Garden City, NJ: American Museum of Natural History.

Northeast Ohio Areawide Coordinating Agency (NOACA). 2015. "NOACA Strategic Plan: Going Forward Together." http://www.noaca.org/modules/showdocument.aspx?documentid=6639.

Northeast Ohio Sustainable Communities Consortium (NOACA). 2014. "Vibrant NEO 2040: A Vision, Framework, and Action Products for Our Future." http://www.vibrantneo.org.

Orfield, Myron, and Thomas F. Luce Jr. 2009. "Governing American Metropolitan Areas: Spatial Policy and Regional Governance." In *Megaregions: Planning for Global Competitiveness*, edited by Catherine L. Ross, 250–79. Washington, DC: Island Press.

Regional Plan Association. n.d. "America 2050." www.america2050.org.

Regional Plan Association. 2006. "America 2050: A Prospectus."

Todorovich, Petra, and Yoav Hagler. 2009. "America 2050: Strategies for Regional Economic Development." http://www.america2050.org/pdf/2050_Report_Regional_Economic_Development_2009.pdf.

US Census. 2017. "Metropolitan and Micropolitan Statistical Ares." https://census.gov/population/metro/.

US Department of Housing and Urban Development. n.d. "Docket No. FR-5396-N-03, Notice of Funding Availability (NOFA) for HUD's Fiscal Year 2010 Sustainable Communities Regional Planning Grant Program." https://portal.hud.gov/hudportal/documents/huddoc?id=DOC_35393.pdf.

US Department of Transportation, Federal Highway Administration. n.d. "Tools and Practices for Land Use Integration." https://www.fhwa.dot.gov/planning/processes/land_use/land_use_tools/thetools.pdf.

Vey, Jennifer. 2007. *Restoring Prosperity: The State Role in Revitalizing America's Older Industrial Cities*. Washington, DC: Brookings Institution.

Yaro, Robert D., and Armondo Carbonell. 2004. *Toward and American Spatial Development Perspective*. Cambridge, MA: Lincoln Institute of Land Policy and the Regional Plan Association.

CONCLUSION

The Future of Legacy Cities

STEPHANIE RYBERG-WEBSTER AND J. ROSIE TIGHE

The conditions of decline demand that policymakers and planners either modify existing strategies or adopt new strategies that respond to these unique circumstances. In the short-term, legacy cities will continue to be complex spaces facing decline and contestations over the benefits of stabilization and revitalization. In recent years, legacy cities in the Northeast have had modest population growth and even the most distressed midwestern legacy cities (Cleveland, Detroit) have experienced population growth in the downtown core and select neighborhoods. Yet these positive markers do not overshadow the larger forces of population decline, extreme racial segregation, inequitable distribution of benefits, and vacancy and abandonment. Understanding the history of decline, the current, complex conditions, and these cities' short-term future provides a sound basis for urban policy and planning strategies that establish the groundwork for a more equitable future. At the same time, accurately predicting the long-term future of legacy cities is nearly impossible. It is reasonable to expect some measure of spatial reorganization as abandoned buildings, vacant land, and underutilized industrial facilities become repurposed for twenty-first-century needs. Unknowns, though, range from climate change impacts on coastal cities, immigration trends, and interregional migration as resources (e.g., water) become increasingly constrained.

For the most part, legacy cities are built-out spaces. While vacant land poses an opportunity for new development, the root form and structure of these cities is unlikely to change in drastic ways. The authors who contributed to this volume, including Kinahan (chapter 4), Hatch (chapter 5), and Simons and Lee (chapter 6), explored the multiple ways that planners, policymakers, developers, and others can address legacy cities' built environments. Central to thinking about the future of legacy cities' built environment is an understanding, as Mikelbank described in chapter 10, that vacancy, in and of itself, demands a policy and planning response. Solutions to chronic vacancy, however, remain contested. For instance, demolition of vacant housing can reduce oversupply, but produces more vacant land without a clear market for redevelopment in many cases. As Krumholz mentioned in chapter 7, demolition policies must be partnered with viable, realistic plans for vacant land reuse, which Cleveland, along with other legacy cities, currently lacks.

Furthermore, the dominant issues facing legacy cities (segregation, vacancy, economic and population decline, etc.) do not disappear outside of municipal boundaries. Regional manifestations of decline demand regional solutions. At the same time, the regional spatial distribution of the negative impacts of decline are highly uneven. As Meghan Rubado argued in chapter 1, to build a more equitable for future for legacy city regions, collaborations among local governments and special districts are imperative. Due to the high level of jurisdictional fragmentation, incentives or mandates must be instituted to build intraregional collaboration. Regional growth controls are warranted, yet the political reality in many states home to legacy cities (e.g., Ohio, Michigan) are highly resistant to this level of public control over private property. To move beyond this seemingly impenetrable barrier, planners, policymakers and legacy region advocates should document the financial burden of decentralized development in regions with nearly zero population growth, including the costs to all taxpayers of building new infrastructure without new revenues to cover costs and other policies that emphasize the fiscal irresponsibility of sprawl within the context of decline and stagnation.

While regional collaborations are essential, the forces that caused decline are not merely local. Nearly a century of federal policies supported decentralization (Jackson 1987; Squires 2002; Weiwal and Perslay 2015), deindustrialization (High 2003, 2013; Mah 2012), and racial segregation (Hirsch 1983; Massey and Denton 1993; Rothstein 2017; Sugrue 1996). When forces beyond local control are partially at the root of decline, it is unreasonable to expect that cash-strapped municipal governments will miraculously spur a turnaround on their own. Rather, there is a key role of federal and state governments, particularly in terms of housing, anti-poverty, and anti-discrimination policies, to provide heightened incentives for housing or other investments in severely distressed cities, funding formulas for programs such as community development block grants could be redesigned to provide more assistance to cities in decline, where the need for incentives and stabilization funds is greatest.

POPULATION DECLINE AND ECONOMIC RESTRUCTURING

A key outcome of sustained, decades-long population and economic contraction is the proliferation of vacant and abandoned buildings and land. As manufacturing jobs left legacy cities, large swaths of underutilized industrial urban space were left behind, much of which is environmentally contaminated. Decentralization compounded central city population decline, leading to "a pernicious pattern of no-growth sprawl in outlying rural areas and on prime agricultural land, coupled with abandonment and disinvestment in cities at the center" (Morrison and Dewar 2012, 117). Population decline resulted in an oversupply of buildings, vacant and abandoned homes, commercial buildings, and other community facilities (e.g., churches, schools). The national average for vacant housing units is 12.5 percent. In St. Louis, New Orleans, Detroit, and Cleveland, more than one in five homes is vacant. According to Hackworth (2014), "supply far outstrips demand in many American Rust Belt cities and the presence of thousands of redundant housing units only serves to drag house prices well below the replacement value" (13). The recent recession and foreclosure crisis compounded these issues and, in many cases, reversed progress made toward neighborhood stabilization in the 1990s and early 2000s. The oversupply of housing drives down property values, as well as the associated property tax revenue for local governments. The oversaturated market offers plentiful affordable housing, albeit one that consists of many low-quality units as landlords have little ability to raise rents to cover even basic investments in routine maintenance, as Megan Hatch illustrated in chapter 5.

Steep and continuous population decline had massive ramifications on legacy cities' fiscal health and associated urban service provisions. As these cities' property, income, and sales tax bases eroded, infrastructure deteriorated, and households lost access to amenities and key services (Hoornbeek and Schwartz 2009; Schilling and Logan 2008). Vacancy and abandonment escalated, yet the scale of roadways, sewer lines, and other physical infrastructure remained the same, creating an imbalance in maintenance and operation costs relative to the new reality of much-reduced populations. The cumulative result is that legacy cities struggle with neighborhood instability, blighted properties, high service demands, cash-strapped municipal budgets, and poor school quality (Immergluck 2010).

If the future of legacy cities will be one of stabilization and regeneration, then the legacy of population decline and economic restructuring may actually offer cautious opportunities. These places have a clear advantage over high-growth cities when it comes to housing affordability, although decades of disinvestment and deferred maintenance make housing quality a pressing issue, particularly for low-income residents (Silverman, Paterson, and Yin 2013). Thus, while the relative low cost of legacy cities offers many opportunities, those opportunities are by no means equal across neighborhoods and communities. Race continues to determine access to opportunity, and as legacy cities continue to be racially segregated, it will take targeted and intentional government policies to ensure that the spoils of any renewal is shared by all.

While gentrification and a lack of housing affordability in high-growth cities escalates, the legacy of population decline offers a window of opportunity to work toward revitalization without the damaging impacts of gentrification. This will require planners, policymakers, elected officials, and others to boldly champion equitable development and face head on the persistent causes of segregation and discrimination. Additionally, cheap land and buildings can provide space for entrepreneurial activities, artists' space, or other innovative experiments, while large swaths of vacant land may be repurposed for new green and/or blue infrastructure systems. Although industry will never return in the form that existed during legacy cities' early twentieth-century heyday, many legacy cities are well-positioned to be centers of health care, advanced manufacturing, and other emerging economic drivers.

PRODUCTION OF URBAN SPACE AND THE BUILT ENVIRONMENT

Over the course of the twentieth century, the drivers of urban development evolved, as did definitions and ideas about who has a right to the city, the roles of citizens and powerbrokers, and forms of civic engagement. While these transitions are not unique to legacy cities, their occurrence within the context of decline has produced a unique contemporary landscape where fundamental questions of value arise: Are legacy cities failed economic spaces? Are they home to strong community and social ties that need to be preserved? Are they grand opportunities for a new urban future built on equity? Are they relics of the past that we—as a society—should let go? Is the best choice demolition, preservation, consolidation, contraction, abandonment, or some other combination of options? Furthermore, who gets to decide?

Legacy cities such as Cleveland retain strong and active growth machines (Logan and Molotch 2007) in which civic boosters promote a pro-growth agenda despite the realities of decline. Growth-oriented strategies predicated on firm attraction, rebuilding a strong manufacturing base, or promoting the industrial sector remain and reflect an ingrained belief that industry is not a thing of the past for legacy cities, but a core part of their future. In Cleveland, for instance, organizations such as Team NEO and

Cleveland Plus promote the region as a sound business investment, with their efforts supported by the Downtown Cleveland Alliance (a business-improvement district), new investments in stadiums and convention centers, and other traditional growth-focused urban development.

Contestations over the production of urban space remain a prominent issue in legacy cities. Contemporary civic engagement strategies range from mundane, public meetings to innovative initiatives that put everyday citizens' ideas about the future of spaces into action, including those described by Liggett in chapter 11. The new growth machine, which includes municipal government, foundations and community development funders, decide which neighborhoods receive the scarce funding that exists.

Today, many community development corporations (CDCs) are leaders of neighborhood development, providing affordable housing, home rehabilitation assistance, and restoring historic buildings (e.g., Cleveland's Detroit Shoreway Community Development Organization). Others focus on gentrification-based strategies in downtown or core neighborhoods (i.e., Pittsburgh Downtown CDC, Cincinnati Center City Development Corporation), while many are low-capacity entities struggling to make an impact. Overall, the diversity of CDCs in terms of focus and capacity results in varied outcomes, wherein some neighborhoods are clear winners—benefitting from well-funded and high-capacity organizations, while others continue to struggle. Many cities, including Cleveland, have an array of home rehabilitation assistance programs. For instance, in Cleveland the Cleveland Housing Network, Neighborhood Housing Services, Cleveland Housing Solutions, the Home Repair Resource Center, and the Cleveland Restoration Society all provide some form of low-interest loans, grants, and/or technical assistance for work ranging from exterior paint to whole-home weatherization. When appropriate, this assistance should be offered to both homeowners and renters.

Furthermore, the system of neighborhood development also reflects the fact that cash-strapped municipal governments struggle to provide basic services and nonprofit CDCs are often the first—and sometimes only—alternative. For example, since the mid-1980s, Cleveland has contracted with the neighborhood CDCs to provide code-enforcement services, although recent HUD interpretations of appropriate use of Community Development Block Grant (CDBG) funds has created an uncertain future for the Neighborhood Code Enforcement Partnership (Frater, Gilson, and O'Leary 2009). While these nonprofit organizations may possess better on-the-ground knowledge, they also vary in capacity and resources, leading to uneven outcomes across the city.

Amid these fiscal realities, civic boosters continue to promote stadium development, the building of convention centers, and attracting national events (such as the 2016 Republication National Cleveland in Cleveland and the 2016 Democratic National Convention in Philadelphia), which shine a positive light on these cities, but mask ongoing struggles and divert funds that could be used in other ways. Certain neighborhoods, including most downtown cores, have recently revitalized with new development and/or building restorations; new residents; new restaurants, nightlife, and other amenities; and rising property values. Yet these improvements, while a welcome change for legacy cities, have not benefitted all residents, and questions about gentrification loom. The future production of legacy cities' urban space remains an open question. From a visionary standpoint, there is an opportunity to rethink how we, as a society, value cities, neighborhoods, and people. The sheer quantity of vacant land and buildings, combined with low market values can be reframed as a grand opportunity to produce cities of the future that mimic the best aspects of the past while championing equity, justice, and legitimate opportunity for all residents.

ARTS AND CULTURE

Today, arts and culture of many varieties remain prominent legacies of legacy cities. These cities are endowed with long-standing arts and cultural institutions, often housed in grand architectural masterpieces, and retain works of public art that date to an era when art figured prominently in city building. More recently, the role of artists in transforming neighborhoods has gained prominence, with neighborhoods devising artist-attraction strategies and cities turning to the arts as a basis for community and economic development (Currid 2009; Phillips 2004; Markusen and Gadwa 2010). When planning for the future of neighborhoods, traditional cultural practices—often harkening to cities' immigrant heritage—form the basis for festivals, community events, and marketing materials (Ryberg-Webster 2016). As explored by Dennis Keating in chapter 12, the arts continue to provide one core basis for urban development and civic engagement within legacy cities. However, legacy cities also struggle to maintain and retain their cultural icons. Recently, the Detroit Institute of Arts, one of the nation's most prominent art museums, made headlines for exploring the possibility of selling off pieces of its collection as the city faced bankruptcy.

As legacy city decline became more widespread in the latter half of the twentieth century, large public investments in public art and culture waned, while the importance of artists and grassroots arts-based development increased. While some institutions stood on solid financial ground, others became vulnerable to the tide of decline. Cleveland's once-vibrant Playhouse Square theaters, for example, were all nearly vacant by the late

1960s and threatened with demolition soon after (Playhouse Square 2017). By the 1970s, though, a new wave of arts-based development was emerging nation-wide with implications for the future of legacy cities. Artists, rather than large arts institutions, occupying "gritty" urban spaces led a wave of neighborhood improvements that continues to this day.

JURISDICTIONAL FRAGMENTATION

Jurisdictional fragmentation is common for legacy cities and their regions, which results in higher infrastructure and other costs than would exist within a more cooperative structure. Such fragmentation is particularly harmful to legacy cities, given dwindling revenues to support maintenance and service provision. Furthermore, many legacy cities are completely surrounded by other incorporated municipalities, preventing them from physically expanding their boundaries as is common in growing cities such as Houston, Phoenix, or even Columbus, Ohio. Tellingly, Cincinnati has not significantly annexed since 1914; Detroit since 1926; Pittsburgh since in 1930; and Cleveland since around 1932.

Regional fragmentation has created a zero-sum game for legacy cities and their surrounding municipalities. It is common, for instance, for suburban municipalities to engage in economic development strategies that use tax breaks and other incentives to encourage firms to relocate out of the core city or first-ring suburbs. While this may result in a net job increase for the destination jurisdiction, it does nothing for job creation in the overall region or state. At the same time, firms avoid paying much-needed property taxes and/or are the recipients of financial incentives that cash-strapped regions and states desperately need (Hill et al. 2012). A prime example was American Greetings' recent decision to relocate from Brooklyn, an inner-ring suburb of Cleveland, to Westlake, a fast-growing outer-ring suburb. The financial package for American Greetings amounted to about $93.5 million in state aid (over fifteen years), a thirty-year tax increment financing package from the city of Westlake and Westlake City Schools, and a fifteen-year income tax credit from the city of Westlake (Jarboe 2011). Although heralded by some as a win for the region and the state, as American Greetings had threatened to leave completely, the net result for the region included the vacated headquarters in Brooklyn and duplicative office and retail development in the outlying suburbs.

In response to such interjurisdictional competition, some municipalities have consolidated activities. For instance, in 2016, four Cleveland east side suburbs—Cleveland Heights, University Heights, Shaker Heights, and South Euclid—created a consolidated fire and police dispatch center (Uldricks 2016). The agreement provides cost-savings to participating communities and perhaps indicates an incremental approach to more efficient coordination within legacy regions. Significantly more efforts are necessary to reduce overlap in service provision, provide efficient infrastructure, coordinate environmental management, ensure regional distributions of affordable housing, and promote regional economic development. The need for regional solutions to legacy challenges speaks to the need for multiple forms of collaboration and has resulted in large-scale planning efforts, such as those described by Hunter Morrison and Mark Salling in chapter 14.

ENVIRONMENTAL ISSUES

The federal and state governments provide limited funding for cleanup, but responsibility for environmentally contaminated sites is highly contested—companies that caused the pollution may no longer exist (and were often not breaking any laws or violating nonexistent regulations at the time of contamination); new developers are leery of purchasing potential brownfields due to the possibility of exorbitant remediation costs; and cash-strapped legacy cities have little internal capacity to fund cleanup. Lead poisoning, which has received increased attention as of late due to the Flint, Michigan, water crisis, stems from the deterioration of century-old infrastructure and failures of the public sector to adequately maintain aging water pipes (Morckel 2017). Lead paint poses additional risks, particularly in legacy cities where market values, concentrated poverty, and a lack of municipal funding has resulted in systemic building deterioration.

Legacy city environmental issues are intricately linked to race and concerns about social justice. Commonly referred to as *environmental racism*, many environmental threats—lead poisoning, toxic air, living near brownfields—disproportionately affect communities of color. Poor, minority households are more likely to live in deteriorated housing, with renters particularly vulnerable as they lack the resources and power to ensure proper maintenance. Poor and minority communities are also more likely to be situated near highways and industrial sites. In total, the result is shameful: African Americans, particularly children, have higher rates of lead poisoning and long-term health issues—chronic asthma, high blood pressure, childhood obesity, and diabetes—than their white counterparts (Dissell and Zeltner 2015).

Unfortunately, as many legacy cities struggle to attract new development, residents, and jobs, environmental concerns may be placed on the back burner. Much needed remediation—overwhelmingly concentrated in poor and minority neighborhoods—has become a much less pressing priority amid fears that regulations or clean up requirements may scare off development.

RACIAL INCLUSION AND SOCIAL JUSTICE

While there is considerable scholarly research and large public policy forums on addressing the challenges of legacy cities, public policy has done little to address the issue of racial inequality and segregation. In fact, public policy and planning interventions have often exacerbated racial and class inequality. In St. Louis the 1970 "team four" plan explicitly divided up the city along racial lines—limiting revitalization efforts in the largely African American north side (Tighe and Ganning 2015). In Baltimore school siting choices were intrinsically race-based, even after *Brown v. the Board of Education* (Baum 2011). In Cleveland tax-abatement strategies to spur development overwhelmingly favored white neighborhoods, doing little to encourage development in African American communities (Krumholz 1991, 1999). The result is that legacy cities comprise the vast majority of the most segregated metropolitan areas in America (US Census 2010).

Each of the other key issues facing legacy cities discussed in this book both produce and result from racial segregation, disinvestment in minority neighborhoods, and public policies that failed city residents for decades. As younger residents begin to "rediscover" urban neighborhoods in legacy cities, tensions flare over the potential for gentrification and conflicts over who "belongs" in the city. A spate of recent racial incidents in legacy cities highlights how contested space can harm nonwhite residents. From the arrest of two black men for sitting in a Starbucks in Philadelphia, to the deaths at the hands of police of Freddie Gray (Baltimore), Tamir Rice (Cleveland), and Michael Brown (St. Louis), it continues to be clear that being black in what is perceived to be a "white space" is deserving of harassment, arrest, or death. As Dunn, Allen, and Whitt pointed out in chapter 8, these incidents are by no means outliers, and they highlight the responsibility that public policymakers, politicians, business owners, and the public have in promoting equity, inclusion, and social justice—particularly in cities experiencing racial change and transition.

CONCLUSION

Even though the construct *legacy city* provides a useful organizing framework, it does not and should not imply that there are one-size-fits-all solutions to common legacy city issues and problems. Nor does it mean that all legacy cities have the same histories, legacies, or current opportunities. Local context, conditions, politics, history, and so forth all matter and must be factored in when devising policy responses and future plans. Broad narratives of decline and ruin are becoming increasingly pervasive, yet they mask the nuanced, on-the-ground reality in these cities. In chapter

7 Norman Krumholz described how planners influenced policy and popular mindsets through writing, and we argue that local actors (planners and beyond) should embrace their role as tellers of their own cities' stories. Local control over the robust story of legacy cities, including framing and storytelling, are essential to advocating for equitable and locally rooted governing, planning, and policymaking.

So what have the chapters in this book told us? How do we move forward and combat the ways that population decline and economic restructuring impact the production of space, jurisdictional fragmentation, arts and cultural revival, environmental protection, and racial segregation and social justice? While the likeliest scenario for the future of legacy cities is one of incremental change, we urge readers to consider the possibility of radical approaches to change as well. We certainly do not have all the answers, nor do we purport to know what will work best. But we do hope that in reading this book, readers will come away with a better understanding of the conditions of decline, the prospects for mitigating decline, and the possibilities for the future.

What would megaregional consolidation do for core legacy cities and their hinterlands? What if all students in a region—regardless of race, income, or neighborhood—attended a single school district that was not funded by ultra-local property taxes? How would strong physical growth boundaries stem the tide of decentralization and fragmentation? What if cities and foundations funneled money to the most distressed communities instead of the most marketable ones? What if legacy cities required a percentage of all new housing in revitalizing neighborhoods to be affordable for those most in need? While the future outlook for legacy cities has been a bleak one for decades, there are countless residents and advocates—ourselves included—who live in these cities and believe in their future. It is our hope that this volume illuminates not only the challenges but also the nuances, meanings, and opportunities of our legacy cities.

Furthermore, it is essential to acknowledge that the issues highlighted in this book do not comprise an exhaustive list. Numerous chapters could have been included that focus on additional challenges facing such cities, including public education, public health, workforce development, transit and walkability, and income security and inequality. We hope this volume spurs additional work in these areas and look forward to continuing to learn about how these and other issues manifest in a context of decline.

We firmly believe that all urban policy and planning for legacy cities must start with a framework of advancing equity, social justice, and inclusivity. The legacy of segregation and discrimination demands solutions that place race in the foreground. Furthermore, inclusive policies and strategies must be informed by a thorough understanding of the history and the current status of income disparities, the spatial dynamics of race, and housing tenure, among others. Equitable planning and policymaking must also be predicated on a holistic agenda that includes housing, health, workforce development, education (at all levels), and transportation and access. Above all else, legacy cities remain home to millions of people, who are disproportionately African American and economically disadvantaged. Thus, all planning and policy solutions must be grounded in the pursuit of equity and work to improve the quality of life and opportunities for all residents.

REFERENCES

Baum, Howell S. 2011. *"Brown" in Baltimore: School Desegregation and the Limits of Liberalism*. Ithaca, NY: Cornell University Press.

Currid, Elizabeth. 2009. "Bohemia as Subculture; 'Bohemia' as Industry: Art, Culture, and Economic Development." *CPL Bibliography* 23, no. 4: 368–82.

Dissell, Rachel, and Brie Zeltner. 2015. "Race, Racism and Lead Poisoning: Toxic Neglect." *Plain Dealer* (Cleveland, OH), October 22, 2015.

Frater, Mark, Colleen M. Gilson, and Ronald J. H. O'Leary. 2009. "The City of Cleveland Code Enforcement Partnership." http://www.communityprogress.net/filebin/pdf/CLE_C.E._Partnership.pdf.

Hackworth, Jason. 2014. "The Limits to Market-Based Strategies for Addressing Land Abandonment in Shrinking American Cities." *Progress in Planning* 90: 1–37.

High, Steven. 2003. *Industrial Sunset: The Making of North America's Rust Belt, 1969–1984*. Toronto: University of Toronto Press.

High, Steven. 2013. "'The Wounds of Class': A Historiographical Reflection on the Study of Deindustrialization, 1973–2013." *History Compass* 11, no. 11: 994–1007.

Hill, Edward W., Harold L. Wolman, Katherine Kowalczyk, and Travis St Clair. 2012. "Forces Affecting City Population Growth or Decline: The Effects of Interregional and Inter-Municipal Competition." In *Rebuilding America's Legacy Cities: New Directions for the Industrial Heartland*, edited by Alan Mallach, 31–79. New York: American Assembly.

Hirsch, Arnold R. 1983. *Making the Second Ghetto: Race and Housing in Chicago 1940–1960*. Chicago: University of Chicago Press.

Hoornbeek, John, and Terry Schwarz. 2009. "Sustainable Infrastructure in Shrinking Cities: Options for the Future." Kent State University Center for Public Administration and Public Policy, in association with the Cleveland Urban Design Collaborative, Kent, OH.

Immergluck, Daniel. 2010. "Neighborhoods in the Wake of the Debacle: Intrametropolitan Patterns of Foreclosed Properties." *Urban Affairs Review* 46, no. 1: 3–36.

Jackson, Kenneth T. 1987. *Crabgrass Frontier: The Suburbanization of the United States*. New York: Oxford University Press.

Jarboe, Michelle. 2011. "American Greetings to Move Headquarters to Crocker Park in Westlake in 2014." *Plain Dealer* (Cleveland, OH), May 20, 2011.

Krumholz, Norman. 1982. "A Retrospective View of Equity Planning, Cleveland, 1969–1979." *Journal of the American Planning Association* 48, no. 2: 163–74.

Krumholz, Norman. 2011. *Making Equity Planning Work: Leadership in the Public Sector*. Philadelphia: Temple University Press.

Logan, John R., and Harvey Molotch. 2007. *Urban Fortunes: The Political Economy of Place*. Berkeley: University of California Press.

Mah, Alice. 2012. *Industrial Ruination, Community, and Place: Landscapes and Legacies of Urban Decline*. Toronto: University of Toronto Press.

Markusen, Ann, and Anne Gadwa. 2010. "Arts and Culture in Urban or Regional Planning: A Review and Research Agenda." *Journal of Planning Education and Research* 29, no. 3: 379–91.

Massey, Douglas S., and Nancy A. Denton. 1993. *American Apartheid: Segregation and the Making of the Underclass*. Cambridge, MA: Harvard University Press.

Morckel, Victoria. 2017. "Why the Flint, Michigan, USA Water Crisis is an Urban Planning Failure." *Cities* 62: 23–27.

Morrison, Hunter, and Margaret Dewar. 2012. "Planning in America's Legacy Cities: Toward Better, Smaller Communities after Decline." In *Rebuilding America's Legacy Cities: New Directions for the Industrial Heartland*, edited by Alan Mallach, 31–79. New York: American Assembly.

Phillips, Rhonda. 2004. "Artful Business: Using the Arts for Community Economic Development." *Community Development Journal* 39, no. 2: 112–22.

Playhouse Square. 2017. "History." http://www.playhousesquare.org/about-playhouse square-main/history.

Rothstein, Richard. 2017. *The Color of Law: A Forgotten History of How Our Government Segregated America*. New York: Liveright.

Schilling, Joseph, and Jonathan Logan. 2008. "Greening the Rust Belt: A Green Infrastructure Model for Right Sizing America's Shrinking Cities." *Journal of the American Planning Association* 74, no. 4: 451–66.

Silverman, Robert, Li Yin, and Kelly L. Patterson. 2013. "Dawn of the Dead City: An Exploratory Analysis of Vacant Addresses in Buffalo, NY 2008–2010." *Journal of Urban Affairs* 35, no. 2: 131–52.

Squires, Gregory D. 2002. "Urban Sprawl and the Uneven Development of Metropolitan America." In *Urban Sprawl: Causes, Consequences, and Policy Responses*, 1–22. Washington, DC: Urban Institute Press.

Sugrue, Thomas J. 1996. *The Origins of the Urban Crisis: Race and Inequality in Postwar Detroit*. Princeton, NJ: Princeton University Press.

Tighe, J. Rosie, and Joanna P. Ganning. 2015. "The Divergent City: Unequal and Uneven Development in St. Louis." *Urban Geography* 36, no. 5: 654–73.

Uldricks, Rick. 2016. "Four Cities to Consolidate Fire and Police Dispatch Services." *Cleveland Heights Patch*, May 6, 2016. https://patch.com/ohio/clevelandheights /four-cities-consolidate-fire-police-dispatch-services.

Wiewel, Wim, and Joseph J. Persky. 2015. *Suburban Sprawl: Private Decisions and Public Policy*. London: Routledge.

ABOUT THE CONTRIBUTORS

Dr. TERRENCE ALLEN is an assistant professor in the School of Social Work at the University of Texas at Austin. Before joining the faculty at the University of Texas he was on the faculty at North Carolina Central University and Wayne State University in Detroit, Michigan. He has a combined twenty-eight years of practice and research experience. His general interest is social issues that impact the quality of life for children and families. His specific areas of expertise are the intersection between the child welfare, juvenile justice, education and mental-health systems, and the interaction between police and juveniles in urban communities.

CANDI CLOUSE is the interim director of the Center for Community Planning and Development at the Maxine Goodman Levin College of Urban Affairs at Cleveland State University. Dr. Clouse concentrates on anchor-based development, business-site selection, place image, industry research, economic-impact modeling, and data analysis. Dr. Clouse received her master's and doctorate degrees in urban studies with a focus on economic development from Cleveland State University. She received her bachelor's in psychology from Wittenberg University. She is a member of the Urban Affairs Association and Pi Alpha Alpha.

KIRBY DATE, AICP, is a community planner and landscape architect based at the Center for Community Planning and Development at the Maxine Goodman Levin College of Urban Affairs at Cleveland State University. As a practitioner, she has provided technical assistance and decision support to local governments and community organizations for many years.

She holds a bachelor's in landscape architecture from Cornell University, and a master's in community and neighborhood development from Cleveland State University. Her areas of interest include urban neighborhood and small town main street redevelopment, and community land use, housing, zoning, and landscape policy.

Dr. RONNIE A. DUNN is an associate professor of urban studies at the Maxine Goodman Levin College of Urban Affairs at Cleveland State University. As an urban sociologist his research interest includes issues affecting minorities and the urban poor, with particular expertise in race, policing, and racial profiling. Dr. Dunn provided written testimony to President Obama's task force on twenty-first-century policing and was appointed by Governor John Kasich to the Ohio task force on community-police relations and the Ohio Collaborative Community-Police Advisory Board, which is establishing statewide standards in policing based on the recommendations of the task force.

Dr. TATYANA GUZMAN is an assistant professor of public administration at the Maxine Goodman Levin College of Urban Affairs at Cleveland State University. Her research interests are in municipal bond market, budgeting, tax preferences, and education finance. She has published articles in peer- and author-reviewed journals, and has authored book chapters and reports. Dr. Guzman has taught undergraduate and graduate-level courses in budgeting, general public finance, research methods, statistics, and economics at Indiana University, Indiana University-Purdue University Indianapolis, and Cleveland State University.

MEGAN E. HATCH is an assistant professor of urban policy and city management at Cleveland State University. Her research focuses on the causes and consequences of policies that disproportionately affect vulnerable populations. Her current research centers on two main types of equity-related policies: rental housing and state-level redistribution via taxes and spending. Her research has been published in *Policy Studies Journal*, *Housing Policy Debate*, *Journal of Planning Literature*, *Political Research Quarterly*, and *Urban Affairs Review*. She has a PhD in public policy and administration from George Washington University and a Master's of Public Administration from Cornell University.

W. DENNIS KEATING is a professor emeritus at the Maxine Goodman Levin College of Urban Affairs at Cleveland State University and a Levin College Distinguished Scholar. He held several administrative positions at the Maxine Goodman Levin College of Urban Affairs, including director of the graduate urban planning program. He has taught and published widely in urban planning, urban policy, neighborhood development, and housing. His latest book is *A Brief History of Tremont: Cleveland's Neighborhood on a Hill* (2016). He is a past president of the Housing and Built Environment Council of the International Sociological Association, and has served on the board of the Urban Affairs Association.

WENDY A. KELLOGG obtained her PhD in city and regional planning from Cornell University. She is currently a professor of urban planning and environmental studies at the Levin College of Urban Affairs. Her research areas include urban and regional sustainability, watershed governance, and Great Lakes water quality. Her current research focuses on governance networks for watershed management, drawing on resilience theory and environmental history. Her teaching areas include urban sustainability planning, environmental landscape planning, and planning studio. Dr. Kellogg also directs the program on water-resilient cities, a topic on which she hosted an international conference 2016. She serves on the technical advisory committee for the Cleveland EcoVillage and other environmental organizations.

KELLY L. KINAHAN is an assistant professor in the Department of Urban and Public Affairs at the University of Louisville, where she teaches courses in the Master of Urban Planning program. Her research focuses on urban revitalization, historic preservation, and community and economic development, often in the context of legacy cities. She holds a PhD in urban studies and public affairs from Cleveland State University. Dr. Kinahan is a member of the American Institute of Certified Planners.

NORMAN KRUMHOLZ is a professor emeritus at the Maxine Goodman Levin College of Urban Affairs at Cleveland State University. He served as planning director of the Cleveland City Planning Commission from 1969 to 1979, where he championed the idea of equity planning. Professor Krumholz has published numerous books and in many professional journals. His research has been supported by the Cleveland Foundation, the George Gund Foundation, and the Ford Foundation. He served as the president of the American Planning Association from 1986 to 1987, and president of the American Institute of Certified Planners in 1999. He was awarded the Rome Prize in 1987, is a fellow of the American Institute of Certified Planners, and the American Planning Association has honored his Cleveland Policy Plan as a "Planning Landmark." He was recently named one of the top one hundred urbanists of all time by the website Planetizen.

EUNKYU LEE is a research associate at the Newman Real Estate Institute within the Zicklin School of Business at Baruch College–City University of New York. His research topics include green buildings and affordable housing. While a doctoral student at Cleveland State University, he worked with Dr. Robert Simons for a CBRE green building project, where the research team developed a nationwide green office building index. His current project examines the effect of municipal bond financing on affordable housing development.

HELEN LIGGETT is an adjunct professor at the College of Architecture and Environmental Design at Kent State University and professor emeritus at the Maxine Goodman Levin College of Urban Affairs at Cleveland State University. Her interests are in the related fields of spatial theory and urban design, visual culture, and photography. Recent projects include research on structures of governance in legacy cities and photo documentation of Design/ReBuild and Making Our Own Space at Kent State University's Cleveland Urban Design Collaborative.

BRIAN MIKELBANK is an associate professor of urban studies at Cleveland State University. He earned his undergraduate degree in economics and geography from SUNY Buffalo, and his master's and doctorate in geography from The Ohio State University. An urban geographer, his research focuses on the dynamics of urban-suburban change and spatial analysis of metropolitan housing markets, with a recent focus on the relationship between the housing crisis, rehabilitation, and preservation. Brian teaches classes in housing analysis, quantitative and spatial data analysis, urban spatial structure, urban geography, and urban development.

HUNTER MORRISON is a senior fellow in urban studies at the Maxine Goodman Levin College of Urban Affairs at Cleveland State University, where he teaches and writes on legacy cities and regions in the Great Lakes megaregion. In 2014 he coauthored "Vibrant NEO 2040," a vision and policy framework for the northeast Ohio region. He previously served as director of the Youngstown State University Center for Urban and Regional Studies (2002–2012) and as Cleveland city planning director (1980–2002), and coauthored the Cleveland Civic Vision 2000: Downtown and Citywide Plans (1990) and the Youngstown 2010 plan (2005).

MERISSA C. PIAZZA is a program manager at the Center for Economic Development at the Levin College of Urban Affairs and specializes in economic development, entrepreneurship, workforce development, metrics and indicators, and survey research. She is an economist with vast experience conducting academic and applied research studies, and her research portfolio includes projects on entrepreneurship, investigating high-growth firms, analysis of the adoption of technologies in industries, navigating industry workforce development issues, and overall industry analysis. Piazza earned her master's degree from the Graduate School of Public and International Affairs at the University of Pittsburgh and earned her PhD from Cleveland State University in urban studies and public affairs.

MEGHAN E. RUBADO is an assistant professor of public administration and city management at the Maxine Goodman Levin College of Urban Affairs at Cleveland State University. Her research focuses primarily on state and local politics and governance, with particular interests in collaborative governance, urban policy, and environmental policy.

STEPHANIE RYBERG-WEBSTER is an associate professor in the Department of Urban Studies at Cleveland State University's Levin College of Urban Affairs, where she also directs the Master of Urban Planning and Development Program. Her work addresses the intersections of historic preservation and urban development. She has published research on preservation and community development, African American heritage, historic rehabilitation tax credits, and preservation amid urban decline. She holds a PhD in city and regional planning from the University of Pennsylvania, a master of historic preservation from the University of Maryland, and a bachelor of urban planning from the University of Cincinnati.

MARK SALLING is a senior fellow and research associate at the Maxine Goodman Levin College of Urban Affairs at Cleveland State University. A former urban planner, he is a certified GIS Professional (GISP) by the Geographic Information Systems Certification Institute, and holds a bachelor's and doctorate in geography from Kent State University, and a master's in geography from the University of Cincinnati. He has authored papers on computer applications in planning, data dissemination, geographic information systems (GIS), public-participation GIS, voting rights, redistricting, poverty, residential mobility, environmental equity, and demography. He has taught courses on GIS, urban geography, statistical and computer methods, and demography.

ARITREE SAMANTA is currently a postdoctoral research associate in the Department of Forestry and Natural Resources at Purdue University. She is an interdisciplinary scholar specializing in the areas of collaborative watershed management, urban and resource governance, and interpretive theory and analysis. She earned her PhD in urban and public affairs from the Maxine Goodman Levin College of Urban Affairs at Cleveland State University, and her master's degree in social work from the University of Delhi. She has held fellowship and research positions with the Alliance for the Great Lakes in Chicago and the Northeast Midwest Institute in Washington, DC.

ROBERT A. SIMONS is a professor at the Maxine Goodman Levin College of Urban Affairs at Cleveland State University. Dr. Simons was a Fulbright scholar in South Africa and a Lady Davis scholar in Israel. Dr. Simons received his PhD from the University of North Carolina at Chapel Hill in city and regional planning. He is a former president of the American Real Estate Society. Dr. Simons has authored over seventy-five journal articles, and is the lead author of four real estate books. Dr. Simons has served as an expert witness in over eighty cases related to housing markets and environmental contamination. He is the editor of the *Journal of Sustainable Real Estate*.

J. ROSIE TIGHE is an associate professor in the Department of Urban Studies at Cleveland State University's Levin College of Urban Affairs. She was previously an assistant professor in the Department of Geography and Planning at Appalachian State University. She holds a PhD in community and regional planning from the University of Texas at Austin and a master's degree in urban and environmental policy and planning from Tufts University. She has published research on affordable housing, gentrification, segregation, shrinking cities, and coedited *The Affordable Housing Reader*. Her work focuses on issues related to affordable housing, social justice, and equitable development.

Dr. AHMED WHITT is an assistant professor at the University of Texas at Austin's School of Social Work and the research director of a national nonprofit organization that provides comprehensive employment services for individuals returning from incarceration. As a social urbanist, Dr. Whitt primarily studies the role of neighborhood on economic decision-making, crime, and access to mental-health services. He is an alumnus of the University of North Carolina at Chapel Hill and the University of Pennsylvania.

JINHEE YUN is a PhD candidate at the Maxine Goodman Levin College of Urban Affairs at Cleveland State University. She studies urban policy development, focusing on community development and economic development. She is specifically interested in poverty and inequality. She has been working as a research assistant in the Center for Economic Development at Cleveland State University for four years. She earned a master's degree in urban planning and real estate and a bachelor's degree in economics from Chung-Ang University in South Korea.

INDEX